Attributes of Memory

Benton J. Underwood
Northwestern University

Scott, Foresman and Company
Glenview, Illinois

Dallas, Texas   Oakland, New Jersey   Palo Alto, California
Tucker, Georgia   London, England

Library of Congress Cataloging in Publication Data

Underwood, Benton J., 1915–
Attributes of memory.

Bibliography: p. 265
Includes index.
1. Memory.   2. Verbal learning.   I. Title.
BF371.U48   1983   153.1   83–2968
ISBN 0–673–15798–9

Printed in the United States of America.
1   2   3   4   5   6 - RRC - 87   86   85   84   83

Preface

For a number of years I have taught two courses dealing primarily with verbal learning and memory. One is an experimental course for undergraduates; the other is a lecture course taken by first-year graduate students. I believe this text can serve as background reading for either of these two types of courses. An integral part of the teaching of both courses in recent years has been the reporting of experiments I carried out for the express purpose of using them as teaching aids to illustrate methods and phenomena. I found they served their purpose well and have reported them here because it seemed to me that others might find the approach useful too.

The title of the book is indicative of my current approach to the study of learning and memory, an approach that views memory as a collection of different types of information, or attributes. This approach can comfortably contain the classical associationistic views while at the same time recognizing that for some phenomena, nonassociative attributes may dominate memory functioning. Although the coverage of the phenomena of learning and memory is quite broad, the book cannot pretend to be a complete review of the vast literature that has grown up in the area during the past one hundred years. Topics were selected for inclusion because of their importance for methods of research, for theory, or because they represent enduring issues seeking solution. Illustrations of each in order are methods of inducing maintenance rehearsal, the role of implicit responses in theory construction, and the persistent question of how associations are formed.

The major purpose of a textbook is, of course, to teach the fundamentals of an area of inquiry, and I have tried to keep this objective preeminent throughout. The book assumes no prior knowledge of the field, but it does assume some statistical training and some acquaintance with the experimental approach as applied to psychological questions.

A book such as this requires the reporting of many published research studies. I fear that I may have been quite parochial by emphasizing my own research and that of the many fine undergraduate and graduate students who have worked with me. This book has benefited from suggestions made by Robert A. Bjork, University of California at Los Angeles; Lyle E. Bourne, Jr., University of Colorado at Boulder; and William P. Wallace, University of Nevada at Reno. Katie Steele supervised the development of the book with admirable professionalism. Carrie Dierks did the near impossible when she found ways to smooth my whimsical prose. The final manuscript was typed quickly and accurately by Maureen Cannon. To all I express my gratitude.

Benton J. Underwood

Contents

Attributes of
Memory

1

Introduction

No matter how it is viewed, the capacity we call memory is most remarkable. It is sometimes cursed when it fails at the moment we search for a particular fact, but in its overall functioning it is a storage system containing a personal record of an enormous number of skills, facts, experiences, and so on, which are largely responsible for our current behavior. The human memory system is not a perfect system, perhaps, because we do forget and we rarely establish memories of long duration without some effort. And, the aged seem to deserve a more fitting tribute in their waning years than that given by the loss of memory produced by creeping senility. Still, all in all, one cannot help but be awed by the functioning of memory in its absolutely fundamental role in our behaviors.

When an event is experienced, some relatively permanent representation of that event may remain; we call this representation a memory. Thousands of past events, some repeated but some occurring only a single time, have a contemporary status because of memory. Memories constitute the raw materials of the intellect. When we say we are thinking, we are evaluating and manipulating memories. Most of the events that form memories that are the raw materials of the intellect are symbolic or verbal in nature. The area of verbal learning and memory concerns itself with such memories—how they are established and how they persist.

A systematic study of the learning and retention of verbal materials must certainly presuppose that we acquire, in the natural scheme of things, memories that in one way or another must be described as consisting of words. This is to say that it is unlikely that psychologists have gone about doing research on the learning and retention of verbal materials without fairly good evidence that we are studying processes that go on under the normal conditions of living. Some reflections may assure us of this. The names of many birds are known as well as the names of many animals; we also know the names of many inanimate objects and the names of many people. Even the very young can give the names of many of the states and their capitals. It seems beyond doubt that the names of many things are acquired, names which in some sense stand alone in memory without dependencies upon anything other than the class names that are used to show that the names are in fact in memory. That is, to test for knowledge of the names of birds, we must ask our subjects to name all of the birds possible. The way we interrogate a memory system tells us something about how that system is organized.

Much of verbal knowledge consists of more than relatively isolated names. More birds can be named than can be identified by name in the wild. Those names that are not associated or attached to a particular species may be said to be relatively isolated memories, memories which remain in our repertoire as a result of an attachment to the name "birds." The moment a bird name is attached to a particular species, the verbal repertoire is seen to consist of more than just isolated words. In effect, there now exists a small network of associations, as they may be called, a network which involves an object, its name, its class name, and its description relative to other objects in the class. Oldfield (1966), an English psychologist, said " . . . the average, reasonably young, university educated, kind of person knows the meaning of about 75,000 $\pm$ 3,500 words (p. 341)." Even if Oldfield has overestimated it is still quite obvious that the collection of words and the associative interrelationships among them that are parts of the system represent a stunning achievement of nature.

Memories are constituted of further kinds of knowledge than thus far mentioned, kinds of knowledge that are also essentially verbal in nature because the knowledge is primarily expressed by words. A knife is sharp, an engine needs fuel, a wheel is round, and a snake is slimy. It is apparent, furthermore, that we learn that objects that have the same properties may be grouped together, and the group may be given a name. Thus, objects that fly and have feathers and two wings are grouped under the class name of birds.

Still, memories are even more verbal in nature than described as yet. A memory may be carried as a series of words that can, upon request, be repeated in the same order time after time. Verses, poems, songs, and passages are memorized; the Gettysburg Address and the Star Spangled Banner have been learned by "heart." When a verbatim memory is established for a paragraph or passage, at the same time parallel passages are available in that with but little additional effort we can use quite different strings of words and yet retain the meaning of the original passage. This ability to paraphrase almost of necessity has its roots in the associative relationships implied by synonymity.

The above illustrations do seem to indicate that verbal learning and verbal memories play a substantial role in our day-to-day living. Experimental studies on the topic have been amassing for nearly one hundred years following the lead of the pioneer German investigator Ebbinghaus, and there is therefore a background literature of some depth. As has been true with so many research disciplines, perhaps 95 percent of all of the research on the topic of verbal learning and memory has taken place during the past twenty years. Beginning in the next chapter, it is the intent to examine the methods of research and to study some of the facts that have resulted from the application of these methods. There are still some introductory matters on which attention will be focused in the present chapter.

THE LEARNING-MEMORY SYSTEM

There seems to have been a certain amount of uncertainty when the plans were drawn up for the systems possessed by living organisms. One might surmise that if living organisms were to be, why were we not constructed so that only positive processes were present? Why are there negative processes that are antithetical to the positive ones? Nature produces a beautiful tree and then destroys it with a tornado or with a disease. Physical effort is inevitably overcome by fatigue processes. Each living organism seems to be continually the center of a struggle in which growth processes and decay processes vie for dominance. In a like manner, the momentary intellectual capabilities of an individual represent a balance between the processes that build, which we call learning and memory, and the processes that destroy, which we call forgetting. The negative effects appear to be relatively minor during the early years for the human organism. But, at an advanced age the negative effects do not appear to be minor, and sometimes it seems as if more old memories are forgotten than new ones are learned. These comments direct us toward speculations about the role of forgetting in nature's scheme of things. We have called forgetting a negative process, but perhaps we should try to view it in various ways, including as an adaptive process.

General Models of the Learning-Memory System

Limited storage. The memory system could be viewed as including a storage area or space, and if we interpret storage here as we do in our everyday experiences, the storage area has a finite capacity. There is only room for so many memories, and once that capacity is realized, no further new memories can be stored. To avoid this intolerable state of affairs, nature (it may be speculated) has provided us with a release mechanism in the process we call forgetting. By forgetting we are able to open up storage space and once again new memories may be stored. Therefore, forgetting, although being a negative process, becomes an adaptive one.

The major criticism of the limited capacity model is that it just does not seem to square with our experiences. Although under certain circumstances when we have spent hours learning new material we may feel that "we cannot learn another thing," a relatively short rest will allow us to learn again without serious trouble. If there is a finite limit to the memory storage system, it seems correct to say that with the normal human this limit has not been approached.

Although we do not believe that the limited-capacity model should be given serious consideration, by way of looking ahead it should be noted at this time that when models are built around different characteristics than those being considered here, some use of the limited-capacity idea may have value. For example, it is not unusual to speak of long-term memory and short-term memory, and to build models around this distinction. A short-term memory is usually characterized as having a sharply limited capacity, and, having such a limited capacity, if new material is to be inserted in the system, some of the old must be eliminated from the short-term store.

No Forgetting. A somewhat radical model starts with the assertion that there is no forgetting. What we call forgetting, according to the underpinnings of such a model, is due to inappropriate retrieval cues. The memory which seems lost is in fact not lost, and this could be demonstrated (according to the model) if we could find the "right" retrieval cue to release the memory from the storage state. One's initial reaction to such a model might be to scoff. But, if we reflect on the matter, we will probably come to the conclusion that such a model is incorporating certain facts that cannot be denied. Let us look at some of the facts that could be marshalled in support of the no-forgetting model.

Each of us has had the experience of trying to remember a particular name or fact, only to be frustrated by our inability to find it in memory. Yet, perhaps an hour or a day later, seemingly without reason, the name or fact suddenly pops into our head. Such an event should show that the particular memory had not been erased or eliminated from the storage system.

Consider another experience which most of us have had. We try to remember a name, but to no avail. Then, a friend says to us: "Was the name you are trying to recall George Albritton?" Immediately we recognize the name as being the one for which we have been searching. So, the memory has not been eliminated from the storage system that mediates *recognition* memory as opposed to recall memory.

To comprehend fully a third illustration, we should try to do something along the following lines. First, we recall all of the bird names we can, but if three minutes go by without recalling a name, we stop trying to remember further names. Then, a day later we try again to recall more names. We continue this search each day until we can no longer remember any new names. It is very likely that we will be able to recall new names each day for several days. This does not mean that we have recovered all of the names we know, but it does mean that to conclude that we have forgotten something because we cannot recall it at the moment is probably not a correct conclusion when the issue has to do with general properties of the learning-memory system.

The outcome of trying to recall bird names over days is similar to that of an experiment carried out by an investigator at the University of California at San Diego (Williams, 1976). This investigator asked his subjects to recall as many of the names of classmates from their high school graduating class as possible. The subjects were given an hour a day for ten days to recall the names. The subjects had all graduated several years earlier from large high schools. It was found that even on the tenth day the subjects were able to recall names they had not recalled during the previous nine days. Furthermore, the correctness of the names recalled was verified by use of the yearbooks from the schools.

Such evidence does not allow us to characterize as absurd models which assume that no forgetting occurs. As a matter of fact, if one is attracted to such models it leads to certain types of experiments that might not have been done under other models. In particular, it leads to studies dealing with the effectiveness of various types of retrieval cues. Still, we must recognize that we cannot deny two propositions which are incompatible with no-forgetting models. First, there is at least functional forgetting in the sense that at a given point in time we cannot either recall or recognize an event which we could remember at an earlier point in time. Such a fact requires an explanation and it may or may not turn out that the loss can be understood by studying retrieval cues. Second, there is no way to deny the possibility that some memories are completely lost in that no trace of them remains in the system (see Loftus and Loftus, 1980, for a full discussion of this issue).

Forgetting Is Adaptive.   In this general model, the critical assumption is that forgetting, which we may curse, is in fact an adaptive process. The argument would take something like the following approach. First, of course, it would accept the proposition that forgetting does occur, and that the longer the interval between learning and the test for forgetting, the greater the forgetting. In a sense, forgetting is viewed as being the opposite of learning. As learning trials increase, the memory gets stronger; as the time since learning increases, the memory gets weaker. The adaptive nature of forgetting can only be argued after a description is given of the situation that would develop if we never forgot anything, and that our memories remained as strong and available and accessible as at the time they were acquired. How would we manage our use of memories under such circumstances? It would seem that we would have a very difficult time in determining the appropriate memory for a given moment. Would we dial the telephone number which had been appropriate ten years ago but which is no longer appropriate? Would we tell our students the experimental facts in an area as they were known a number of years ago because of our inability to discriminate between the old and the new? It would seem that if there was no forgetting, we would have to develop a lot of new learning that would allow us to discriminate between the appropriateness of one memory and that of another. As it is, one can view forgetting in an adaptive sense by indicating that in a probabilistic way the most recently formed memories are most likely to be appropriate and also stronger than older memories. In other words, as a consequence of forgetting, we have a crude dating system whereby old memories can be discriminated from newer memories.

There are problems with the above model as there have been with the others. The most obvious flaw is that age and strength are not always negatively correlated. A memory that was formed many years ago can be said to be very strong at present. Thus, a dating system would require some discriminating device other than strength. Still, the number of such exceptions may not be large; a memory that has not been "used" for many years will usually be a weak memory. It is also likely that in some cases our memories are dated by means of associative learning which will also serve to keep the potential confusion among memories to a minimum. Associative learning in this case means only that a given memory is known to have been established on a certain calendar date.

The matter of general models based on the relationships between learning and forgetting will not be pursued further at this time. Let us recognize that model building in the study of memory is widespread, and we will need to keep before us the fact that we should not become confused between the two domains which are a part of the research enterprise. The empirical world or domain is constituted of the outcome of experiments in which independent variables are manipulated. The second, or theoretical domain, includes many different theoretical approaches, including even such generalized models as described above. Many models are characterized as metaphors. For example, to speak of a memory storage area is clearly a metaphor, and it is not a very good metaphor. When objects are stored in a warehouse, the removal of the objects vacates space. This is not true with the memory store. To recall a memory does not vacate the area where that memory "resided." In fact, in the sense that the recall of a memory strengthens that memory, the storage space required may actually expand.

It is always our intent to bring the theoretical and empirical domain in to some sort of juxtaposition. The data need to land on the model or on the theory, so to speak. The theory must assimilate available laws relating independent and dependent variables as well as suggest new relationships. This is what we say the goal of theory is when we speak of it in the idealistic world; in the real world of the study of memory, such tidiness between fact and theory simply does not prevail.

LEARNING, MEMORY, AND PERFORMANCE

A common procedure in studying the learning and memory for verbal materials is to present the subject a list of unrelated words, each word being presented one at a time. The list is usually presented for several trials, with a test being given after each study trial. Within this simple paradigm, we ask about the influence of certain independent variables on the rate at which the list is memorized, or about the influence of certain variables on the retention of the list after, for example, one week. In any such experiment we record certain performance measures. In a so-called learning experiment such as just described we might record the number of correct responses produced by the subject on each test trial. Changes in the magnitude (increases) of this performance measure are the basis for inferring that certain changes have taken place in the organism. We identify these changes as learning. Others may choose to look at this situation with a slightly different perspective. This perspective would note that the increase in the performance scores over trials can only occur because of increased memory for the items on the list. The performance scores are thus taken as *prima facie* evidence that a memory for the words has been established.

The above matters should not be taken too seriously; let us not become paralyzed by such issues. We may speak of learning trials or acquisition trials at least in a procedural sense, fully recognizing that the consequences of such trials are to produce learning or to establish memories. Both learning and memory are first-order inferences from performance scores. An extreme empirical approach would insist that we should never use the terms such as learning and memory. According to this approach, an experiment only produces performance scores; why, then, should we go beyond this? Most investigators do not find this extreme position valid. At the very least, the use of such terms as learning and memory identifies an area of research. If one is asked what area of research engages his interest, it is quite simple to respond with "verbal learning" or "human memory." It is a little awkward to reply: "Performance scores over a series of trials with verbal material."

A distinction that *is* of some importance is that between the performance scores and the inferential changes in the organism called learning or memory. The reason for this has become quite evident in recent years, although it has antecedents in other areas of research which has always made it a useful distinction. This may be illustrated. A subject is given a series of trials on a motor task followed by a rest period of a few minutes. After the rest period the subject returns to the task. The performance scores will usually show a marked increase over those recorded just prior to the rest interval. Such evidence makes it highly probable that the subject had learned more than he was capable of exhibiting in his performance just preceding the rest interval. We assume that he did not learn during the rest interval, but that the rest interval allowed some process to occur that reduced the discrepancy between what the subject had learned and what he was able to demonstrate in his performance. Indeed, it is generally assumed that both positive and negative processes build up with practice; nature is again seen to be in conflict.

We have already seen that we must accept the possibility that there may be discrepancies between performance scores and what is stored in memory. That we cannot recall a particular name at one moment does not mean we will not be able to at a later moment. It was this type of observation that gave some authenticity to the model that assumes that forgetting never occurs. What we are doing now is accepting the need for the distinction between learning and performance without at the same time assuming that no forgetting occurs.

THE PLAN

In the next two chapters we will describe various tasks which are frequently used in studying verbal learning and memory in the laboratory. Included in these descriptions will be the results of a number of experiments conducted to accompany the task descriptions. Looking at the data from these experiments will introduce us to the types of response measures used, and will give an initial look at some of the phenomena of memory which will engage us in later chapters. When we move to Chapter 4 we will look at conceptual reflections of differences in tasks, by which is meant that different tasks may emphasize different types of information, or as we will speak of this, different attributes of memory.

Chapter 5 evaluates the relationship between study time and learning. There is, of course, a positive relationship between study time and amount learned under most circumstances, but the exceptions are of special interest. We will also examine how the sharpness of the relationship between study time and learning is influenced by the nature of the study.

Chapters 6 and 7 attempt to organize certain phenomena by use of theories. The theories are relatively simple but generally speaking are given considerable support by the data. At the present stage of the development of the research areas there may be justification in maintaining theories at a simple level in spite of the fact that there may be some findings which the theory fails to handle. Too frequently, the attempt to elaborate a theory to account for some discordant results produces a vastly complicated theory that may fall because of its own complexity.

Chapter 8 discusses task variables with particular emphasis on the difficulties of identifying the underlying bases for the effects of the variables. Chapter 9 on transfer and interference then follows, and this leads rather naturally into Chapter 10 which is concerned with forgetting and in which much of the discussion revolves around interference among memories. Finally, Chapter 11 takes a look at basic mechanisms believed to be involved in associative learning and a special case of associative learning, namely, free-recall learning.

2

Tasks: Recognition Memory

The discussion of tasks used in studying verbal learning will be divided into two sections, one dealing with recognition learning and the other with associative learning. In recognition learning the subjects are not required to recall or retrieve or produce words from memory; in most associative learning tasks the production or retrieval is required. Although such a division need not imply anything fundamental about differences in learning processes, in this case it does. As will be seen in due time, we believe the data argue for a basic difference between associative learning and recognition learning.

Before undertaking a description of recognition tasks, some remarks about laboratory tasks in general seem necessary. Tasks are sometimes spoken of as being standard tasks. All this means is that the tasks are used frequently in various experiments. However, that a task is used frequently may mean that it is serving some analytical purpose that other tasks do not serve. There is, perhaps, some value in using a task that others have used also because it does aid in making comparisons of results across laboratories. Generally speaking, therefore, investigators will use a so-called standard task unless they have specific reasons for not doing so. Still, we must remember that a task has certain characteristics that make it different from other tasks and because of these differences, tasks must be thought of as representing an independent variable. Whether differences between tasks influence performance is something for the experimenter to investigate. In discussing various tasks we will sometimes include some of the evidence which has been gathered on such matters.

OLD-NEW RECOGNITION

In recognition learning the subject or observer or learner is asked to learn to identify an event as belonging to one of two classes of events. For many recognition tasks the two classes of events are referred to as an *old* class and as a *new* class. The members of the old class are those given to the subject to learn; the new items are those that are used in testing for recognition learning (in ways to be described shortly) and are seen for the first time by the subjects during the test. The learning in recognition learning, then, acts to discriminate between the two classes of items.

Discrete Study and Test Trials: Forced Choice

The methods used in the forced-choice procedure are easy to understand because they tie in with a technique that we are all familiar with as used in the multiple-choice test to evaluate course performance. In the laboratory the subject is first given a study trial on a list of words. More particularly, let us say the subject was presented with eighty four-letter words, such as *menu, bred, onyx, desk, jail,* and so on, each for two seconds. We could, perhaps, present the eighty words on a sheet of paper in columns and allow 160 seconds to study the list (two seconds per word), but this method of complete presentation is not frequently used. Complete presentation is believed to be less desirable than item-by-item presentation because presenting each item individually is more likely to spread study time equally over all items than is the method of complete presentation. This is a conjecture, however; it does not appear that anyone has studied comparatively the properties of the two methods for recognition.

What do we tell the subjects before presenting the eighty items for study? This depends to some extent upon the purpose of the experiment. At one extreme we might inform them that after the list is presented a memory test will be given, but the nature of the test will not be described until after the study phase. Laboratory lore has it that subjects, given such instructions, usually believe that a recall test will be given. At the other extreme, the instructions may be quite specific. We did in fact test thirty-six subjects on an eighty-item list of four-letter words.* The instructions read before presenting the list for the single study trial were explicit, as follows:

> I am going to show you a rather long list of words, by slides. There will be one word on each slide and each will be shown for two seconds. Your task is to remember as many of the words as possible. After I have shown the list once, I will test your memory. To do this, I will show you a series of pairs of words. In each pair one of the words was on the study list, one was not. You will be asked to identify the word which was on the study list. So, study each word carefully so that you can identify it later.

Immediately after the last word was presented for study, the forced-choice test was given, in this case being a two-alternative forced-choice

---

*All nonreferenced experiments were carried out by the author for inclusion in this book.

test. Each of the old words was paired with a new word (one that was not in the study list) and the subject was asked to circle the old word in each pair. The test might be paced, or it might be unpaced. If paced, each pair is presented for a constant period of time (perhaps three or four seconds) and during this time the subject must make a decision by choosing what he thinks is the old word. If unpaced, the pair are shown in columns on a test booklet and the subjects are allowed essentially unlimited time to complete the test. Regardless of which method is used, the instructions usually inform the subjects that they must make a decision for each pair, guessing if necessary.

It would seem obvious that the positions of the old and new words in the pair should be varied randomly so that the subject will not have any information other than the words per se with which to make his decision. It is also customary to have the order of the pairs differ from the order represented by the old words on the study trial, but we will shortly see that that is not always done. It would be possible, of course, to have a second study and test trial, or even a third, but this is rarely done, primarily because performance reaches a high level very quickly.

A question may be raised about including new words on a recognition test. Why not simply present the old words and ask the subject to indicate which ones were on the study list? It apparently has been presumed that subjects might "catch on" to the fact that only old words are on the test and would therefore mark all of them as old. Wallace (1980) has argued that using only the old words on the test is a perfectly appropriate procedure. Nevertheless, because there are very little data available on recognition performance without the use of new or distractor items, the experiments we will cover in this volume will all use new items on the tests.

The dependent variable or response measure for the forced-choice experiment is the number of errors, or the number of correct responses. We would not know from a simple experiment such as described just how the correct decisions were reached. On the one hand, the subject might have chosen the correct word in a pair because he remembered it as being on the study list. On the other hand, subjects may choose a correct word because they are quite sure that the incorrect word—the new word—had *not* been in the study list. These are matters for theory which we will get to later. For our experiment, the thirty-six subjects obtained an average of 83.1 percent correct responses on the first list they were given. Immediately after the test on the first list we said to the subjects:

> I will now show you another list; the words are different from the first list, but otherwise we will do everything exactly as we did for the first list. Study the list in preparation for a recognition test.

On the second list the mean proportion correct was 81.3 percent.

We will now consider a matter associated with the order of the items on the test relative to the order on the study trial. It was earlier noted that it is common to have the order of the test pairs random with respect to the order of the study words. What this does is make the retention interval short for some items and long for others. These differences occur because we must consider the time involved in taking the test to represent a retention interval; therefore, items tested early will have short retention intervals, those tested late will have long intervals (assuming that randomization on the test trial would result in the mean study position to be about equal for subgroups of items tested at different points in time following the study trial).

There is another approach to handling the relationship between positions of items on the study and test trials. We might make the retention interval constant for all items. This can be done by using the same order on the test as was used on the study trial. Perhaps we do not want the subjects to realize that the order is the same because they might begin to use order as a type of information in making their decisions (see Light & Schurr, 1973). In the present case, we simply reversed the order of the first ten test pairs relative to the study order of the ten old words. Then, the test order of the remaining seventy pairs was exactly the same as the study order of the old words. We believe that with the reversal of the first ten items the subject was not likely to recognize that the study order was the same as the test order for the seventy items. Given the above, the retention interval for all old items would be about the same, providing the time taken for each item on the retention test is about the same as the time given to the study of each item.

Now, given that we have roughly equalized the retention interval for all items, we may ask about changes which occur in performance as the subjects take the test. For present purposes, we examined the number of correct responses in each successive fourth of the test list, each fourth containing twenty pairs. Since the words were assigned randomly to position in the study list, there is no reason to believe that the difficulty of the subsets of twenty items would differ.

The mean percentage correct for each fourth of the test for each list is shown in Figure 2.1. The finding is clear; with each successive section, performance decreases. It is as if there was forgetting, but because we have roughly equalized the retention interval, we are not dealing with differences in forgetting. In fact, however, the interpretation is not unambiguous. Other investigators have noted similar decrements, and Schulman (1974a) in particular has systematically examined various experiments for the decrements. Such losses do not always occur, but the critical differences between studies that show the decrement and those that do not is unknown. The loss, when it occurs, might be due to something happening during the testing or it might be due to the fact that during the study trial the level of learning decreases across items. Just what is involved is not a point at issue for the moment. What we must recognize is that the amount of the decrement may differ as a function of certain independent variables.

Figure 2.1.

Percent correct recognition on forced-choice tests as a function of stage of testing (fourths of list). The subjects were given two unrelated lists in immediate succession.

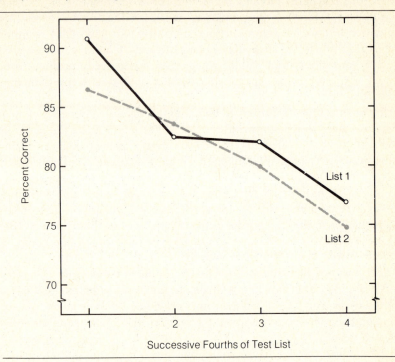

Thus, to fully represent the data from a recognition experiment we should indicate whether or not differences produced by an independent variable resulted in differential losses associated with testing. Or, to say this another way, we need to report whether there was an interaction between stage of testing and our independent variable.

Discrete Study and Test Trials: YES-NO Tests

In the YES-NO recognition test the subjects are given a series of single words (assuming the study list contained single words) of which there are two classes, old and new. The instructions request the subjects to make either a YES decision (the word was in the study list) or a NO decision (the word was not in the study list), and if in doubt, to guess. In the usual experiment the number of old and new words will be equivalent, although as we will see, the proportion of old to new words on the test as a whole may have some influence on the subjects' decisions.

It seems obvious that when using either the forced choice or the YES-NO test, the relationship between the old and new items will be a very prominent variable. Indeed, as will be discussed at length in a subsequent chapter, some tests of recognition theories are made by manipulating the relationships between the old and new words. If this variable is not being manipulated in an experiment, the old and new items are normally chosen randomly from a given pool of words. In addition to such randomization (or in lieu of), the experimenter may interchange old and new items across two subgroups of subjects.

Two different types of errors may be made by subjects on the YES-NO test. First, they may call an old item "new," and secondly, they may call a new item "old." To call an old item new is a *miss*; to call a new item old is commonly referred to as a *false alarm*. Given these two types of errors, how is a single score for a subject to be derived? To answer this question requires a bit of a diversion to discuss what is called signal-detection theory, a theory not originally concerned with recognition memory but which has been applied directly by a number of investigators.

The theory recognized that two factors are involved in making a recognition decision in the YES-NO test. There is first whatever it is that allows a subject to discriminate a difference in familiarity (or newness, or oldness, or strength) of the old and new items. This sensitivity or discriminability is symbolized as d' in signal detection measures. The second factor is a little more difficult to understand. Assume that in a YES-NO study two subjects make the following errors:

	Misses	False Alarms
Subject 1	2	10
Subject 2	10	2

Both subjects make the same number of errors (twelve) but they certainly differ in the nature of the errors made. To understand this difference in the nature of errors, let us examine the extreme cases. Suppose a subject responded YES to all items on a YES-NO test. This would produce false alarms for all new items but would also produce perfect performance on all old items. On the other hand, if a subject said NO to all items, there would be no false alarms but all old items would be missed. The data for the two subjects above have these same tendencies but not to such extremes. The first subject seems to require less evidence of oldness to call an item old than does the second subject. Or, it might be said that the second subject is more conservative than the first subject in that the evidence for oldness must be strong before a YES response is given. As a consequence, the second subject has many misses, but few false alarms.

This second factor recognizes that subjects may have differences in the criterion they set for calling an item old, even though they have equal discrimination ability (d'). This implies that if we could derive an index to measure the criterion differences among subjects, the index would not correlate with d'. The signal detection approach in its full regalia uses rather complex procedures to calculate d' and a measure of criterion differences (commonly called *beta* differences). The full story can be found in Green and Swets (1966).

For present purposes, we will simply note that for the usual recognition experiment our response measures can be more direct than those implied by signal detection. It has been shown by a number of investigators that the correlation between measures of d' and the simple sum of the misses and false alarms for a group of subjects is very high. Further, several simple measures of *beta* can be obtained. Perhaps the simplest of all is the percentage that the total of the false alarms of a subject is of the total of the misses plus the false alarms, or for this poor-man's *beta*, false alarms/ misses plus false alarms $\times$ 100. The greater the proportion of false alarms to the total errors, the lower the criterion of the subject.

One further matter about response measures needs to be considered at this point. It can be seen that criterion differences cannot influence performance on the forced-choice test. In the forced-choice test, the subject makes a choice as to which alternative is older; by the nature of the test there is no way to establish an absolute criterion of oldness and then let that criterion determine the response as in the YES-NO test. This seems to suggest that if a recognition experiment is to be done in which a *beta* difference across conditions would adversely affect the outcome, or in which the investigator is simply not interested in *beta*, the forced-choice procedure is to be recommended.

Another procedure is sometimes used to eliminate *beta* differences. In the usual YES-NO test we ask the subjects to make a decision on every item, guessing if necessary. As a substitute procedure we might ask the subject to identify a certain number of the words as being old. Thus, given fifty old and fifty new items on the test, the subjects might be asked to identify forty of the one hundred items as being old. This avoids a criterion problem, but there is a drawback in that if there are a large number of items on the test, the subject must spend a considerable amount of time counting the number of items checked. And what do we do if in fact only thirty-eight are checked?

An Illustration. For this illustrative study, sentences were used. The sentences came from a number of different sources and varied considerably in the degree of abstractness. A total of 144 sentences was used of which every tenth one is shown in Table 2.1. Seventy-two of the sentences were chosen randomly as study sentences with the remaining seventy-two used as new items on the test. The sentences were presented aurally (on tape) for study at a ten-second rate. The subjects were fully informed from the beginning as to what was expected of them. They knew that there would be seventy-two sentences in the study phase and that these seventy-two old sentences would be mixed with seventy-two new sentences on the test. At the end of the study phase there was a slight pause as the test instructions were repeated, and then the 144 test sentences were presented

Table 2.1. A Sample of the Sentences Used in the YES-NO Recognition Study

The auction of the period furniture produced a substantial sum of money.
It is imperative that we keep the system as streamlined as possible.
Taxes on income from horse racing did not cancel the deficit.
Guns began spraying everything in sight including a squadron of fighters.
Mere age has ceased to be an indispensable condition of leadership.
The subcommittee was given a week to report back to the full committee.
He wondered how he would cope with the refugees when the trickle became a flood.
His philosophy is so constructed as to insure the ultimate reality of the individual.
A man who cannot control himself will never control others.
An exchange of managers might be in the best interest of both organizations.
It is likely that the fire started when a small can of gas exploded.
It consists of a central plateau and a high mountain fringe on the north.
The hero of the play is a young man who has settled on being an inventor.
Military engineers are charged with facilitating the movement of friendly troops.
Lengthy classes are sometimes interrupted for short meditation breaks.

at a ten-second rate with the subjects required to make a decision for each sentence, guessing if necessary. The subjects were tested in groups. The decisions on the test were recorded by the subjects on a test sheet having the numbers 1 through 144 listed in columns with each number followed by YES and NO. The subjects circled the appropriate word. A total of forty subjects was tested.

As an independent variable, differences in the length of the retention interval were introduced. The first thirty-six sentences presented for study were said to be in the first half of the study phase; eighteen of these were tested in the first half of the test phase and eighteen were tested in the second half of the test phase. In the test phase, of course, the seventy-two new sentences were mixed with the seventy-two old ones. Each of the four retention intervals can be indentified by two numbers, with the first number indicating where the sentences were studied (first half or second half) and the second number indicating the test locus (first half or second half). Thus, Condition 1-2 represents the eighteen sentences studied in the first half and tested in the second half. The average retention intervals for the sentences in each condition were as follows: Condition 2-1, nine minutes; Condition 1-1, fifteen minutes; Condition 2-2, twenty-one minutes, and Condition 1-2, twenty-seven minutes.

The average subject had 18.33 misses and made 10.68 false alarms. We have earlier spoken of the fact that subjects may differ in the criterion they set for responding; some subjects are conservative, some "radical." Figure 2.2 illustrates this for two subjects, Numbers 27 and 28, both of whom had a total of twenty errors. However, subject Number 28 had only 10 percent false alarms and 90 percent misses, while Number 27 had 75 percent false alarms and 25 percent misses. These two subjects are said to have about equal sensitivity or discriminability, but they certainly differed in the way

Figure 2.2.

Differences in the frequencies of misses and false alarms for two subjects (No. 27 and No. 28) whose total errors were equivalent. The experiment used sentences as the memory unit and a YES-NO test of recognition.

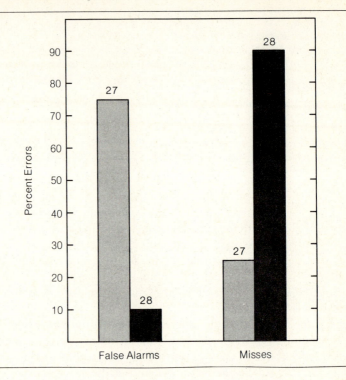

the errors were distributed—they differed on the criterion set or established to differentiate between YES and NO items.

As a next step we will look at the consequences of studying items in different sections and testing them in different sections. Figure 2.3 gives the data which result from combining the misses and false alarms for all forty subjects. As can be seen, the sentences tested in the first half were better recognized than those tested in the second half (2-1 and 1-1 are better than 2-2 and 1-2). But there is also another factor involved; sentences studied in the first half were better recognized than those studied in the second half.

The data are examined in a different way in Figure 2.4, where successively longer retention intervals are plotted along the baseline and the misses and false alarms are shown separately. We see that the false alarms and misses rise and fall in concert. A little thought will indicate that we were not prepared for this finding because the thinking about criterion differences would lead to the expectation that the gross correlation present in Figure 2.4 should not be present. Rather, misses and false

Figure 2.3.
Recognition errors as a function of position of sentence in the study list and in the test list.

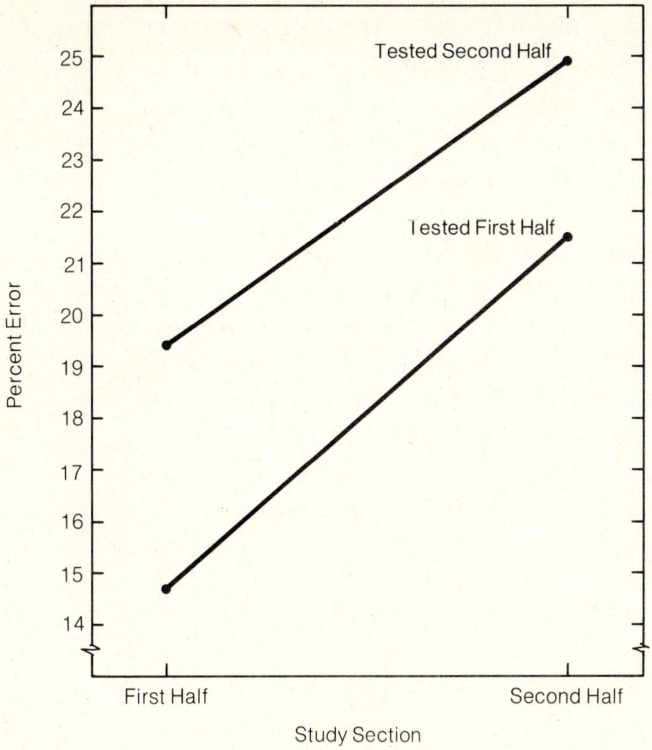

Figure shows plot with "Percent Error" on y-axis (ranging 14 to 25), "Study Section" on x-axis (First Half, Second Half). Two lines labeled "Tested Second Half" and "Tested First Half".

alarms might be negatively correlated. The data for the two subjects plotted in Figure 2.2 show this reciprocal relationship between misses and false alarms, but apparently these two subjects do not represent all forty subjects very well. The correlation between the number of false alarms and the number of misses across the forty subjects was .31, a low positive relationship. What then is going on? There are several factors that must be considered.

If a subject is making a number of misses because he actually cannot remember old sentences, it is likely also that he will have a number of false alarms; if the old sentence is weak in the memory, any sentence may seem correct. This would tend to produce the yoking seen in Figure 2.4.

There is a phenomenon called *probability matching*. Suppose you are presented a green light and a red light and you are asked to indicate on each of a great many trials which of the two lights will be lit. The experimenter will have programmed the lights to come on equally often in a random manner. What happens is that you, as the subject, will come to guess that the lights will be lit equally often. If the lights are programmed

Figure 2.4.
Misses and false alarms in recognition memory for sentences as related to the length of the retention interval.

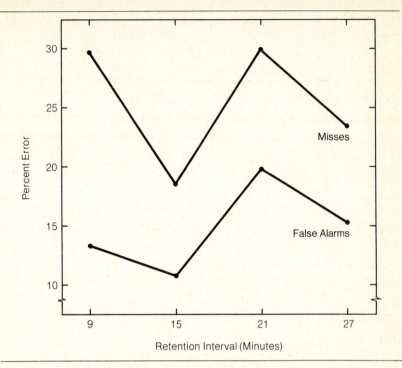

for 75 percent red and 25 percent green, your guesses as a subject will come to approximate those values. This phenomenon is called probability matching.

The subjects in the sentence experiment knew that old and new items were to occur equally often on the test. Further, they had their recording sheets before them so that the proportion of YES and NO responses they had recorded could be roughly estimated. Given these conditions, the subjects may have tended toward probability matching when they were quite unsure of a given item. Thus, if NO had been circled for several items in a row, and if on the next item the subject was quite unsure, YES would probably be circled. It appears that more than sensitivity and criterion differences may enter into recognition decisions of the YES-NO type.

Both Figures 2.3 and 2.4 show forgetting, but the forgetting is not a simple relationship between time and performance. The amount of forgetting is counteracted by a positive factor. This positive factor is related to the study section. Sentences studied in the first half are better remembered than those studied in the second half. This is the same finding reported earlier for the forced-choice test for single words. Perhaps the simplest interpretation is that the sentences occurring in the first half are learned better than those studied in the second half. Why should there be differences in the level of learning? Perhaps attention or effort are stronger in the first half than in the second. Perhaps there is some interference from sentences presented in the first half on the learning of those presented in the second half. This experiment is not analytical with respect to such matters. But, the data seem to show that the apparent simplicity of the method is not always matched by a simplicity of the results.

Running Recognition

This task, developed by Shepard and Teghtsoonian (1961), does not have discrete study and test trials. Rather, the subjects are continually studying items on which they may be tested later, and they are also being tested on items which they may or may not have studied earlier. The instructions to the subjects simply indicate that a long series of items will be shown and as each item is presented they are to decide whether the item had (YES) or had not (NO) been presented earlier in the list. Within the list, of course, are items which occur twice. As is true with the YES-NO procedure used with discrete study and test phases, both misses and false alarms may occur as errors, hence the earlier discussion of the response measures for the YES-NO technique is applicable.

An Illustration. The materials used in this illustrative study were two-word phrases, such as *soil-erosion, ancient-history, vice-squad,* and *public-opinion.* A total of 216 such phrases was used. Of these, 144 occurred twice and 72 occurred once. The details of the list construction will not be described. It is sufficient to indicate the critical matters. In the initial part of the list, repeated items were used with increasing frequency so that between positions 90 and 108 the number of new phrases and old (repeated) phrases became equal. Furthermore, this 50:50 split between old and new was maintained throughout the remainder of the list. A total of 360 positions was required to present all phrases.

An obvious variable in running recognition is the time between the two occurrences of an item. This time is usually expressed as *lag,* which is the number of items which fall between the two occurrences. In the present experiment, lag varied between 7 and 310.

The list was presented by audio tape at a five-second rate so that thirty minutes were required. The subjects used a four-page booklet in which the numbers 1 through 370 occurred, with the words YES and NO after each number. The subjects circled YES if they judged the phrase presented to represent a second occurrence (an old item) and circled NO if they judged it to be a new item. A total of forty-four subjects was tested.

The subjects reported rather universally that they felt confidence in their decisions; this is to say that they felt the task to be an easy one and that they made few errors. The results do not give strong support to these feelings. Of the 144 repeated items, the average subject made errors (said

NO) to the second occurrence of 23.11 of them (16 percent). These are called misses, of course. There were 216 phrases on which the subjects could make a false alarm by saying YES to the first occurrence of an item. The average subject made 9.5 false alarms (4.4 percent).

We may ask about changes which may have occurred throughout the thirty minutes of testing. To determine this, the 216 first occurrences of the phrases were divided into six successive groupings of thirty-six phrases each. For each grouping the mean number of false alarms was calculated. These values are plotted in Figure 2.5 and although they suffer somewhat from the lack of aesthetic appeal, it is patent that the false alarms increased across the test period. That the number should increase seems quite reasonable; the greater the number of phrases presented, the greater the likelihood that a phrase presented in the past will be sufficiently similar to the one being presented at the moment to produce a YES. There are competing hypotheses, of course. For example, it is possible that the subjects' criterion for responding YES became looser (lower) as testing proceeded. There is no way to tell from the present data which of these two hypotheses (or others) best account for the changes with testing.

To examine the influence of lag on misses we will turn to items as the unit of analysis rather than subjects. The 144 items occurring twice were placed in five lag groupings, the mean lags for the groups being 28, 74, 121, 172, and 253, with the number of items in each group being 21, 32, 47, 25, and 19. For each group the mean numbers of errors were determined, and these are shown in Figure 2.6. The mean misses increased sharply as lag increased between 28 and 74, but increased very slowly beyond that. What causes the change? Again, there is no easy answer. Lag increases inherently have two components which increase together: time and number of items. To establish the underlying basis for the losses shown in Figure 2.6 would require initially that we manipulate lag without confounding time and number of items.

ARBITRARY EVENT CLASSES

Verbal-Discrimination Learning

In the tasks discussed thus far, the items were divided into two event classes based on age (so to speak). Items that had been presented for study (or presented earlier in running recognition) formed one class, those that had not been presented for study formed a second event class. We will now consider recognition learning when the two event classes are quite arbitrarily designated. The most frequently used task of this nature is the verbal-discrimination task. Subjects are presented successive pairs of words. For each pair the experimenter has arbitrarily designated one as the correct word, the other as the incorrect one. Thus, the two event classes are *correct* and *incorrect*, and one word from each pair fits into each class.

Figure 2-5.
False alarms in YES-NO running recognition of two-word phrases as a function of stage of testing.

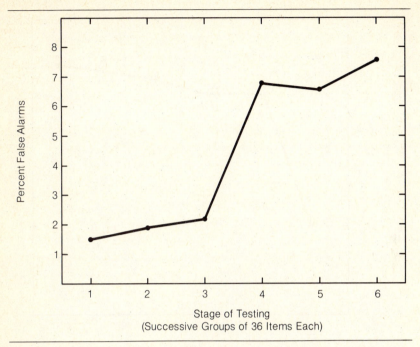

Obviously, the immediate question is how the experimenter tells the subject about these two classes. How does the experimenter tell the subject as to which class each item belongs? Two methods have been commonly used, the study-test method and the anticipation method.

In the study-test method there are alternate study and test trials. On the study trial the pairs are presented successively with the correct word in each pair underlined. The subjects are informed, of course, that the underlined words are the correct words. On the test trials, the pairs are presented without the underlining and the subject is to inform the experimenter which word in each pair had been underlined on the study trial. The timing is a rather arbitrary matter, of course, but a common plan is to present each pair for two seconds on the study trial, and also allow two seconds for the subject to make his choice for each pair on the test trial. Subjects may be instructed to make a choice for each pair, guessing if necessary. The order for presenting the pairs on the test trial differs from that used on the study trial, and if several study test trials are used, the order constantly changes across the trials. The left-right positions of the paired items also change randomly from trial to trial to prevent the subject from learning that the correct word always occupies a given position.

It should be persistently recognized that there is nothing magical about methods. We need not be bound by what others have done. For example,

Figure 2.6.
The effect of the "distance" (lag) between the two occurrences of items on the number of misses in the recognition memory for two-word phrases.

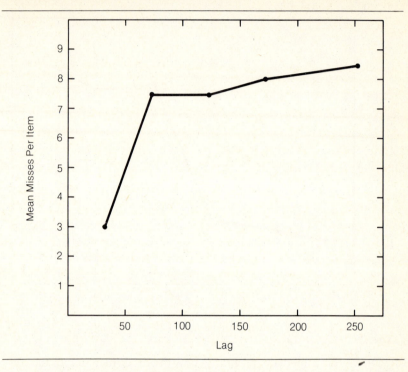

the study phase of the study-test method might be given by complete presentation. Or, the test might be unpaced rather than paced. This is not to imply that the different methods will give the same results, but it does imply that different ways of presenting materials for a learning experiment simply represent a class of variables, and, like all variables, their influence may be assessed empirically, perhaps with the help of a pointed theory.

The response measure for verbal discrimination is perhaps obvious. If the subjects are asked to respond to all items, the number of correct responses and number of incorrect responses are complementary. Also, as is true with the tasks used to study forced-choice recognition with two alternatives, the chance level of responding is 50 percent so that to demonstrate learning the subject must get more than 50 percent correct. We recently gave twenty-eight subjects forty pairs of four-letter words to study, each pair presented for two seconds on the study trial, with one word in each pair underlined. This was followed by an unpaced test in which the forty pairs were listed on a single sheet and the subjects were asked to underline the word in each pair which had been underlined on the study trial. Of the twenty-eight subjects, the best score of any subject involved thirty-nine correct responses. Two subjects scored at a chance level, getting twenty and twenty-one correct responses, but for the twenty-eight subjects as a whole, the mean number of correct responses was 31.82 (79.6 percent). The subjects were given a second list immediately after the first, and the mean number correct was 33.29 (85.3 percent). Only one subject scored at a chance level, and there were six subjects who attained perfect scores. The correlation between the scores on the two lists for the twenty-eight subjects was .60.

The second method of presenting verbal-discrimination lists, the anticipation method, is a little more complicated than the study-test method. Studying and testing occur simultaneously. The subject is shown a pair of items, for perhaps two seconds, and then the correct word in the pair is shown alone for two seconds. In this way the subject is informed as to the correct response for that pair. Then, another pair is presented, followed by the correct word alone, and so on down through the list of pairs. The trial as just described is really only a study trial. It is not until the second trial that the subjects can knowingly respond, and they do this by trying to anticipate the correct word in each pair. When a pair is presented on the second trial, the subjects have two seconds to choose the correct word from the pair and say it aloud to the experimenter before the pair is replaced by the correct response alone. The subject always gets feedback of the correct response immediately after the anticipation interval. Immediately after the feedback interval for one pair is over, another pair is presented and so on. Again, order of the pairs changes across trials as well as the left-right position of the items in a pair. It was noted that the first trial is really only a study trial. However, some investigators request the subject to respond to the pairs on the first trial by guessing, just as if they had already studied the pairs. The performance should be at a chance level if the guessing occurs.

These two methods of presenting the verbal-discrimination task produce differences in the rate of learning the lists, at least for longer lists (Underwood, Shaughnessy, & Zimmerman, 1972b) with the study-test method producing the more rapid learning.

Two-Category Classification Task

This task has not been used frequently, but perhaps it should be. In many respects it is like the verbal-discrimination task but at the present time it is by no means clear that the two tasks involve the same basic learning processes. Indeed, the two-category task might be classed as an associative task. In conforming to a two-category task, items are presented singly. Each item is identified as belonging to one of the two arbitrary event classes. Thus, half the items might be underlined, half not, this being determined randomly. After a study trial, the items are presented for a test trial in which the underlining is removed, and the subjects must identify which items had been underlined on the study trial, which had not. Any means of identifying the two classes other than underlining would be quite satisfactory, and there could be more than two classes of events. If more than one study-test sequence is given, the order of the items should be changed from trial to trial.

The use of arbitrary event classes to form either verbal-discrimination lists or two-category classification lists may be easily related to studies involving concept recognition. For example, if all of the underlined words in the two-category list were animal names, and all others were bird names, it seems quite likely that the subject would use these well-known concepts rather than the underlining to make his decisions on the test. That is, the subjects would use the concept information if they had noted the perfect correlation between the underlining and animal names. In the same vein, if all correct items in a verbal-discrimination task were printed in red ink, and all incorrect items in black ink, it seems beyond doubt that the two event classes would quickly become red ink and black ink rather than underlined and nonunderlined. Learning either task requires a form of disjunctive concept learning in which there is no initial similarity among the items in the same class. They become similar in a sense as learning proceeds because all those belonging to the class have the same function.

MINIATURE TASKS

Investigators will always develop new tasks if they find that those available do not meet their demands for the study of psychological processes. About 1960 there was a clear move toward the development of tasks which were felt to be more appropriate for studying short-term memory than were the available tasks. We must come to some understanding about short-term memory when it is contrasted with long-term memory. As a beginning, two different lines of thought may be identified which contrast short- and long-term memory.

The first line of thought looks at procedural differences only. In the tasks we have discussed thus far, the number of items or units making up a list was "large." By this is meant that the numbers of items in the lists were perhaps ten or more, and in many cases there have been scores of items. The tasks which are said to deal with short-term memory are essentially miniaturized versions of the long tasks. This is not precisely true, but it is close enough to the truth to be useful in describing the miniaturized tasks as counterparts of the long lists. In short-term memory tasks the number of items is small, sometimes consisting of only a single letter, but usually no more than five or six items.

Two other differences are sometimes noted between the tasks used to study long-term memory and those used to study short-term memory, but they have less generality than does the difference in terms of number of items. One of these is that long-term memory tasks frequently involve multiple trials whereas the tasks for short-term memory involve a single study trial. However, as we have already seen, some long-term recognition tasks may involve a single study-test trial just like short-term memory tasks. A third difference is that if forgetting is being studied, the length of the retention interval is shorter for the short-term memory task than for the long-term memory task. The retention interval may be measured in seconds for the short-term task, in minutes and hours and days for long-term memory tasks.

The second line of thought ignores procedural differences entirely, and appeals to allegedly more fundamental factors to maintain a distinction between short- and long-term memory. Thus, some believe the short-term system has some functional properties that are quite different from the properties of the long-term system. Most importantly, the short-term system is said to have a sharp limit on capacity and that there is no permanent storage in the system. There is still another conception which might be called working memory. Working memory refers to the memories being used at the moment. No critical or fundamental distinction is made between long-term and short-term memories. Working memory will usually consist in part of information that enters the system from the outside at the moment (short-term memory) and in part of information that has already been acquired and is merely retrieved for use at the time (long-term memory).

We need not take positions on these matters for the time being. It is sufficient to comprehend that, for whatever reason, tasks have been developed which are miniaturized versions of the tasks we have already discussed, and that some investigators speak of these versions as dealing with short-term memory. Actually, most of the miniaturization has occurred with recall tasks and will be described later. However, two tasks will be identified as representing miniature tasks for recognition.

Probe Technique

The subjects are presented a short list of items, and immediately after the last item is shown, a probe item is displayed. The subject must decide whether the item was or was not in the study list. Thus, only a single item is tested from each study list, although the subjects may be given a rather large number of short lists. It might seem wasteful to test only one item from a list. However, for analytical purposes it may be desirable to test only the one item. There is some belief that interference may occur if successive items are tested, but that the first items tested will escape the interference. Why would anyone want to use this task? The answer of course depends upon what theories might be tendered and what independent variables are manipulated as a consequence of the theory. Certain independent variables are obvious, such as the length of the retention interval, the similarity between an old probe and a new probe, the number of items in the list, and so on.

A modification of the probe technique has been used by a number of investigators, but probably most successfully by Sternberg (1969) as he set about to try to understand how a subject makes his decision as to whether the item had or had not been in the study list. He set up a situation so that the subject only rarely made an error to the probe. The primary dependent variable therefore became the latency or reaction time in responding to the probe. Suppose that there were three items in the list, and that each item was presented for a one-second study period before the probe occurred. Suppose further that the reaction times to the probe increased directly as the position of the item increased; i.e., the reaction time to the first word is shortest, that of the third word the longest. One interpretation of this result is that the subject, when presented the probe, makes a serial scan of his memory for the three items in succession. If this is true, it seems reasonable that the reaction time to each successive word would be longer and longer. It can also be seen that if the subject does scan his memory in the order indicated, a probe which was not in the list (a new item) would produce a longer reaction time than would any probe from the list. This is to be expected because the subject would be assumed to make a serial scan of the items in memory as a means of determining whether the probe was old or new. If it is not identified as old by the scan, then it surely must be new.

An Illustration. In this illustrative experiment, the subjects were presented five items aurally in fairly rapid sequence. Then an item appeared and the subject was required to make a YES-NO decision, YES meaning that the item was in the list of five items, NO meaning that it was not. Each item within the short list consisted of a number and a letter, the numbers always being 1, 2, 3, 4, or 5, and the letters always being B, F, H, K, or L. The subjects were tested on 120 lists and the items in each list always consisted of number-letter pairs made up of the numbers and letters as indicated just above. The letters were always in a random order, but the order of the numbers constituted one of the independent variables of the experiment. For half the lists the numbers were in order 1 through 5, and for the other half, they were ordered randomly. Thus there were sixty sequential lists, e.g., 1L, 2H, 3F, 4K, and 5B, and there were sixty random-number lists, e.g., 5F, 3B, 2H, 1L, and 4K. On the tests, a YES probe consisted of one of the five number-letter pairs which was in the list presented, and a NO probe consisted of a number and letter from the list but which were not paired in the list.

The idea behind the study is that position of the item gets associated with the item and represents a part of the memory for the list. When the numbers are in sequential order, the numbers are in some sense redundant although they may serve as well-learned cues for the five positions. When the numbers are in random order, the numbers and positions are not coordinated and interference in the memory for position may occur. Given this line of reasoning, it is necessary to predict that performance will be better when the numbers are in sequential order than when they are in random order. One may wonder why the subjects encode position as a part of the memory. The answer is not known but apparently the subject has difficulty *not* encoding the positions at least for the initial items in the list.

As noted earlier, the subjects received 120, five-item lists. The letters were in 120 orders as determined by random numbers. For sixty of the lists the numbers were also in random order, whereas for the other sixty, the numbers were in sequence. Of the sixty items, thirty were tested by a YES probe, and thirty were tested by a NO probe. The probes for the thirty YES tests came equally often (six times) from each position. The lists and probes were presented aurally by tape, with the items being presented at a two-second rate and with the probe presented two seconds after the fifth item. The subjects were then allowed six seconds to make a decision (circling YES or NO on the data sheet), and two seconds later the signal was given to be ready for the next list. Several practice trials were given prior to initiating the experimental lists. There were twenty-one subjects in the experiment which had a complete within-subject design, i.e., each subject was tested under all conditions. The random-sequential variable was balanced across blocks of trials so that the subjects always knew whether the list was to have the numbers in sequence or in random order.

We will look first at the results for the sixty YES items, asking what percentage of the times the subjects failed to say YES and hence were in error (miss). To review, thirty of the lists involved sequential numbers, thirty random, each position within each being tested six times. The results are seen in Figure 2.7. Performance was poorer when the numbers were in random sequence than when they were in the sequence 1 through 5. Position per se had a very distinct effect, with items at the end of the list having the fewest errors when probed, and those in the middle of the list having the greatest number of errors when probed. The data suggest that the largest difference between sequential and random lists occurred on the initial position and the smallest difference on the last position. However, the statistical interaction between position and type of number sequence was far from being reliable. This means that we probably should view the differences between random and sequential ordering as being constant across positions.

There were sixty probes for which the correct answer was NO. When the numbers were sequential, the percentage of errors (false alarms) was 8.7, and when random, 21.0. This indicates in another way the fact that the memory for the items was simply not as crisp when the random sequences of numbers were used as when the numbers were in sequence.

Figure 2.7.

Errors (misses) in a probe recognition task where there were five items in each list. Each item always consisted of a letter (B, F, H, K, or L) and a number (1, 2, 3, 4, or 5). For half the lists the numbers and letters within a list were paired randomly; for the other half the numbers were always in sequence, with the letters being random.

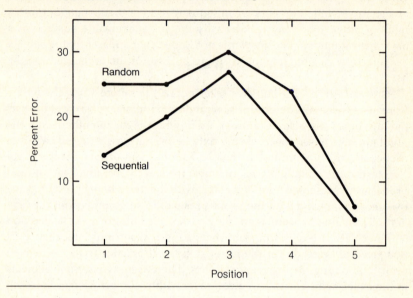

String Matching

Memory span procedures have been primarily associated with recall (see later). The subject is given a series of items, such as digits or letters, and is asked to repeat the string immediately in exactly the same order. The average college student can correctly reproduce a string of seven to eight numbers (the memory span), but performance deteriorates quickly as the number of digits increases beyond this level. In string matching, the subject hears or sees two series of items in immediate succession and is asked to decide whether the two series were or were not identical. To be judged identical the two strings must contain exactly the same items in exactly the same order. An experiment using string matching could be set up so that both the items and the order of them differ for the two strings, or where the items in the two strings are the same but the order differs. Although very little work has been done using string matching, it has good potential for examining a number of problems. An illustrative study was conducted.

An Illustration. The subjects heard two successive ten-digit strings, both strings using all of the numbers from zero through nine once. The subjects had been told that both strings would have the ten digits and that they were to judge whether the two strings had the same or different orders of the digits. The independent variable concerned the nature of the differ-ence when the two strings were in fact different. The second string was altered by interchanging two of the numbers in the first string, with all other numbers maintaining the same positions in both strings. The two interchanged numbers were separated by 0, 1, 2, 3, or 4 other numbers. This variable may be called lag, referring to the number of other numbers which separate the two critical numbers, critical in this case meaning the two interchanged numbers. The lags are illustrated in Table 2.2, with the arrows indicating the numbers that are interchanged.

There were twelve sets of strings for each lag, where a set consists of the two strings about which the subject makes a judgment. The order of the numbers in the first string in a set was random, and the particular strings used at each lag were assigned at random. It seemed necessary to include also sets in which both strings were identical. We used thirty-six such control sets. The control and experimental sets were randomized within blocks of eight sets, each block having each of the five lags, and three being control sets. A given subject was presented all sets so that the design was a complete within-subject design.

All of the strings were presented aurally by tape. Each string required 4 seconds to read. The end of the first string in a set was signalled by a bell-like "cling." The second string began immediately after the signal for the end of the first string, and its end was signalled by "cling, cling." At this point the subject had five seconds to make his decision by circling "Same" or "Different" on a prepared data sheet. At the end of the five-sec-ond period, the word "ready" was heard and the first string of the next set was read. A total of twenty-three subjects completed the experiment.

The influence of the independent variable may be seen in Figure 2.8. As a response measure, the mean number of correct decisions for the exper-imental sets was used. The results were quite unambiguous; as lag in-creased, the number of correct responses increased. Chance performance would be six correct. It can be seen that with a lag of zero, performance is

Table 2.2. Illustration of the Lag Variable Used in the String-Matching Experiment

	First String									
	9	1	4	3	5	2	7	0	8	6
					Second Strings					
Lag 0	9	1	4	3	2	5	7	0	8	6
Lag 1	9	1	4	3	7	2	5	0	8	6
Lag 2	9	1	4	7	5	2	3	0	8	6
Lag 3	9	1	4	0	5	2	7	3	8	6
Lag 4	9	1	0	3	5	2	7	4	8	6

Figure 2.8.

The effect of lag (distance between two interchanged numbers in ten-digit strings) on recognition memory for order of the numbers. The subjects heard two successive strings and had to judge whether they were the same or different. When the second string differed from the first it was by an interchange of two numbers.

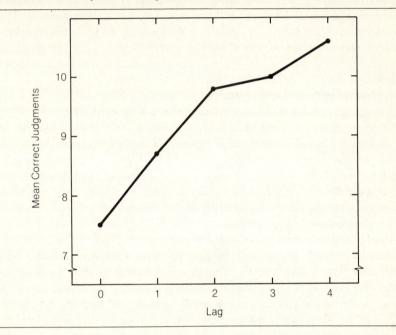

above chance, and at the highest level of performance (lag 4), the mean number correct was equivalent to 88.4 percent. The mean number correct for the control sets was twenty-three out of thirty-six, or 63.9 percent.

These two types of tasks (probe and string matching) which have been discussed here as representing short-term memory tasks using recognition procedures must be viewed as illustrative only. There is almost no end to the variations that might be introduced for a given task. For example, in the probe recognition task, in which each of the five items in the list consisted of a number and a letter, associative learning was required. The subject had to learn that 3 and H went together, 1 and G went together, and so on. In the Sternberg task, an item is made up of a single unit and the associative learning is less obvious. The lesson to be learned, as we have said before, is that there are many, many potential variations that may be made on a modal task to fit the demands of a particular experiment.

SELECTION OF MATERIALS

To one who has never conducted an experiment in verbal learning, there are undoubtedly many questions that may arise in preparing materials for the first experiment. How long should the list be? Where does one get words? Should the words be easy or difficult? Should the words be common words, or relatively uncommon? In reply to such questions, it is first important to realize that there are many, many arbitrary decisions made in selecting materials. One might use the lists brought together by another investigator. Or, one might arbitrarily decide to use five-letter concrete nouns. A second point has somewhat more substance to it. It has long been realized that because our subjects have such an extensive verbal repertoire, there will be interactions (in a psychological sense) between the verbal materials used in an experiment and the verbal knowledge possessed by the subject. New learning takes place "on top of" old learning. Because of this, many studies have been done to scale words on various characteristics (e.g., affectivity, synonymity, concreteness) and in determining the associative interrelationships among words, usually through the use of word-association tests. We will make no attempt to go over this rather extensive literature, although as we report various experiments where choice of material is crucial, we will most certainly get involved in sources of materials. However, a very excellent summary of the extensive literature is available (Brown, 1976). Brown reports the essentials of 172 studies in which verbal materials have been classified along either objective or subjective dimensions. If one wants a particular type of words, it is highly probable that someone has brought together a group of words of this type and has scaled them along at least one dimension.

SUMMARY

The purpose of this chapter was to describe some of the major tasks that are used to study recognition memory by experimental procedures. For most of the tasks, illustrative experiments were reported as a means of examining the response measures used, the methods for analyzing the data, and a "feel" for the type of results to be expected from recognition-memory experiments. The following tasks were described and most were illustrated by experiments.

I. Old-New Recognition
   A. Discrete study and test trials
      1. Forced choice
      2. YES-NO
   B. Running recognition
II. Arbitrary event classes
   A. Verbal-discrimination learning
   B. Two-category classification tasks
III. Miniature Recognition Tasks
   A. Probe tasks
   B. String matching

3

Tasks: Recall Learning

By recall learning is meant only that the nature of the task requires that the subjects produce, retrieve, or recall items. This contrasts with the tasks described in the previous chapter where the subjects had only to recognize the items as belonging or not belonging to certain event classes. Four different tasks will be described as representing recall learning and this will be followed by examining some of the miniaturized versions.

FREE-RECALL LEARNING

The free-recall task is an extremely simple one, procedurally. The subjects are given a list of words for study under instructions that they will be asked to recall the words in any order they choose. These are all the instructions needed for single-trial free recall. If multiple trials are given, the order of presenting the items on study trials will differ from trial to trial, although the subjects always write or speak the words in any order they wish on recall.

Rates of presentation on free-recall study trials are generally no more than a few seconds per item. Sometimes complete presentation of the list is used, so that a given amount of time is allowed to study all the items in any way the subjects choose. Recall may be paced or unpaced, although it is most common to use unpaced tests. On a paced test the subjects are presented a neutral cue over and over at a given rate, and each time it is presented they try to recall a word not recalled earlier. For example, an asterisk might be the neutral cue that is shown every three seconds with the subjects instructed to recall a new word each time the asterisk appears. The asterisk occurs as many times as there are items in the list.

For the unpaced test the subjects are usually allowed a given amount of time, such as 90 seconds or 180 seconds, to recall as many items as possible. Of course, the longer the list the longer the time allowed to recall. Sometimes no particular time is set; the experimenter simply tries to get the subject to recall all items possible, and when it seems that no more are going to be recalled, the attempts are stopped. The act of free recall has certain characteristics that are fairly common across subjects. When the signal for recall is given the subjects write or speak the words from the list as fast as they can as if they believe that if they do not emit them at once they will be forgotten. So, one sees a rapid spewing of the words followed by a gradual increase in the time between successive responses until the subject apparently decides that no more can be recalled.

Single-trial free recall produces some distinguishing characteristics between recall probabilities and the position held by the item in the study list. Figure 3.1 shows one such relationship. This figure evolved from the recall of eight different lists by two hundred subjects. Each list contained twenty-four words, and each word was presented for study at a four-second rate with two minutes allowed for recall. The relationship between the recall and position for the first few items in the list is called the primacy effect, and a fairly comparable relationship between the last few items in the list and recall is spoken of as the recency effect. Figure 3.1 shows a near

Figure 3.1.
Single-trial free recall as related to the study position of the twenty-four words. The data were combined for eight different lists learned by two hundred subjects (Underwood, Boruch, & Malmi, 1978).

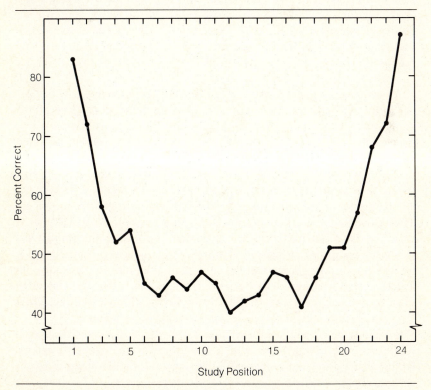

symmetrical curve, but this need not be expected in all cases. Among other variables which will influence the nature of the relationship is the length of the list, the number of lists given to the subjects, and in particular, the delay between study and recall. A number of investigators have shown that even a relatively short delay, e.g., thirty seconds, between the study trial and recall will cause the recency effect to disappear. This simple fact has been heavily weighed by those who choose to proceed on the belief that there is a short-term memory system that is distinct from the long-term system. The last few items in the free-recall list are believed to be held in short-term memory and these are lost with a short delay.

Under some circumstances (e.g., Cohen, 1970) the recency effect is not only lost, but recall of the last few items of the list is poorer than the recall of the items in the body of the list. This is spoken of as *negative recency*.

Historical Note

Tulving (1968) has provided a brief history of free-recall learning, and certain of these facts should be mentioned. Free-recall learning was only rarely represented in the literature of verbal learning before 1960. But from 1960 to the present day, the research has been conducted at a furious pace and the number of publications is in the hundreds. Tulving notes several reasons why this upsurge may have occurred, but for our purposes only two need to be mentioned. First, as noted earlier, the data have shown that a short delay between the presentation of the list and recall results in the loss of the recency effect, and this has been taken as indicative of a distinct short-term system.

A second reason why the free-recall task enchanted many investigators lies in the phenomena associated with allowing the subjects to recall the items in any order they choose. Assume the list contains several words from each of several categories (several animal names, several bird names, and so on), and that these words are scattered more or less randomly throughout the list. Under these circumstances it is normally found that the subjects recall the names from the same category together. That is, the animal names are recalled together, the bird names together, and so on. This phenomenon is called *clustering*, and much has been written about the various ways to quantify clustering as well as speculations about what clustering means when viewed in broad ways. To assert that clustering occurred it must be shown that the subject recalled related items together at a level that is above a chance level. Indeed, that is the way clustering must be defined. It may be said that if the words within a free-recall task are obvious instances of categories, clustering will be heavy.

Related to clustering is a phenomenon called *subjective organization*, first described in Tulving's work (1962). Tulving presented lists of unrelated words, being unrelated in the sense that they did not belong to the same categories nor were they related in any other apparent ways. The lists were presented for a number of study-test trials, the order of the items being different from study trial to study trial. When Tulving studied the order of recall across trials he found that a given subject tended to recall the words in the same order on successive trials, and these constancies increased across trials. It was as if the subjects had "organized" the items in the list based on some rather idiosyncratic relationships. One might anticipate that it would be impossible to get words for a list which are entirely unrelated (whatever that might mean), and therefore that subjects would perceive some similarities among the words which would be reflected in the developing constancy of the order of recall. This seems to be the case. Furthermore, although some subjects do seem to develop idiosyncratic orders of recall, overall there will be a considerable agreement across subjects indicating that they have perceived the same similarities among the words.

Clustering and subjective organization represent effects that do not occur with any other tasks because recall order in the other tasks is always fixed. In addition, it is sometimes found that across subjects the greater the subjective organization or the greater the clustering, the better the recall. Such a correlation seems to fit certain predilections about learning, predilections which point to the role of organization in learning and remembering. This has been a powerful lure for many investigators for the use of the free-recall task.

PAIRED-ASSOCIATE LEARNING

In this task the subjects are shown pairs of words and then are asked to learn to be able to respond with one member of the pair when the other is shown. It is common to symbolize the paired-associate task as A-B, where A indicates the left hand or stimulus term to which the subject must respond, and where B represents the right hand or response term with which the subject must respond. This task is the one most commonly thought of when associative learning is to be involved; when the subject learns to say B when A is shown, an association is said to have been established. To learn to give the B terms to their appropriate A terms is the most frequently used form of the paired-associate task. The learning in this case is said to be unidirectional in that the subject is only required to learn to give the B terms to the appropriate A terms. In bidirectional learning, the subjects are tested in both directions—A to B as well as B to A.

As was true with some of the tasks discussed in the previous chapter, two techniques are commonly used to present the lists to the subjects. In the anticipation method, a stimulus term (A) is shown alone for a short period of time (such as two seconds), and then both items (A-B) are shown together for a like period of time. During the first trial, the subjects simply observe the items, but for the following trials, they are asked to say (anticipate) the response term for each stimulus term during the two seconds in which the A term is shown alone. Thus, when A is shown alone, the subjects try to give B before the A-B pair is shown; when C is shown alone, they try to give D before C-D is shown, and so on down through the list. The subjects are not normally forced to respond to each stimulus term. Rather, they are asked to give the correct response if they can, but they may choose to remain silent until they develop some confidence that they know the correct right-hand term.

The second common method of presenting a paired-associate list for learning is called the study-test method. The subjects study the pairs as they are presented successively on the first study trial. On the first test trial, each left hand or stimulus term is shown alone, and the subjects are asked to supply the appropriate right hand term for each. The alternating study and test trials proceed until the experimenter stops the subject at some given level of performance, or until a given number of trials has been completed. With the study-test method as well as with the anticipation method, a different order of the items is used on each trial so that serial learning (see later) will not occur. In practice, to say that the order of the items differed from trial to trial may mean that there were three or four different orders, these orders reoccurring if necessary.

A rather substantial literature has grown up in which the anticipation method and the study-test method have been compared. Generally speaking, learning has been found to occur more rapidly with the study-test method than with the anticipation method, but there are some puzzling exceptions. Battig (1965) argued persuasively that the study-test method is to be preferred because it clearly separates the learning trials (study trials) from the performing (test) trials. With the anticipation method, these two functions are thoroughly muddled in that on any trial after the first the subject tries to show what has been learned (by anticipating response terms) as well as to develop new learning. Nevertheless, because available data do not show consistently that there are interactions between method (anticipation versus study-test) and other independent variables, we probably can feel reasonably secure in summing across the two methods when asking about the effects of various independent variables.

The dependent variable for measuring the course of learning is usually the number of correct responses. Error measures may be used, but in reporting errors, distinctions must be made between four different classes of errors. First, because subjects are not forced to respond, we may call a failure to respond an error. Second, the subject may produce a response term from the list, but produce it to the wrong stimulus term. These are sometimes spoken of as misplaced response terms. Third, the subject may respond with a stimulus term. Fourth, the subject may respond with a word which is not in the list, making what is called an *extralist error* or *intrusion*. Such errors are rare except under special circumstances.

Let us now examine the paired-associate list as it is used and analyzed in an experiment.

An Illustration

There were twenty pairs in each of two lists. One of these lists, the Number-Word List, was as follows: 5-minnow, 14-rabbit, 11-wallet, 7-supper, 9-fellow, 20-paddle, 13-lesson, 1-fiddle, 6-pepper, 18-mallet, 19-rubber, 10-bullet, 8-cellar, 3-willow, 16-butter, 12-garret, 2-ladder, 17-cattle, 15-sorrow, and 4-galley. The numbers and words were paired randomly subject to the restriction that contiguous numbers were not assigned to words having the same first letter. The other list was the Word-Number List, which was the "turned-over" version of the Number-Word List so that the pairs were minnow-5, rabbit-14, and so on. In the Word-Number List the subjects had to respond to the words by giving the numbers, whereas in the Number-Word List they had to respond to the numbers by giving the words.

There were two groups of twenty-five subjects each, assigned to the two lists randomly. The subjects were fully instructed in that they knew there were twenty pairs, that the numbers 1 through 20 were used, and that there would be four study and test trials. They were also instructed that they should not be afraid of making errors on the test trials, but that they should not guess wildly. On each study trial each pair was presented for four seconds. On the test trials, the subjects who had studied the Number-Word List were given a list of twenty numbers (in random order), each followed by a blank, and the instructions asked that as many words as possible be filled in opposite their appropriate numbers. The test for the Word-Number List consisted of the twenty words in random order with a blank after each; the subjects were instructed to fill in as many of the correct numbers as they could. Ninety seconds were allowed for each test trial, and there were four study-test trials. Immediately after the fourth test trial the subjects were given (unexpectedly) a fifth test which was a backward test trial. If the subjects had learned the Word-Number List, they were tested by being given the numbers and asked to fill in the appropriate words; if they had learned the Number-Word List they were given the words and were asked to assign each its appropriate number.

The mean numbers of correct responses on each trial are shown in Figure 3.2. It is obvious that the Word-Number List was easier to learn than the Number-Word List, and the reason is probably equally obvious. Because the subjects were told that the numbers 1 through 20 were used, there was no problem in producing these numbers as response terms. On the other hand, for the Number-Word list, the subjects had to learn to recall (produce) the words in addition to associating each with its appropriate number. In essence, the subjects learning the Number-Word List had to learn to recall the words as well as to learn to associate each with its

Figure 3.2.

Paired-associate learning across four trials using the study-test procedure. One list consisted of twenty word-number pairs, the other of the same items in reverse order (number-word pairs). On the "backward" test the subjects were unexpectedly given the response terms and were asked to produce the stimulus terms.

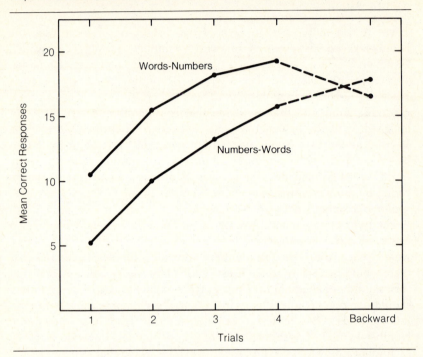

appropriate number. The subjects who learned the Word-Number List had only to learn to associate each word with its appropriate number.

Let us examine next what happened on the backward tests. When the subjects who had learned the Word-Number List were asked to produce the words to the numbers, performance fell. These subjects, in learning the list, had not learned to recall the words. Apparently, therefore, associations between a number and a word can be formed without the subject being able to produce the word when the number is shown. In a manner of speaking, the association is strong enough to produce a correct pairing when the word is shown, but not strong enough to produce the recall of the word when the number is shown.

The backward tests for the subjects who learned the Number-Word Lists again indicate differences between associations producing recall of a word and associations not strong enough to do this. Thus, when the requirement to recall the words is lifted in the backward test, performance "jumps" appreciably higher. It must be remembered that there was no study trial between the fourth test trial and the backward tests.

The two groups of subjects produced about the same relative numbers of intralist errors (misplaced responses). For subjects learning the Word-Number List, the overt responses made resulted in 91.9 percent correct responses and 8.1 percent intralist errors. The corresponding values for the subjects given the Number-Word List were 91.7 percent and 8.3 percent. There were, of course, many blanks in which the subject failed to insert a word or number, but there were no intrusions.

The data allow an answer to a further question: Do the differences in difficulty among the word-number pairs correspond to the differences in difficulty among the number-word pairs? To determine the answer to this question, we calculated the number of times a correct response was given for each pair, summing across the four trials and across the twenty-five subjects. This was done separately for each of the two groups and the totals for the two lists for the twenty pairs were correlated. The resultant value was 0.69. A correlation of this magnitude indicates that the relative difficulty of the pairs in the two lists is not influenced much by the order of the units (number-words versus word-numbers). The correlation also indicates, of course, that there is consistency among the subjects as to easy and difficult items. Such a finding has been reported many times. The implication is that a difficult item for one subject is likely to be difficult for another, and there is very little influence on the difficulty that can be attributed to the idiosyncracies of the subjects.

There is one final matter to mention about item difficulty. It would not be unreasonable to expect that learning of pairs containing certain numbers, numbers such as 1, 5, 10, 15, and 20, might be acquired more rapidly than pairs in which the numbers are relatively nondescript. As may be seen in Figure 3.3, this does not seem to be a strong factor although there is some evidence in support of it. The total correct responses given for each pair involving the numbers 1 through 20 are shown separately for the two lists. The correlation of 0.69 reported above can be inferred from the fact that the peaks and valleys for the two lists generally go together.

In the description of the paired-associate technique as given above there have always been as many different response terms as stimulus terms in the list. There may be times when the number of response terms will be less than the number of stimulus terms. When such tasks are used they become like the classification tasks described in the previous chapter.

SERIAL LEARNING

When the German pioneer, Hermann Ebbinghaus, first brought verbal learning and the laboratory together in the late nineteenth century, the task he devised to represent verbal learning was the serial task. The subjects are presented a series of items and they must be recalled in the order presented. To say this another way, the study order and the order of recall must match. In some variants of the procedure, the order of recall

Figure 3.3.
Learning of paired associates as related to the numbers 1 through 20 which occurred in the pairs.

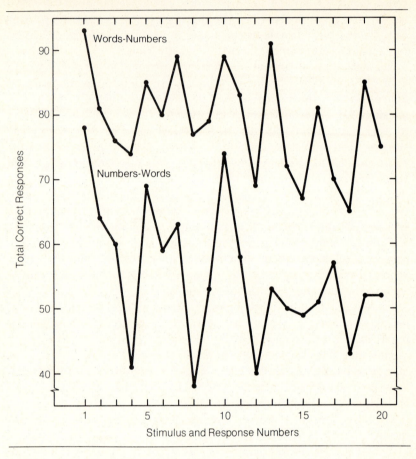

need not match the study order, but the items must be ordered to correspond to the study order regardless of the order of emission. Under this method the subject might recall the fourth presented word first and this would be called correct if the word is placed in the fourth position. The anticipation method applied to serial learning requires the subjects to be able to call out the second word in the list when the first is presented alone, to call out the third when the second is shown, and so on, thus keeping one jump ahead of the items as shown. The study-test method requires the recall of the items in their proper positions but may or may not include the additional requirement that the order of emission of the items must match the study order. The test is probably most simply presented by giving the subjects a sheet having a series of blanks on it, the number of blanks equalling the number of items in the list. The task is to fill in the blanks with the items appropriate to each.

Such a procedure was used in a study in which two hundred subjects learned two successive serial lists, each consisting of twelve common words (Underwood, Boruch, & Malmi, 1978). On the study trials, each word was presented for two seconds; on a test trial, sixty seconds were allowed to write down as many words as possible in the correct order, there being twelve blanks. The data in Figure 3.4 show the percentage of correct responses at each serial position, summing across both lists, for each of the first two trials. It is apparent that learning was acutely influenced by the position held by an item. Items at the beginning and end were readily learned; those in the middle were most poorly learned. In general, this is what has been shown for free recall (see Figure 3.1), but there are differences. The poorest performance of the serial list is shown on items that occur just past the middle of the list, and this does not occur consistently with a free-recall list.

SERIAL SYNTACTICAL

In the previous chapter an experiment was described in which sentences were used as recognition targets. Sentences are also used in recall tasks, either as separate, unrelated sentences, or as parts of a longer passage. A

Figure 3.4.
Correct responses as related to position of the items in the serial lists. Two trials were given using a study-test procedure. The data were combined for two lists of twelve common words learned by two hundred subjects (Underwood, Boruch, & Malmi, 1978).

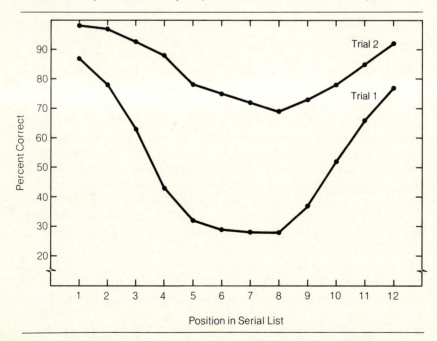

Table 3.1. Sentences and the Random Ordering of the Words in Those
Sentences Used for Serial Learning

Sentences

the loyalty and devotion of those who worked for him were universal
we seem to have developed a distribution system that works rather well
loans should be made at a price high enough to discourage borrowing
free and open discussion of the emotional issues is an absolute necessity
scores of heavily armed soldiers patrolled streets far beyond the city center

Random Orders of the Words from the Sentences

worked were for devotion universal him who the and loyalty of those
rather than have to system developed seems a works distribution well we
should to loans discourage made be enough high borrowing a price at
absolute of open free is an necessity emotional an discussion issues the
streets far patrolled heavily armed scores soldiers city the center beyond of

---

sentence has some of the properties of a serial list if verbatim recall is
required. The major difference is that whereas in serial learning the items
are put together in a more or less random order, the sentence is a series of
items in which many are restricted (by grammar or syntax) as to where
they can occur in the list. If the first two words in a sentence are "The boy,"
the probability is high that the third word will be a verb. All words in a
sentence do not have equal probabilities of occupying each position in the
sentence, as is the case in a serial list. This matter needs some further
comment.

The sequence of letters in a word have, so to speak, a syntax or grammar. If there are two successive consonants in a word, the probabilities are
very high that the immediately following letter will be a vowel. Two
vowels, on the other hand, are usually followed by a consonant. The letter
q is only followed by u. Likewise, the rules of syntax governing sentence
generation give probabilistic structure to a string of words so that in
learning a sentence verbatim the subjects have already acquired habits
which determine the position of some of the words. Furthermore, certain
pairs of words which are adjacent in a sentence may already have preestablished associations between them. And, of course, the sense of a sentence must be useful in both recalling the words as well as placing them in
their proper positions in the sentences. It would appear, then, that learning
the words in a sentence in serial order would be easier than learning the
words in random order. To make sure of this, a simple experiment was
carried out.

One group of twenty-four subjects learned five sentences, one at a time,
each for two trials. A study-test method was used. Each sentence contained twelve words as may be seen in Table 3.1. The words were pre-

sented at a three-second rate on the study trials, and sixty seconds were allowed to recall the words after each study trial. Two trials were given on each list. As a control, twenty-four subjects learned five serial lists which consisted of the words from the sentences, arranged in random order (Table 3.1). The procedure for learning the strings was exactly the same as for the sentences.

To no one's surprise, learning the sentences was easier than learning the same words in random order. Perhaps it is a bit surprising that the magnitude of the difference was so large. As may be seen in Figure 3.5, where mean total errors for the five sentences and five strings are plotted, out of a possible sixty errors the mean for the sentences was 5.6 on the first trial while nearly six times as many errors were made by the subjects given the strings of random words.

There is no reason not to expect that performance on the random sequences would be very similar to that shown for serial learning. The best index for that would be learning as a function of serial position. The errors made at each serial position, summed across trials, subjects, and strings was determined, and the errors at each position were calculated as a percent of total errors. The position curve seen in Figure 3.6 clearly indicates the usual position effects for serial learning. There were too few errors made in learning the sentences to give stability to errors at the various positions. However, it can be said that most of the errors occurred

Figure 3.5.
Errors made on two trials in the serial learning of five, twelve-word sentences, and the learning of the same five sets of twelve words when ordered randomly.

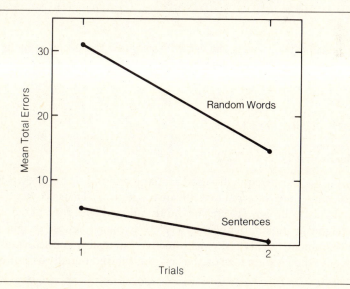

Figure 3.6.

Errors as a function of position in the serial learning of the random orders of the words referred to in Figure 3-5.

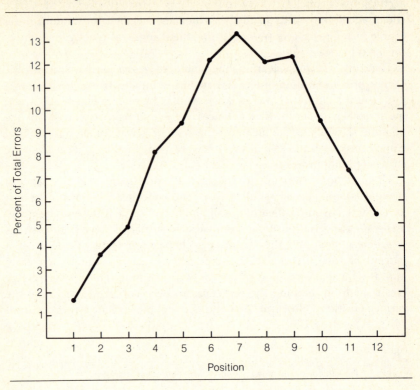

in the latter positions in the list, with very few errors occurring in the first five positions. The greatest number occurred for the last word in the sentences.

MINIATURIZED TASKS

The Brown-Peterson Task

By far the most frequently used miniaturized task is the Brown-Peterson task, sometimes referred to as the distractor task. This task was devised in England by Brown (1958) and quite independently by Lloyd and Jean Peterson at Indiana University (1959). It seems almost certain that the development of this task was directly responsible for scores of studies because the performance on the task was viewed initially as a direct index of some short-term memory system. Even after the initial exuberance over this aspect of the task waned, investigators found it to be very effective for many different purposes.

Basically the Brown-Peterson task as developed originally was a miniaturized version of the free-recall task. The subjects were told that the examiner would speak some letters and then a number. They were further told that when they heard the number they were to repeat it and then to count backwards by threes in time with a metronome. Thus, if the examiner said BCD 309, the subject was to say 309, 306, 303, and so on. This backward counting continued until a red light came on at which time the subject was to recall the three letters. The independent variable in the first experiment conducted by the Petersons was the length of the retention interval (the time between speaking the letters and the point at which recall of the three letters was requested), these intervals being 3, 6, 9, 12, 15, and 18 seconds.

The procedure should be examined in still more detail. The unit of study and test was the three letters, and these three letters are called a consonant syllable. The abbreviation CCC is frequently used to designate such units. Meaningfulness values for CCCs have been determined by a number of different investigators. One procedure is to determine the number of subjects who "get an association" to the syllable within a limited period of time, such as three or four seconds. The fewer the number of subjects who can get an association the lower the meaningfulness is said to be. Meaningfulness is expressed as a percent, the value simply indicating the percentage of the subjects who reported an association. Units such as QJF, BQJ, and KXB have very low meaningfulness, while units such as DNT, SLW, and FRM have very high meaningfulness. As will be discussed in Chapter 8, ease of learning CCCs is directly related to meaningfulness.

Another method that has been used to scale meaningfulness is to determine the number of associates elicited within a given period of time, e.g., sixty seconds, or the rated number of associates expected to be elicited. The greater the number of actual associates elicited or the greater the number of rated associates, the higher the meaningfulness. These procedures can be used with words as well as nonwords. Perhaps the most frequently used units which are nonwords are three-letter units with a consonant-vowel-consonant (CVC) structure. When a description is given of units as being nonsense syllables it is very likely that the reference is to CVCs.

Returning to the Peterson-Peterson procedure, we may ask why the subjects were required to count backward following the study of the CCC. The purpose of this was to keep them mentally busy so they would not be able to rehearse or think about the three letters they were to remember.

The backward counting was aimed at distracting attention away from the consonant syllable so that the memory for it would be based only on the initial brief exposure when read by the examiner.

The design of the study was a complete within-subject design. That is, each subject was tested at all retention intervals. In fact, each subject was tested eight times at each of the six intervals. The forty-eight CCCs were used equally often for each interval when viewed across all of the subjects. Across the forty-eight tests given each subject, each interval was represented once in each successive block of six tests. This is called block randomization; a block consists of one occurrence of each condition, and the order of the conditions within the block is random. In this particular experiment there were eight blocks of six conditions each.

The results for the Peterson-Peterson experiment showed that correct recalls fell precipitously as a function of the retention interval so that after eighteen seconds only a few of the syllables were remembered. It appears now that this rapid loss over the short interval was due to the nature of the experimental design. The recall of an item is heavily influenced by the number of previous items tested in that the greater the number of previous items tested, the poorer the recall. This phenomenon is known as *proactive interference* or *proactive inhibition*. To demonstrate this phenomenon we would use a single retention interval, say twenty seconds. The subjects are given a series of tests, each with a different CCC, each being tested for recall after twenty seconds. If recall decreases with successive tests, proactive inhibition is demonstrated. This implies that items presented and tested earlier interfere with the learning or retention of items presented later.

In recent years, investigators using the Brown-Peterson technique have most commonly used word triads as the unit for study rather than CCCs. Thus, rather than trying to learn and remember RZL, the subject tries to learn and remember *rag-dog-pie*. If then, the investigator requires the subjects to recall the three elements in the order they are presented, the task is a miniature serial-learning task. If the investigator allows the subjects to recall the three elements in any order they choose, it is like a miniature free-recall list.

It was noted above that if a within-subject design is used, proactive interference may occur. Now, proactive interference differs in magnitude as a function of the similarity among the items used in the experiment. Generally speaking, the higher the similarity the greater the interference. What do we mean by similarity in these cases? If we are dealing with nonwords of low meaningfulness, such as CCCs, the similarity is identified with repeated letters across units. Thus, HQX will interfere more with DXQ than will RZL. This is said to represent formal similarity; that is, when similarity is manipulated by repetition of letters across units, formal similarity is said to be involved. On the other hand, if we are dealing with word triads, the investigator would be most interested in similarity produced by semantic overlap among the units. For example, if we give one group of subjects a series of word triads, all made up of names of animals, the buildup in proactive interference would be more rapid than if the words in the triads represented many different categories. The fact that similarity produces proactive interference has been used as a basis for determining the characteristics of the memory for a word triad. This is done by using proactive interference changes as a basic measure. Some elaboration is required.

Release From Proactive Interference.   When a word triad is studied for two or three seconds, it is assumed that certain dimensions or characteristics of the words become represented in memory. But what are these dimensions, or characteristics, or attributes? Wickens (1970) perceived that answers to such questions might be obtained by utilizing the empirical relationship between similarity and proactive interference in the Brown-Peterson task. His reasoning may be illustrated. Assume that a series of word triads are all made up of animal names, and that these triads are studied and tested after a given retention interval as described above. With each successive triad, performance becomes poorer and poorer. It has been presumed that this decrement is produced by interference from a common code established for each word, namely, the code that each word is the name of an animal. If this is true, then, following the presentation of the series of animal triads, the presentation of a triad which has words that are not names of animals, but perhaps names of flowers, should result in high performance because there should be no interference from the previously presented animal names. In a manner of speaking, the flower triad should produce a release from proactive interference. By this is meant that recall should be higher for the flower triad than for the last given triad of animal names. Furthermore, and speaking again in general terms, the reasoning leads to the conclusion that the greater the release, the less the overlap in the memory codes for the two types of triads.

In carrying out such experiments, experiments designed to determine the nature of the memory codes for words, it is necessary to use two groups of subjects. Both groups are treated exactly the same during the buildup of proactive interference. Customarily, three or four buildup trials are given, and for illustrative purposes we will assume four trials. On all trials words from the same category are used in order to produce the buildup. A hypothetical buildup is shown (Figure 3.7) for the first four trials for the two groups. The fifth trial, then, becomes the critical one. One group, the Control (C) Group, receives a fifth trial using names from the same category as used for the first four triads. The other group, the Experimental (E) Group, is given a triad of words from quite a different category. If recall of the E Group on this fifth triad is statistically higher than the recall of the C Group on the fifth triad, release from proactive interference is said to have occurred. If the recovery of the performance

Figure 3.7.
Schematic picture of the release from proactive inhibition in the Brown-Peterson short-term memory paradigm.

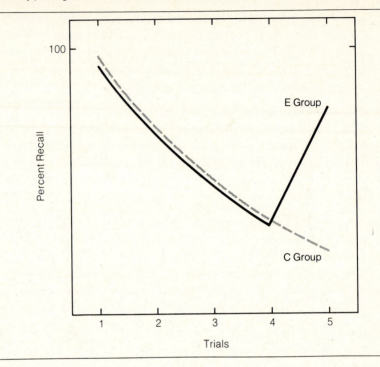

for the E Group is complete—if performance rises to the level shown in the recall of the *first* triad, it is concluded that there was zero overlap in the memory codes for the fifth triads for the two groups. In Figure 3.7, partial release has been indicated with the difference in the recall between the two groups identified as the amount of release from proactive interference.

A wide variety of semantic and nonsemantic dimensions have been explored and most have shown a release effect. Perhaps the most novel study involved a simulated television news program (Gunter, Clifford, & Berry, 1980). Subjects were presented triads of news items, with each triad being recalled after one minute. Four such trials were given. One group, the C Group, had all political items on all four trials or all sports items on all four trials. The results for the C Group would presumably describe the buildup of interference across the four trials. The second group, the E Group, had the same type of news triads (sports or politics) for the first three trials, and then on the fourth trial saw the other type. Obviously the idea is that if sports news items are encoded differently (at least in part) than are items on politics, release should be observed on the fourth trial.

The results are shown in Figure 3.8 where the data have been summed

Figure 3.8.
Observed release from proactive interference using news items as the learning material.
Data from Table 1 of Gunter, Clifford, and Berry (1980).

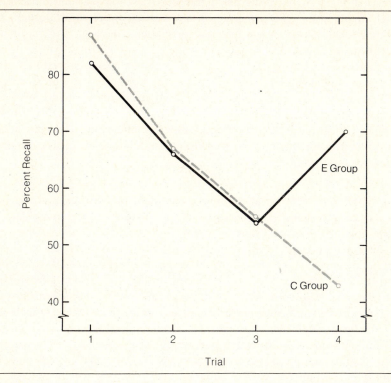

for the subgroups given the different orders. The results must be considered a smashing success if the goal was to produce a set of results that might be called ideal. The buildup in proactive inhibition is sharp across the three trials, and the release is crisp. The Brown-Peterson method has been a very valuable addition to our methods, and the Wickens modification to study release from interference has been of enormous worth in developing ideas about the bases for memory codes. We will examine this in detail in the next chapter.

Memory Span

The memory span was mentioned earlier when a recognition test was described. Strictly speaking, the memory span procedure is a recall procedure which is the miniaturized version of serial learning. The subjects hear or see a string of numbers or letters (the most commonly used items for studying memory span) and they attempt to produce immediately the items in the order presented. Only a single trial on a given string is involved. The memory span procedure appears to be a true miniaturized version of serial learning, yet it is not at all certain that the same processes are involved in the two tasks, i.e., in multiple trial serial learning and single trial memory span. For example, in one study (Underwood, Boruch, & Malmi, 1978) it was shown that the correlations between memory span performance and serial-learning performance were so low as to indicate at best only weak relationships. Observed commonalities in procedures and requirements of the long and short tasks do not necessarily mean commonalities in the underlying processes involved in learning and remembering. This does not mean that one task is more important than the other; it simply means that they are tapping different underlying characteristics of the learning process. We need to know about both kinds of tasks; that is the long and the short of it.

An Illustration. In this illustrative experiment the subjects were given strings of letters which they were to write in the proper order immediately after hearing the string. There were three independent variables. One was the number of letters in the strings, these being either six, seven, or eight letters in length. A second independent variable was the rate at which the strings were read. In one case the letters occurred at the rate of two per second, and in another case the rate was one per second. Because this variable had no influence on performance, nothing more will be said about it. The third variable was the letter to letter associative strength as inferred from the frequency with which two letters occur in succession in words. This is often identified as bigram frequency. The associative strength was either low or high, and each may be illustrated with eight-letter strings:

B P J W F G C M   (low association)

C R N S O D Y L   (high association)

The low-association string consists of successive bigrams BP, PJ, JW, and so on, bigrams which rarely occur in words. On the other hand, the high-association string consists of successive bigrams which occur quite frequently in words.

There were twenty-three subjects in the experiment, and each subject was exposed to all conditions by using a complete within-subject design. Each subject was given twenty strings at each length for each level of associability. The strings were presented by audio tape and the subjects recorded their strings on a prepared data sheet in which the length of the string was signified by the number of blanks. After the last letter in a string was heard, the subjects were allowed ten seconds to record the string. In scoring, an error was called if the correct letters were in an incorrect order.

The results are seen in Figure 3.9 where the string length is plotted along the baseline and the percentage error on the ordinate. The data indicate

Figure 3.9.
Errors in the recall of letter strings as a function of string length and level of association (low and high) between successive letters in the strings.

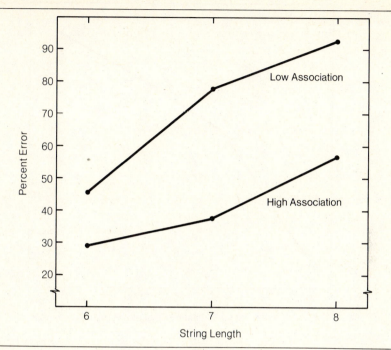

that the bigram frequency was a highly relevant variable, with far more errors made on the strings when the letter to letter association was low than when it was high. Although these data were not intended to provide a measure of the memory span, a rough index of the span can be obtained by dropping a line from the 50 percent level on each curve. Thus, with low-association strings, the average span for these strings was approximately 6.1 letters. What this means is that strings having a greater number of letters would produce errors of more than 50 percent, those strings having a fewer number of letters would produce less than 50 percent errors. For the highly associated letter strings the memory span would be about 7.6 letters.

The subjects were tested on a total of 120 strings. Testing was continuous except for a two-minute rest after the sixtieth trial. We may ask if any changes in performance occurred across the testing period. The percentage of errors was determined for each successive grouping of thirty trials, with the results seen in Figure 3.10. The number of errors increased successively across the testing period. Subjects reported that their attention lagged as the number of strings increased.

Figure 3.10.
Performance in the recall of letter strings as related to stage of testing.

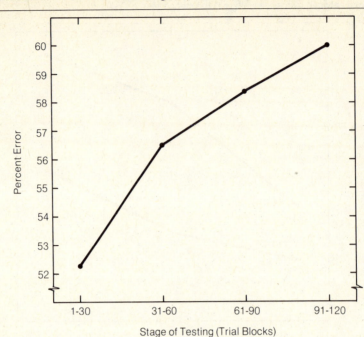

OTHER TASKS

Of course, other tasks are used occasionally. Some are long, and some are short. We have not attempted to be exhaustive. A running recall task is sometimes used in which paired-associates are presented by the anticipation method. In this task, the subject tries to anticipate the response term for each stimulus term. Unlike the usual paired-associate task, however, the response term paired with a stimulus term is changed across the many presentations, and the subject must try to give the response term most recently paired with each stimulus term. Probe recall procedures have also been used. For example, a short paired-associate list may be presented once, followed by a single stimulus term as the probe. Across many lists each position is probed several times, and delays may be introduced between the presentation of the last pair on the study trial and the occurrence of the probe. A serial probe task has also been used. This requires a short serial list, and the subject's task is to give the item which followed when a probe from the list is given as a cue. Remember that the use of a single probe after each list is a means of avoiding output interference which some believe may occur when all items are tested.

RESPONSE MEASURES

In describing the tasks and reporting the illustrative experiments, the response measure was described as consisting of the number of correct responses, or number of errors, or some combination of the two. However, we must recognize that the investigator may be interested in the development of knowledge other than that represented by the ability to recall an item or to recognize an item. Some examples follow.

1. A list of items may be presented in a manner comparable to that for free-recall learning except that some items are presented once, some twice, some three times, and perhaps some even with greater frequency. On the test the subjects are given all of the items presented and are asked to fill in a blank for each word indicating the number of times it appeared in the list. Such a procedure measures the assimilation of frequency information. Another measure of frequency assimilation would be to present pairs of words from the list and ask subjects to indicate the word in each pair that occurred most frequently.

2. After presenting a long list once, subjects may be asked to identify the position each item holds in the list. The subject does not have to be able to recall the items, but only has to make a judgment on the item's position. This measure is said to deal with recency information.

3. Latency measures are sometimes taken as auxiliary to correct responses, or they can be used as the prime measure. In the Sternberg paradigm the arrangement was such that the subject rarely made an error. The critical measure was the latency in producing the correct response.

An investigator chooses a response measure as a means of getting at what he or she wants to get at. This is determined by the investigator's conception of those memories the particular tasks will establish. In many cases, merely to have the subject learn to recall a task perfectly, or to learn to recognize a list without error, will not do the job.

SUMMARY

Tasks for which recall or production of the items is required were described. These tasks included free recall, paired associates, serial lists, and sentences. The miniature tasks described were the Brown-Peterson task and the memory-span procedures. For most of the tasks experimental illustrations were given which indicated the nature of the response measures commonly used, the reliability of item difficulty, and, for serial- and free-recall learning, the relationships between the position of an item during learning and its probability of recall. These are spoken of as serial-position curves. For the Brown-Peterson task, illustrations were given of the development of proactive inhibition (poorer recall with successive testing) and also of its release.

4

Attributes
of a Memory

In Chapters 2 and 3 we examined the tasks which have been used in laboratories to study the learning and forgetting of verbal materials. We will now describe a conception of memory that will form a background against which, all of the remaining material in this book will be set. Sometimes this background dominates, sometimes it recedes, depending upon the particular phenomena being discussed. This conception of memory was first published a number of years ago (Underwood, 1969a), and it appears to have maintained its usefulness. This chapter represents an extension and elaboration of the original paper.

A memory is viewed as consisting of a collection or set of different types of information, each type being called an attribute. Thus, the constituents of a memory are attributes. In the original paper some evidence was available to support the "reality" of some of the attributes. These data will not be reproduced here. Rather, the attributes as they are viewed now will be listed and described, and in some cases further experimental evidence will be introduced.

Several dimensions could be used to differentiate among the attributes. None alone, nor a combination, has been found highly satisfactory as a scheme for the organization of the attributes. However, it may be worthwhile to indicate two of the dimensions along which the attributes may differ.

1. Certain attributes appear to be an inevitable part of the stimulus input and we have little if any control over them; i.e., we cannot prevent them from becoming a part of the memory. Such attributes are sometimes said to be obligatory or automatic. Other attributes appear to result from an effort by the subject to produce them, which is to say that whether they are or are not present as a part of a memory depends upon the activity of the subject. In general, the listing of attributes in this chapter will follow from the obligatory to the volitional.

The question should be raised as to how we know whether an attribute is automatic or not. Essentially, if an attribute becomes a part of the memory whether or not the subject tries to make it a part of the memory, it is said to be automatic. If the attribute becomes a part of the memory only because the subject sets out to make it a part of memory, it would be considered nonautomatic or volitional.

2. It is assumed that attributes serve two basic functions, namely, to distinguish between memories and to be involved in producing (recalling) them. To distinguish between the attributes on these grounds can present a bit of a problem in the study of memory, but such a division has some usefulness.

It is common to speak of coding mechanisms or coding processes. One may view the collection of attributes that constitute a memory as its code, a code which results from the coding mechanisms. In a somewhat more elaborative manner, we may speak of the encoding and decoding of memories, words which imply that the subject may transform the material to be learned (encode) and then retransform it (decode) when given a memory test. The exposition will be built around coding mechanisms assumed to be operative when a word or a series of words is presented and the subject correctly perceives each of them. To say that the subjects correctly perceive the words means that if the subjects were asked to repeat each word immediately after it was shown they could do so. The act of perception is sometimes spoken of as the representational response. We ask about the composition of memory that may result from both automatic and volitional coding mechanisms.

The basic criterion for establishing the existence of an attribute of memory is to demonstrate that it has been coded as a part of the memory. We are frequently in the position of concluding that an attribute was present only when it did influence performance on a memory test. The negative cases—the presence of an attribute which did not influence performance—are more difficult to detect.

We will now identify and discuss the various attributes of memory.

ACOUSTIC ATTRIBUTE

An experimenter, using the memory-span procedure, asks a subject to produce in order a series of letters or numbers immediately after they are read. If the subject is a willing one with an intact auditory system, there is no way to avoid the acoustic input and surely the acoustic differences among the items must become a part of the memory, no matter how fleeting. Additional attributes may be added (e.g., Drewnowski, 1980), but the acoustic attribute is fundamental and obligatory.

It is obvious that we can discriminate at some level among the acoustic signals making up consonants or words; otherwise speech communication would be impossible. But the discrimination is not perfect, and if the acoustic attribute is a dominant part of the memory there may be breakdowns in the discriminations. The role of the acoustic attribute has been a central issue in the arguments concerning short-term versus long-term memory systems with the acoustic attribute often said to be dominant in the short-term system.

In an earlier publication it was stated:

> Only if attributes other than the acoustic attribute are minimized at the time the material is presented for learning does it appear that the acoustic attribute plays a dominant role in memory (Underwood, 1969a, p. 567).

The evidence at that time indicated that with relatively low meaningful material (where other attributes are likely to be weak), the acoustic attribute would be important. Common words, therefore, would be relatively uninfluenced by the acoustic similarity. It should be noted that this conclusion did not imply that the acoustic attribute was not a part of memory for the words; rather, it presumed that other attributes were dominant so that the acoustic similarity effects (breakdown in discrimination) were minimized. Data now available indicate that some modification of this conclusion is required. (Nelson, Peebles, & Pancotto, 1970; Runquist, 1970). Heavy use of a few letters (maximum similarity) among common words as stimuli in a paired-associate list will retard learning. That is, if there is high similarity among the acoustic properties of several stimulus words, e.g., *ham, hum, ram, rum*, the acoustic component appears difficult to "keep down" in the collection of attributes. Nelson, Peebles, and Pancotto, (1970) have summarized the situation:

> The particular constraints . . . (e.g., time pressure, stimulus pronunciation, response characteristics) may have increased the saliency of the phonetic at the cost of the unique semantic and associative properties of the words (p. 119).

And:

> This result would suggest that words may be encoded along any number of dimensions, the salient one being determined by the particular task demands (p. 119).

One issue that will periodically arise concerns the control the subject may exercise over coding or over the selection of attributes from among those constituting a memory. Some initial observations relative to this matter will be made. It must first be recognized that the acoustic attribute has a representation in the memory for common words. Again, to understand the spoken word without this representation would be rather difficult. For example, that we may easily propose a rhyming word for another word indicates that the memory for the word includes an acoustic component. Puns, as an instrument of humor, frequently require the listener to translate the sound of one word or phrase to a word or phrase with similar acoustic properties but with a different meaning as when the parishioner, being grateful to the minister for some act of kindness, says "sanctuary much."

In a study by Forrester and Spear (1969), subjects learned two successive paired-associate lists in which the stimulus terms were identical (single-digit numbers), and the two response terms paired with the common stimulus term—numbers in this case—had the same acoustic properties, e.g., 3-ake, 3-ache. The data show almost perfect transfer in learning the second list when the requirements were to pronounce the response terms. Similar findings have been reported by Laurence (1970). Can we conclude from such studies that the acoustic attribute was the major attribute of the response term in the learning of the first list? Probably not. Clearly, the acoustic attribute was a part of the memory for the first list, but it may have become dominant only when it was appropriate for performance on the second list. If this is a reasonable explanation, it indicates that the subject has some control over the utilization of the attributes which constitute a memory.

Although there may be just a bit of overkill here, let us look at one more technique to show that the acoustic attribute is a "working" part of many memories. This study, using free recall, was conducted by Long and Allen (1973). They constructed an eighteen-word list in which there were six groups of three words each which rhymed (e.g., Ted, Red, Head; Jack, Black, Back). These eighteen words also formed six groups of three words each which were conceptually related (e.g., Ted, Jack, Jean; Red, Black, Green). The question posed was whether subjects would cluster their recalls based on the acoustic attribute or upon the conceptual attribute. The results, as inferred from the clustering, show that the acoustic attribute dominated the organization.

There is no way to know from the Long-Allen study whether the conceptual similarity of the groups of items was greater or less than the acoustic similarity. For the present purpose that is not a critical issue. It would probably be quite possible to construct other lists in which the conceptual attribute would dominate the acoustic attribute. Nevertheless, the study shows that even for groups of words in which anyone could identify the conceptual relationships, this attribute was less favored as an organizational dimension than was the acoustic similarity among groups of the same words. The acoustic attribute obviously had to be a part of the memory for the words in order for clustering along the acoustic dimension to occur.

ORTHOGRAPHIC ATTRIBUTES

Different letters obviously have different forms or shapes. So also, when letters are placed in sequence to form a word, differences in the visual structure among words appear. Words differ in length or number of syllables, in number of repeated letters, and in terms of unusual or infrequently appearing sequences. Lower case letters may extend above (e.g., *b*) or below (e.g., *g*) the base line. All such characteristics by which words may differ are called orthographic attributes. Subjects can rate words reliably in terms of their orthographic distinctiveness (Zechmeister, 1969). A word such as *phlox* is rated as being very distinctive, a word such as *parse* not distinctive, and these differences have been shown to have an influence on memory (Zechmeister, 1972; Hunt & Elliott, 1980).

The structural features of a word are, like the acoustic properties, given in the perception of a word and are therefore obligatory. They must become a part of the memory for that word, at least momentarily. Furthermore, each word has a unique structure. The orthographic attributes have the potential for at least distinguishing among memories. We will examine some illustrative studies.

In the previous chapter we discussed a technique for examining differences in coding between two sets of a material. This was called the release-from-proactive inhibition (PI) technique. Before proceeding, some comments about the technique need to be made. It may be argued that the release technique is too sensitive to changes in coding (Underwood, 1972). This may produce problems with regard to generalizing the results to other situations. For example, if one asks about the attributes coded for a single word in a free-recall list of unrelated words, it is likely that the release technique will overestimate the number of attributes involved. The technique essentially "instructs" or primes the subject to code a given attribute for the units used in the buildup. When the materials are changed on the test trial, the change becomes obvious. This is not to deny the reality of the change that occurs, but it does suggest that some caution must be exercised, and that perhaps we should not assume that the attributes identified by the release technique are omnipresent in other tasks.

There is a further problem. How does one view the results when a buildup occurs but no release is evident on the change? It would be assumed that some common attribute (or attributes) was responsible for the buildup, but the lack of release may indicate that the particular attribute of interest to the experimenter was not involved in the buildup. Yet, if not, what produced the buildup? The failure to obtain a release does not mean that the attribute of interest was not encoded. Rather, it means that if it was encoded it was not a dominant attribute of memory. The technique cannot be used to determine the presence of an attribute which did not influence memory performance in this situation.

Within this context, let us examine a particular study in which the orthographic feature of interest was the length of the words (Lachar & Goggin, 1969). Four-letter words and ten-letter words defined the length variable. The subjects were presented four successive triads, each triad being recalled after eighteen seconds. The first three triads were used to produce the buildup of PI, the fourth to determine the release as a function of the change in the length of the words. It should be clear that the semantic characteristics of the words were not involved in any critical way.

There were four groups of subjects. Two control groups, long-long and short-short, had the same length of words on all four trials. The two experimental groups were short-long and long-short. The results for the two groups within each class have been combined for the display in Figure 4.1. The response measure was the mean number of words recalled out of three possible for each successive triad. Proactive inhibition built up over the first three triads for both groups; on the test trial, performance improved appreciably for the change groups, with performance approaching that shown on the first triad.

This evidence indicates that word length may be an attribute of memory. The meaning of this finding should be explained. It is not known at all that word length was the dominant attribute in memory for the first three trials. We can say with confidence that word length was carried in the memories for the first three triads. This must have been true, or the change in the length on the fourth triad would not have influenced the memory for it. Presumably the change in length on the fourth triad produced an added attribute which reduced interference at recall, either because learning was better, forgetting was less rapid, or both.

One more study will be reviewed. Hintzman, Block, and Inskeep (1972)

Figure 4.1.
Release from proactive interference using the Brown-Peterson procedure when word length is changed (E Group) or not changed (C Group) between trials 3 and 4. Data from Table 1 of Lachar and Goggin (1969).

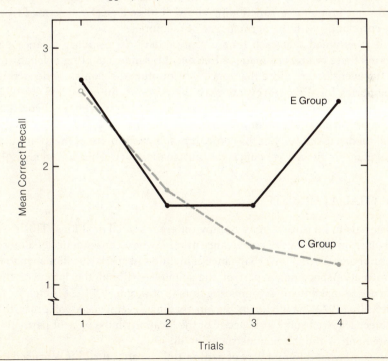

presented subjects with eight successive free-recall lists, eighteen words per list. Half of the words were printed in upper-case block letters, and half were printed in lower-case script letters. The type of print was randomized within the list. Two types of evidence indicated that the orthographic characteristics were a part of the memory for at least some of the words. First, some clustering based on type style occurred. Second, after all of the lists had been presented, the subjects were shown all of the words from the eight lists and asked to identify the type style in which the word had been printed in the list. For this test, half of the subjects had all the words presented in one style, half in the other. The results showed that subjects had some knowledge of the type style; their judgments were 58 percent correct (chance would be 50 percent).

FREQUENCY ATTRIBUTES

For a memory of an event to be established, some representation of that event must have entered the memory system at least once. Generally speaking, the strength or the permanence of a memory is directly related to the number of times the event has been perceived. A central problem in memory theory is to explain the relationship between frequency and permanence. This issue will be set aside for the present because to view frequency as an attribute is not to view it as a vehicle for permanence. Rather, frequency is viewed as an independent type of information whose influence on memory functioning allows it to be logically separated from its correlation with the permanence of memories.

It is assumed that each time a representational response of an event occurs there is a record made of that event by some counting mechanism. If the event occurs more than once the counting mechanism reflects this. Memories for different events may therefore be differentiated by their relative frequencies. This attribute will be used as a primary theoretical mechanism in subsequent chapters, and the problems attending its use will be discussed fully at that time. It is sufficient to say at this point that frequency is viewed as being coded automatically (Hasher & Zacks, 1979).

SPATIAL ATTRIBUTE

Materials to be learned may occupy different spatial positions. This may result from a laboratory contrivance or it may be a consequence of a more natural distribution of verbal material in different spatial locations. Spatial information becomes a part of the memory without the intent of the learner to make it so. Two investigators (Rothkoph, 1971; Zechmeister & McKillip, 1972) have shown that in reading several pages of prose the subject acquired some knowledge of the location on the page of particular statements without being instructed to do so.

A somewhat different way of getting at the spatial attribute was used by

Weeks (1975). The release-from-PI technique was employed, and the subjects were given five successive CCCs, these being spelled. Two speakers (as in radio speakers) were positioned 120 degrees apart. The presentation of the first four CCCs came from one of these speakers but for the fifth one the voice came from the other speaker. There was PI release as gauged by the control group that had all five CCCs spelled in the same location.

It is not unusual for us to remember that a particular bit of information occurred on a given location on the page of a book or a newspaper. However, in the usual verbal-learning studies where lists are used, there are very few opportunities for a spatial attribute to even be present because we frequently balance against this in presenting the materials. Still, in serial learning and in single-trial free-recall learning, it is quite possible to identify a word as occupying a given spatial position in the list, although it is apparent that this may be completely confounded with a temporal attribute to which we now turn.

TEMPORAL ATTRIBUTE

Because memories can only be formed sequentially over time, the memories for different events may have a temporal attribute. It does not seem appropriate to presume that differences in points of time per se can be discriminable. Rather, we must presume that the changing events which index phenomenal time are in some way responsible for the temporal attribute if one exists. To make this more explicit, we assume that one event which occurs in close contiguity with another event which is the nominal target event may have representation in the memory for the target event. If on one's birthday a notice is received that $50,000 has been won in a lottery, the two events (birthday and money) may become associated. Effectively, the memory for the receipt of the money is dated.

It is probably quite apparent that at a gross level memories can be discriminated along a temporal dimension. We know that the memory for the multiplication tables was acquired in grade school and that marriage occurred at a later point in time. Nevertheless, there are data which indicate that, generally speaking, we do not have very good discrimination among memories in terms of their ages. In one study (Underwood, 1977) college students were given a list of eight events, events for which it was sure they had memories, and they were asked to rank order these events in terms of their ages. Roughly the events occurred about a year apart. Out of 108 students, only two correctly rank ordered the events. Thus, it must be understood that when we speak of the temporal attribute of memories we are speaking of a relatively loose set of discriminations.

Three techniques have been used to study temporal discrimination among words in a list. Assume that a long list of words has been presented the subject under the general instructions that some aspect of memory will be tested. One way to measure the temporal discrimination for the words is to present the subject pairs of words from the list and ask the subject to make a judgment as to which word in each pair occurred most recently. These are called recency judgments. Another method is to have the subjects estimate the position held by each item in the list; these judgments are called position judgments. A third method is to show the subject pairs of words from the list with the subject instructed to estimate the number of words which fell between the two words in each pair (lag judgments).

Studies which have asked about the correspondence among the three methods (e.g., Underwood & Malmi, 1978a) have shown that the lag judgments are not valid. They are not valid in the sense that the judgments of lag do not correspond to true lag. Even after the subject has had several trials on the same list, there is only a relatively low increase in the validity of the judgments. However, if the subjects have been given several trials with lag judgments and are then switched without warning to one of the other two measures (recency or position), performance jumps dramatically. What happens is that the subjects, while studying and being tested on lag judgments, acquire a great deal of information about temporal relations among the items which, for unknown reasons, cannot be demonstrated with lag judgments. The moment they are switched to one of the other dependent variables, the knowledge is expressed. This is another illustration of the discrepancy between knowledge and performance.

As indicated earlier, it appears that our usual temporal dating of memories results from associative-learning processes, although in some cases we may reconstruct events in such a way as to arrive at the relative age of two memories. At very short intervals it appears that we have a specialized system which affords recency information directly (Underwood, Lund, & Malmi, 1978). In the experiment subjects were presented a series of ten-item lists. Immediately after the list was presented, paced recency tests were given at varying intervals up to twenty-seven seconds. The critical recency tests included the last item in the list paired with some other item from the list, this later varying for different lists. The results showed that the identification of the last word in the list as being most recent decreased up to about fifteen seconds following its presentation. At that point the judgments of recency involving the last word were no better than the judgments involving the other words. Prior to that point, however, the accuracy of the judgments of recency for the last item were superior to the judgments for the other items. That a recency attribute appeared to cling to the last word for as long as fifteen seconds was made more impressive by the fact that the recency information for the ninth item in the list was no more accurate than that for any of the other items. The last item, and the last item only, was given special information.

One may speculate about the importance of this short recency effect. If we are talking spontaneously, the recency principle implied in the above data allows us to distinguish between what was just said and what was said two sentences ago. It appears that the recency principle allows us to give continuity to a sequence of sentences so that the sentence spoken a moment ago is not confused with the sentence just spoken.

Still other operations may be linked to a temporal attribute which are known to influence memory. Consider the memory-span procedure. If a nine-digit string is presented with a pause between successive subgroups of three digits, performance is better than if the pauses are omitted. In fact, if changes in the temporal patterning of the same string of digits occurs from trial to trial the subjects perceive them as being quite different strings, which indeed they are in terms of temporal patternings (Bower & Winzenz, 1969). Patterning can be produced by other means (e.g., emphasizing certain digits in the string) so the effect of patterning is not unique to temporal variations.

MODALITY ATTRIBUTE

People perceive events through the various sensory registers corresponding to the various modalities (vision, hearing, taste, etc.). Therefore, memory may carry some information about the "port of entry." Insofar as a modality attribute becomes a part of a memory, it may differentiate it from memories established via other modalities. In practice, when verbal learning is involved, only the distinction between auditory and visual inputs is of interest. The evidence is quite conclusive that a discrimination between aural and visual presentation of the material may occur. A bit earlier a study by Hintzman, Block, & Inskeep (1972) was reviewed because it showed the presence of an orthographic attribute. These investigators also tested for the modality attribute in essentially the same way as they had tested for the orthographic attribute. The subjects were tested on several free-recall lists in which half the words were given visually and half aurally. Subsequently, the subjects were asked to identify which words had been spoken and which words had been shown visually. In recall, clustering occurred by input modality, and in identifying which words had been presented visually and which had been presented aurally, the subjects were correct 74 percent of the time.

We must remember that there is a very high degree of interchange among memories established via different modalities. If you are read a long list of words to learn and then your recognition memory is tested by a forced-choice test printed on paper, you do not report that none of these words was read to you. There is an evident interchange between the visual and aural modalities. Consider another example. If I would use my index finger as a printing instrument on your bare back, you will be able to distinguish nearly perfectly all of the letters of the alphabet as they are successively printed. Based upon the assumption that you did not learn the letters by back printing, we would conclude that in some way the tactile stimulation can be translated into a memory system that was formed via the visual system. A large amount of such cross-modality mapping takes place. Any way this transfer is viewed, it can only be considered a fortunate matter. To say that there is a modality attribute; to say that a memory may carry information about the sensory system through which an event arrives, does not mean at all that the sensory systems are unique and independent. The fact that we do remember the input modality to some extent is a relatively trivial matter compared with the implications of the great interchange shown by the different modality systems.

CONTEXT ATTRIBUTES

By context is meant the background for a given learning task. If that background becomes a part of the memory, we may speak of the context attribute. Common observation would suggest that such an attribute is real. We may remember precisely where we first met a person (in a given hotel, at a given meeting) even though we have forgotten the person's name. One of the problems faced in dealing with context is that features on which context is said to vary are essentially unlimited. For example, release from PI can be obtained by changing the size of the background area on which the test words are printed (Turvey & Eagan, 1969) and by changing the speaker's voice from male to female or vice versa (Gardiner & Cameron, 1974).

It would not be correct to leave the impression that context manipulations inevitably produce differences in the composition of memory. There are many, many reports in the journals in which context variables have been used without producing effects of consequence. Whatever, we do know that context manipulations can have an effect, and therefore we must recognize that one constituent of a memory may be background characteristics.

AFFECTIVE ATTRIBUTES

An affective attribute consists of the emotional response produced by the material being learned. If different materials produce different affective responses, the memories for these materials will differ on that attribute. An affective attribute could be viewed as an internal context variable. The positive evidence concerning this attribute has come from the use of the release-from-PI technique (Wickens & Clark, 1968). For example, words rated as being pleasant may be used to produce a PI buildup and then words rated unpleasant will produce the release phenomenon. If the pleasant and unpleasant words do not differ on other characteristics which could produce the release, we can conclude that an affective attribute may be a part of the memory for a list of words.

VERBAL ASSOCIATIVE ATTRIBUTES

The attributes to be discussed for the remainder of the chapter all illustrate what might be called semantic or meaning attributes. When a word occurs in a learning task it may produce (implicitly) a variety of verbal associates. Such implicitly produced words may become a part of the memory for the word which produced them; hence, they must be reckoned with in evaluating the mechanisms responsible for performance on a memory test. Two different types of associates may be distinguished: *parallel* associates and *class* associates.

Parallel Associates

Three types of parallel associates have been studied most intensively. These are antonyms, synonyms, and what may be called functional associates. By a functional associate is meant such pairs as *cup-saucer, table-chair* or *key-lock*. These associative relationships seemed to have developed because of functional contiguity. Speaking at a general level, parallel associates are those in which the associate is at the same usage level as the word which instigated it.

Information as to the expected implicit associate comes from word association tables. This is to say, then, that if we wish to predict the associate that is likely to become a part of the memory for a word in a learning task, we would look toward the most frequently given word as shown in word association tables. Demonstrations that associates of a word in a learning task may indeed become a part of the memory will be given in later chapters.

Class Attributes

When an associate that occurs is a category name that includes the word eliciting it, we speak of the associate as being a class attribute. The most obvious, yet one of the most powerful class attributes is that which identifies the class of material presented. If the subjects are presented a list of CCCs for free-recall learning, a memory test will rarely find them producing actual words. The reverse is even a more unlikely possibility. Usually the instructions supply the subjects with this class attribute in that they specify whether the subjects are being asked to learn a list of CCCs or a list of words. This information is usually repeated if there is a retention test at a later point. But even if these class names were not provided the subjects, they would probably establish the class characteristic on their own initiative.

Of somewhat greater interest among class attributes are those which indicate a hierarchical classification of objects, events, or ideas. If the word *horse* is presented in the learning task, we can be quite confident that some of the subjects will produce the implicit category response, *animal.* There is some reason to believe that at least under certain circumstances, additional implicit class responses may occur. In the case of *horse*, such associates as "domestic animals," "four-footed animals," "method of transportation," may be produced, either to the original word or as by one implicit response producing another. To say that such hierarchical class associates may be produced is not to say that they are always produced by the isolated word in the learning task. But, as will be shown later, it seems beyond doubt that they will be produced under some situations. It is from such situations that we are able to give some procedural meaning to the notion of the organization of memories. One further matter: in the illustration above, particular words have been used to indicate different levels of inclusion. This is not to imply that these words would necessarily be elicited in many cases. In fact, there is reason to believe that subjects may recognize two or more objects as belonging to the same class without in fact using a word to indicate it. It is somewhat like the young child who somehow has reached a conclusion that a dog and a cat and a sparrow are different from a table, a house, and a sidewalk. Verbalization of the hierarchical level is something we may expect from the usual college student but even here the ability to report a name for a relationship which is apparent to them is by no means without flaw.

It was noted earlier that a sentence can be viewed as a serial list with a restriction on the position which may be occupied by a given word. We presume that a sentence must consist of a minimal hierarchical structure of the type described above. Here is a case, however, in which the subject may have no knowledge of the words used to denote these levels. It is as if through experience the subjects have developed a "feel" for the appropriate positions of words carrying different functions. The verbs, the nouns, the adjectives must have some higher-order representation, yet determining this representation is difficult and cannot possibly be thought of as the mediator for appropriate ordering of the words to form a sentence.

TRANSFORMATIONAL ATTRIBUTES

Although specific instances of attributes fitting this category will be given, like the context attributes the transformational attributes are something of a grab bag. As a general class the transformational attributes represent the use of mnemonics in memory storage as will be described in the next several paragraphs.

For all of the previous attributes discussed, the target memory was assumed to have a more or less direct, isomorphic representation in memory, and the attributes represented the additional types of information which were a part of the memory of the target item. In the case of some transformational attributes, changes are produced in the target so that it no longer can be spoken of as a direct representation of the item as presented for learning. Therefore, as a result of the transformation, a part of the memory must consist of information for decoding, and it is this decoding information that constitutes the transformational attribute. Some of these types of attributes are discussed below.

Images

Certain words or ideas may be translated into images. Obviously, the decoding problem for this transformation is of little consequence since one cannot speak or write an image to demonstrate a memory. The class attribute "words" is so dominant that the decoding (image to word) comes quite naturally. Only if the image represents a highly elaborated version of the object signified by a word is it possible that some problem in decoding could occur.

Natural Language Mediators

A variety of transformations may fit into this category, but as the name implies, the critical aspect is that some additional information (mediator) beyond the target becomes a part of the memory to link or tie two verbal units together. Paired-associate learning is most commonly used to study such mediation. The basic notion is that the mediator provides a more meaningful link between the stimulus and response terms than is given directly by these terms. In a sense, if a pair was *cab-taxi*, the relationship is given directly by the common meaning. If the pair was *cab-dip*, a natural language mediator might be *cab-tip-dip*. The meaningful relationship (natural language) is used to generate *dip*. The subject must, however, carry information in memory which allows him to change the first letter of *tip* when trying to produce the correct response.

The presence of natural language mediation is inferred from reports of the subjects. A problem is whether or not such mediators are involved in a fundamental way in establishing the memory. Subjects report all sorts of things that they do in learning. They may report weaving a story out of a serial list by adding implicitly here and there a word of their own. If they do in fact learn in this fashion they obviously must carry information in memory to "subtract" the words they used implicitly. They may not always accomplish this and errors (intrusions) will appear in the experimenter's records of the subjects' responses.

A special case of natural language mediation is called sentential facilitation. In this case a stimulus and response term may be viewed as two words in a sentence with a verb implicitly inserted between them. For example, if a pair to be learned is *dog-car*, the word *chase* may be inserted.

One of the advantages of such mediation for a list of paired associates is that a single decoding rule will fit all pairs.

Order Transformations

Relatively meaningless verbal units such as CVCs or CCCs may be made more meaningful by changing the order of the letters. The unit *rac* becomes *car*, *nep* becomes *pen*. The learning consists, then, of learning words plus a decoding rule or rules. Even the memory for sentences may involve a reordering of the words. A passive sentence may be changed into an active sentence ("The ball was hit by the boy" being changed to "The boy hit the ball"). If verbatim recall is required, decoding must occur to reorder the words.

Others

A little thought will show innumerable other types of transformations that might be used by a subject in learning, whether to link words into pairs, remember ideas, or to recall single units as in free recall. In all cases we must recognize that the transformation rule represents a part of the memory.

SO?

We have listed the attributes of memory. Where has this gotten us? The basic idea is that the fundamental empirical and theoretical tasks involve determining the roles of the attributes in producing the various memory phenomena. We are far from being able to specify all of these functionings, but our purpose later will be to show how certain theoretical approaches have succeeded to some degree in carrying out the task.

At a different level of discourse, the attribute approach naturally leads to various types of research problems. At the developmental level we need to know how rapidly attributes develop as a child grows, which attributes are of major importance at certain ages, and so on. A problem that will be illustrated in a number of cases throughout the book concerns the degree to which the learner can control the attributes. Is there a relationship between the permanence of memories and the number of attributes constituting the memories? How does forgetting occur under the attribute conception? Are differences in forgetting among tasks traceable to differences in the attributes making up the memories? If the attribute approach has generality, what does it tell us about how memory abnormalities develop? These and many other questions flow from the attribute approach. Not all of these questions will be addressed in this book, but if the attribute approach is to endure, they must be faced sooner or later.

SUMMARY

Attributes are types of information which form memories. Because each memory is unique, each one consists of a different collection of attributes. The attributes identified and described were as follows: acoustic, orthographic, frequency, spatial, temporal, modality, context, affective, verbal associative (including various types of word associates and class attributes), and finally, transformational attributes of various kinds.

Part of the theoretical and experimental task of the memory researcher is to determine what roles the various attributes play in memory functioning. In some of the following chapters, we can be very specific about the role of particular attributes. In dealing with other phenomena, the specificity will be missing.

5

Study Time

In graphing biological and physical events, the passage of time is frequently used as a plotting variable. The passage of an electric current through a wire requires time; the sound wave travels at a given rate; the division of a cell takes time, and the action of an enzyme on a food substance also takes place over time. Whether time is accorded more representation than implied by a plotting variable—whether time might be assigned causal properties—is a matter for the theoretician. In studying verbal learning and forgetting, the consensus is that time is best thought of as a plotting variable and should be considered the necessary framework into which processes that necessarily require time to occur do occur. Within this framework it is quite obvious that no experiments were necessary to arrive at a law which asserts that the amount learned is a direct function of study time. Any schoolboy or schoolgirl knows that this law is valid. As long as we admit that learning occurs and requires time to occur, it must follow that the longer the study time, the greater the amount of learning that occurs. No one has ever reported that forgetting or "unlearning" occurs for a verbal task as study time on it increases, nor has anyone ever reported that a task has been learned with zero study time. Therefore, since learning is known to occur, and since learning, like any other process, requires time, learning is some function of study time. An occasional report may suggest that no learning was observed as a consequence of study time, but these are rare and usually some learning will be observed by some kind of test given that there has been study time.

If the relationship between learning and study time is so obvious, why devote space to it? There are several reasons. First, it is worthwhile to know something about the nature of the relationship between study time and learning. Second, because of the importance of study time for learning, it is a potential confounding variable of which we must be particularly aware. Third, there is at least one phenomenon which appears to contradict a law that relates learning and study time. Finally, we would surely be suspicious of a law that said that study time and learning are related in a given way regardless of the nature of the study activities. Surely, we would suppose, that what the subject does with the study time is something to reckon with.

THE TOTAL-TIME HYPOTHESIS

Modern interest in the study time-learning relationship seems to have been a consequence of two events, namely, a research report by Murdock (1960) and a literature review by Cooper and Pantle (1967) that led them to a refined statement of the relationship between study time and learning. Each will be considered in turn.

The Murdock Studies

Murdock's interest initially centered on single-trial free recall as a function of the length of the list. The fact is that as the number of items in a list increases, the number of items recalled increases, although the percentage of items recalled decreases. Murdock was not happy with these generalizations; they did not seem to tell very much. Further, he pointed out that there is a confounding in that as list length increases there is an accompanying increase in study time. In addition, the longer the list, the longer the mean retention interval in immediate recall, providing the study time per item is equal for all list lengths. This difference in length of the retention interval is further exacerbated by the fact that more items are recalled from the longer list than from the shorter, and all items recalled from the longer list beyond the number recalled from the shorter list are recalled after a longer retention interval than are any items from the shorter list. Thus, there were very good reasons for Murdock to change his approach.

The change involved making the total study time constant across all list lengths. In one of his experiments, four conditions were carried out using single-trial free recall of common words. These conditions and the results are shown in Table 5.1. Because the recall differences were not statistically different, it appears that list length per se was not an important variable. Rather, recall seemed to be determined by total study time.

In another experiment Murdock gave subjects twenty-five, fifty, or seventy-five words printed on a sheet of paper and allowed thirty seconds to study the words. The mean number of items recalled from each list did not differ statistically, thus supporting the inference that study time is the critical variable. Murdock concluded from these and other studies that the number of items produced after a single study trial was a linear function of total time given for study.

Table 5.1. Four Conditions Used by Murdock (1960) in His Work on the Relationship Between Study Time and Learning.

List Length	Time Per Word	Total Time	Mean Number Recalled
20	3 seconds	60 seconds	9.3
30	2 seconds	60 seconds	9.3
40	1.5 seconds	60 seconds	9.6
60	1 second	60 seconds	8.4

Cooper-Pantle Review

Seven years after Murdock's work, Cooper and Pantle published a review of studies that provided evidence bearing on study time and amount learned. They found it necessary to draw a distinction between *nominal* and *effective* study time. Nominal study time is clock time—the time provided by the experimenter for study. Effective study time refers to that portion of the nominal time that the subject actually spends rehearsing the items. This distinction, while raising some troubling issues, seemed necessary to handle the basic observation made by many investigators that a subject must try to rehearse if the study time is to be effective. The problem, of course, is that we are likely to conclude that if study time and learning are not clearly related, there must indeed have been a discrepancy between nominal and effective study time. Actually, Cooper and Pantle found the idea of a discrepancy between nominal and effective study time to be necessary only in special cases. For example, varying the length of the anticipation interval in paired-associate learning may not influence rate of learning. However, it can be seen that increasing the anticipation interval would not allow the subjects to rehearse the pair for a longer and longer time unless they already knew the correct response term for the particular stimulus term. The study-test method is appropriate for testing the relationship between study time and learning of paired-associate lists. We should not conclude that the length of the anticipation interval is irrelevant; it clearly is relevant as studies have shown (e.g., Nodine & Goss, 1969), but that is not our interest of the moment.

Cooper and Pantle developed strong evidence for what they called the total-time hypothesis, which states that the amount learned is a direct function of the amount of study time regardless of how that time is divided. The hypothesis would say, for example, that five trials on a serial list with the items presented at a four-second rate will result in performance that will not differ from that observed if ten trials are given on the list at a two-second rate. Cooper and Pantle were careful to point out that the law probably will break down at the extremes—when study time is very short or very long. They also dealt only with recall tasks. Still, the hypothesis had strong support in the literature they reviewed. Furthermore, they proposed that hitherto unexplained phenomena may be indirect manifestations of the study-time law. The von Restorff effect occurs when, in a single-trial, free-recall learning task, one of the items is noticeably different from all other items. For example, the sixth item might have a red background while all others have a white background. The item with the red background will be better recalled than if it has a white background (for a control group). Cooper and Pantle argue that the subjects may redistribute their study time, giving more time to the red or "isolated" item than to other adjacent items.

Cooper and Pantle may not be correct in their account of the von Restorff effect, but the general idea on which the attempt was based should be kept in mind. We should always examine the operations defining an alleged new phenomenon to determine if it could reasonably be produced by differences in study time. It may be noted that some studies speak of high-priority events (e.g., Schulz & Straub, 1972). In terms of the operations, the name of a famous person (high-priority event) might be inserted into a list of unrelated words. The results of such experiments appear to be much the same as those reported under the name of the von Restorff phenomenon or the isolation effect.

To review and amplify, we may state three laws relating to recall tasks, differing in precision:

1. Amount learned is a direct function of the length of study time.

2. Amount learned is a direct linear function of the length of study time.

3. Amount learned is a direct function of the length of study time, regardless of how that study time is divided.

The first statement is true. The second statement is very likely true and may be used in place of the first statement. The third statement (the total-time hypothesis) is the one that has provoked the most work and for which some exceptions have been found.

Other Work

Studies published since the Cooper-Pantle review generally give support to the total-time hypothesis. Indeed, some believe that the support is sufficiently strong that it should no longer be called an hypothesis. To be sure, occasional reports will be published which fail to support the hypothesis (Brewer, 1967; Calfee & Anderson, 1971; Roberts, 1972), but there are many, many that do. It is extremely rare to find that study time and learning show no relationship. That is, even if the results do not support the total-time hypothesis, they usually show that amount learned and study time are directly related, and hence conform to the first law above.

In making tests of the total-time hypothesis, there is a potential confounding that may not have always been avoided. Assume that we plan to test the hypothesis by comparing overall learning time when a serial list is presented at a five-second rate versus the case where it is presented at a one-second rate. These values usually refer to exposure time. However, devices for presenting the lists very likely will require change time, i.e., the time to terminate the exposure of one item and initiate the exposure of the next. The number of change times will be less for long exposure durations than for short exposure durations. Indeed, if the total-time hypothesis holds in the illustration, there would be five times as many changes in the one condition as compared with the other. It can be seen that unless the ratio between change time and exposure time is constant across all exposure times, there may be an error in calculating total time. Total time presumably should include both exposure time and change time on the grounds that the subject continues to rehearse during change time.

It may have occurred to some that study time per item, as governed by the experimenter, is quite an arbitrary matter. The memory drum, the slide projector, or the computer is set at a two-second rate, or a four-second rate, or what not, and the subject is asked to learn the task with the study time per item being imposed by the experimenter. Why not let the subject choose the study time? Why not let each subject tailor the study time to match his or her capabilities? The rather surprising fact is that if this is done—if the subjects are allowed to pace themselves—the mean total time to learn a paired-associate list to a criterion of perfection is not different from the mean total time observed when the rates are imposed by the experimenter (Bugelski & Rickwood, 1963). In a similar manner, Zacks (1972) allowed her subjects to study a paired-associate list in almost any way they chose (i.e., study a pair as long as they wished, take test trials whenever they wished), but the time to learn did not change, and retention one week later did not differ for the groups using the different procedures.

Rundus and Atkinson (1970) showed that subjects could be trained to "learn aloud" in the sense that they overtly rehearsed a free-recall task on the study trial. Because the subjects rehearsed the words aloud, the experimenters had a record of the number of times each word was attended to. Of course, the subjects rehearsed items beyond the one being shown at the moment. This is to be expected when the list is presented at a rather slow rate. A simple and direct fact emerged from the Rundus-Atkinson study: the greater the number of times an item was rehearsed, the greater the likelihood that it would be recalled. Thus, in a somewhat different way, study time and learning were directly related.

We initiated this discussion on study time by indicating that study time and performance had to be related. In a sense, the issue seemed somewhat trivial, and may still seem so to some. However, we sometimes may dream that an investigator will discover some magical variable that will speed up learning dramatically and make all of our educational efforts easy and painless. There are in fact some gimmicks which do have an influence on rate of learning, but we can be sure that study time will remain a fundamental variable. Those who examine the problems of formal schooling and possible solutions to these problems have not overlooked the basic role of study time. Bloom (1974), a professor of education, had this to say:

". . . I have considered differences in learning achievement between nations, states, and communities. I have also considered differences in learning of particular subjects under different classroom conditions. While there can be no simple explanation for all of these differences, it seems to some of us that the percent of time the student spends on a task in the classroom may be a powerful variable underlying most of these differences" (p. 687).

A Summary Graph

Figure 5.1 is a schematic graph representing the various relationships between study time and amount learned. In all cases, linear relationships are depicted. These curves may be used to describe different relationships based on the slopes of the lines, while maintaining a positive relationship between time and amount learned for all. We fully recognize that there are individual differences in the rate of learning. If we gave a group of subjects a constant period of time to learn, we would expect something like that shown in Figure 5.1 where each line represents a different subject or a small group of subjects of homogeneous ability.

If we gave subjects a list of items heterogeneous with respect to difficulty, we would expect the results to be much like that shown in the figure where each line represents the learning of a particular item, from very difficult items (bottom lines) to very easy items (top lines). Or, each line could represent a list of homogeneous items but with the differences in

Figure 5.1.
Possible relationships between study time and amount learned.

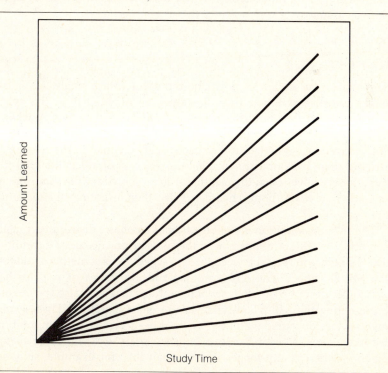

difficulty obtaining across lists. The total-time hypothesis refers to the constancy in amount learned per unit of time for a particular list. We could test this hypothesis by using a very long list (to avoid ceiling effects), giving one group forty trials at a two-second rate, and another twenty trials at a four-second rate. We would also get a performance measure for each trial at the four-second rate and for every two trials at the two-second rate. We could then have twenty points along the baseline representing the study time which at each point is equivalent for the two groups. If the two lines fall on top of each other, we would conclude that the total-time hypothesis is supported.

THE SPACING EFFECT

It now must be said that there is at least one stunning and general exception to the total-time hypothesis, a phenomenon known as the spacing effect. The total-time hypothesis states that amount learned is a direct function of the time regardless of how the time is divided. But, the spacing effect occurs when items are presented twice or more within a given study trial and when, in addition, the occurrences are separated by other items in one case, and not separated in the other. The spacing effect is said to occur if recall of the former type of items is greater than the recall of the latter type. Thinking in terms of free recall, and letting A stand for an item of interest and Xs for other items, we may designate the two types of operations as follows:

Spaced: . . . . . X X A X X X X A X X . . .

Massed: . . . . . X X X X X X A A X X . . .

The above two sequences might be represented in a single list or they might occur in different lists. It should be noted that in the spaced schedule, four other items fall between the two occurrences of A, whereas in the massed schedule, the two occurrences of A are in adjacent positions. If the recall of A is higher in the spaced schedule than in the massed, the spacing effect is demonstrated. That this effect contradicts the total-time hypothesis evolves from the fact that A is presented for the same amount of study time under both schedules. Why, then, is not recall equal under both schedules?

The spacing condition is sometimes spoken of as a distributed-practice condition, or DP, in opposition to the massed-practice or MP condition. The difference in recall between the two schedules is sometimes said to be the MP-DP effect. The terms *massing* and *distribution* of practice have previously described another set of operations that were also spoken of as representing the MP-DP variable in the older literature. These experiments were concerned with the time *between* successive trials in multitrial learning. Thus, a second or two between trials was said to be massed practice, whereas any longer interval than this, for example, sixty seconds, was said to be distributed practice. The interval between trials for the distributed-practice conditions was always filled with an activity to prevent the subjects from rehearsing the items in the list. It was believed that distributed practice would produce faster learning than massed practice. However, a rather large number of studies led to the conclusion that the expected effect occurs only occasionally and that the particular conditions causing it to occur are unknown. In many experiments the common finding was that learning was not related to the length of the intertrial interval.

During the past fifteen years very few studies have had the intertrial interval as the independent variable. Some evidence has been found, though, to indicate that a positive effect of intertrial interval in paired-associate learning is to be expected only with the study-test method, and not with the anticipation method (Izawa, 1971). We mention these classical operations here to contrast them with those used to study the spacing effect, that is, the effect produced by repeating items within a trial. As a further contrast it may be noted that most of the work on the spacing effect has been done during relatively recent years. The first study was reported by Melton in 1967, and, unlike the results from the older MP-DP studies, the spacing effect is extremely robust and pervasive.

An Illustrative Experiment

We will now examine a study to see what the spacing effect "looks like" in terms of data, and also as a means of discussing the various decisions made in designing an experiment, preparing the materials, and executing the study. This will lead into some diversions, most of them rather brief.

What Kind of Task? The spacing effect has been studied primarily by using free-recall and paired-associate lists. For the illustrative experiment, it was quite an arbitrary decision to use a free-recall task.

Many independent variables may be manipulated either *within* a list or *between* lists. Thus, in the present case, we could construct a list that had both spaced and massed items within the list. Or, we could construct two lists, one that had only massed items and one that had only spaced items. It so happens that the choice involved is not a critical one because it has been shown that a spacing effect occurs with either method of manipulating the independent variable. However, the within-between choice is a critical one for certain variables that will be discussed in later chapters. For the present experiment the within manipulation was used.

For many independent variables the experimenter has the option of presenting subjects with several short lists or one or two quite long lists. In the present instance it was decided to use a long list, although again it is known that the spacing effect occurs with either length of list. The list consisted of fifty-four words. The plan was to present this list for a single study trial, and the list was sufficiently long that it seemed quite unlikely, judging from previous work, that any subject would recall all fifty-four items even if some were repeated several times.

Associative learning tasks can be extremely difficult to learn if they are long, and when length becomes a serious issue, the task may be divided into parts, with a new part being learned each day. For example, Sanders and Dudycha (1974) asked their subjects to learn a 720-item paired-associate list, a list which simulated the task that mail sorters have to learn. The subjects learned twenty new associations a day for thirty-six days. Each day the subjects reviewed what they had learned on previous days. The cumulative total study time was a linear function of the number of items learned (the criterion of learning was 95 percent correct).

In the above procedure the list (of necessity) was broken into parts for learning. Another test of the total-time law results from experimentation on the whole-part problem. In the whole procedure the entire list is presented over and over for learning. In the part procedure the list might be broken into halves, with each half being learned separately before being combined into a whole list for final learning. The results of such procedures have shown consistently that time to learn is equivalent for the whole and for the part procedures (e.g., Postman & Goggin, 1966).

In the usual experiment we try to restrict the time required to learn a task in order to fit within the usual fifty- to sixty-minute periods under which university classes are held. Still, we must recognize that the learning is carried out in two basic ways. In one case, the experimenter may ask the subjects to keep at the learning task until a given criterion is achieved. The experimenter may also give a constant number of learning trials. Obviously, in this second method, the time the subject will require can be calculated exactly. This has many advantages over having the subjects learn to a criterion, in which it always seems that a few subjects cannot learn the task within the fifty-minute period.

For the present experiment it was decided that the rate of presentation would be five seconds per item. Many of the fifty-four words were to be presented more than once, but each presentation would last five seconds. All told there were 126 different exposures or different positions in the list presented for learning. Allowing three minutes for recall, it was evident that the task would not be overly taxing. In fact, we tested the subjects in a further experiment after they had been tested in this one.

The spacing effect occurs with either aural or visual presentation. We chose to use aural presentation via a tape recorder. This decision automatically produced other recommendations concerning the type of words to use. In particular, the amount of accoustical similarity among the words needed to be minimal so that a subject would not confuse one word with another. This in turn meant that the words should not be short words because finding fifty-four three- or four-letter words that did not have some similarity in the pronunciation of the words would be virtually impossible. We chose nouns of six or more letters and having at least two syllables. During the presentation each word was said twice during the five-second interval and there was no evidence that subjects failed to understand a word.

List Construction. As noted, fifty-four words were chosen and these were distributed across 126 positions. What was the particular function of each of these words?

1. In the discussion thus far we have spoken of spaced and massed items occurring twice. However, the spacing effect usually becomes greater and greater as the number of occurrences increases. In an illustrative experiment it seemed useful to try to produce large effects; therefore, we had spaced and massed items occurring two, three, and four times.

2. In Chapter 3 we noted that items at the beginning and end of a free-recall list are recalled better (usually, far better) than are those in the body of the list. Investigators customarily fill the primacy and recency positions with buffer items, meaning items that would absorb the primacy and recency effects. In the present experiment there were three buffer items at each end of the list (positions 1, 2, 3, 124, 125, 126), and the performance on these never entered into the calculation of a spacing effect.

3. It is of value to know the probability of recall of items presented once. Sometimes it is observed that a massed item presented twice is no better recalled than an item presented once. Twelve words were assigned frequencies of one and were distributed across the list in positions 4, 13, 25, 30, 43, 52, 64, 70, 75, 93, 118, and 122. The functions of the classes of items are summarized in Table 5.2.

4. The position an item holds in the study list may influence its probability of recall. If we are using a mixed list, then, we must be sure that in putting the list together the positions of last occurrence of massed and spaced items of the same frequency are approximately equivalent. Otherwise, it might be argued that differences in recall between massed and spaced items were due to position differences rather than to spacing and massing. To take an extreme case, it would not seem appropriate to have all of the massed items in the first half of the list and all of the spaced items in the last half of the list. In the present list we were reasonably successful in "matching" the position of last occurrences of the massed and spaced items.

5. The spaced items, to be spaced items, must have at least one other item falling between occurrences. It might be surmised that the number of other items falling between occurrences would be a pertinent independent variable. Evidence is contradictory on this matter. Most of the research on this variable has used only two occurrences of the spaced item. The distance between the two occurrences, as measured by the number of other items falling between, is called the *lag*. When lag does influence recall, it is that the greater the lag (within limits), the better the recall. Why a lag

Table 5.2. Word Functions, Frequency, and Number of Words Serving Each Function

Function	Frequency	Number of Words
Buffers	1	6
Singles	1	12
Massed	2	6
Massed	3	6
Massed	4	6
Spaced	2	6
Spaced	3	6
Spaced	4	6

effect is found in some experiments and not in others seems to be a mystery. It should be understood that it is quite possible to get a spacing effect without obtaining a lag effect. Lags of one and fifty may produce the same recall, but both may be better than the recall with a lag of zero (massed).

Lags of one, five, and ten were used in the present study, and when the frequencies were three and four, the same lag was used to separate all occurrences. That is, if the frequency was four and the lag was ten, the lag between each of the occurrences was ten. Slight deviations were necessary in some cases; i.e., a lag of nine was used instead of ten. Lag differences, of course, refer only to the spaced items. Because there were only six items at each frequency level, there were only two items used for each of the three lags.

6. As was seen earlier, six items were used to serve each critical function. Ignoring lag, the critical comparisons are between the massed and spaced items at each frequency level. The particular function assigned an item was determined randomly. Presumably, differences between the recall of spaced and massed items would not be due to differences in difficulty among the groups of six items. Nevertheless, when only six items are involved for each function, some concern would not seem unreasonable. It would not be highly improbable that two groups of six items, each drawn randomly from a common pool, could be different in average difficulty. To set aside this uneasiness, five forms were used. Essentially, this means that there were five different lists, with all lists having precisely the same structure, but differing in terms of the items serving particular functions. Items were assigned randomly to function for each of the five forms subject only to the restriction that a given item not serve the same function in more than one form. As a consequence, when we summed across forms there were thirty different words that served the same function. This increased confidence immeasurably that differences among functions were not likely to be due to differences in the difficulty of items.

Other Details. A total of eighty-five college students was tested, using group procedures, with seventeen subjects assigned to each form. Note that because the independent variables were worked out entirely within the list there was no issue involved in getting equivalent groups of subjects. Instructions to the subjects emphasized that they were to learn as many words as possible in preparation for a recall test in which the words could be recalled in any order. The subjects were further told that the list was long but that many of the words occurred more than once. Recall sheets, showing fifty-four numbered blanks, were given to the subjects before the list was presented, and recall started immediately after presentation of the word in position 126. After two minutes of recall, the subjects were asked to "dig deep; dredge up all you can." Recall was terminated after three minutes of total recall time.

Results. The first exhibit is seen in Figure 5.2, where frequency of occurrence is shown along the baseline and with the massed and spaced items identified within the graph. Percent correct recall was used as the response measure. The expected difference in the recall of massed and spaced items is apparent, as is the fact that the difference between the recall of the two types of items becomes larger and larger as the frequency increases. It can be seen that a massed item presented four times resulted

Figure 5.2.
Single-trial free recall as related to the number of times a word is studied, and to the spacing or massing of the occurrences.

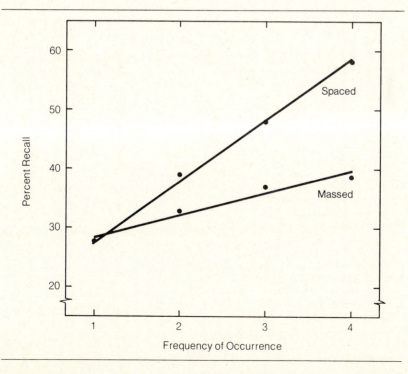

in about the same recall as did a spaced item presented twice. Clearly, the spaced-massed difference represents a violation of the total-time hypothesis.

The data in Figure 5.2 were obtained by summing across lag differences. We may now look at the effects of lag for the spaced items as seen in Figure 5.3. With a frequency of two, there seems to be no clear effect of lag, whereas with frequencies of three and four, recall increased directly as lag increased, although this interaction was not reliable statistically. Statistically speaking, there was a highly significant lag effect and an effect of frequency, but no interaction. That a lag effect occurred in these data when it has not been observed for several very similar studies only deepens the mystery of this phenomenon. The difference between spaced and massed items is highly predictable; the difference in recall of spaced items as a function of lag is not predictable.

The data in Figures 5.2 and 5.3 are based on averages. Did all subjects show a spacing effect? Of the eighty-five subjects, 77.6 percent recalled a greater number of the eighteen spaced items than of the eighteen massed items, whereas 16.5 percent showed a reverse effect, and 5.9 percent had no difference in the recall of massed and spaced items.

Figure 5.3.
Level of spacing (lag), frequency of occurrence, and single-trial free recall.

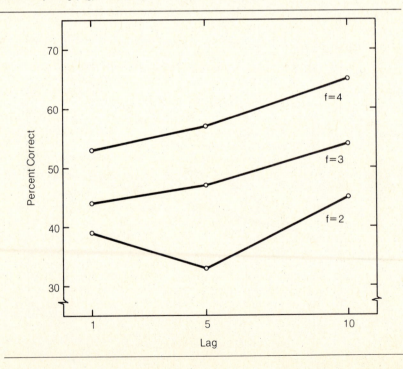

Theory

When we say we have a theory about a phenomenon (or group of phenomena) we mean that we have a proposed explanation. Explanations may take many forms but the basic idea is to describe just how the independent variable(s) produces its effect. A theory should specify a mechanism that is more general than that implied by the independent variable, or else little will be gained from the theory. Theories, as suggested above, may differ in many characteristics (Underwood & Shaughnessy, 1975), and it is to be expected that there is no "standard" way to go about theorizing. In the case of the spacing effect, two different theories have evolved, theories which are distinctly different in their approaches. One is called the attenuation-of-attention theory. This theory has to a large extent been associated with the author's laboratory. To simplify the exposition, we will simply refer to this as attention theory. The other theory has been associated with workers in the University of Michigan laboratory and will be called context theory.

Attention Theory. This theory assumes that the difference between massed and spaced recall results from a reduction in recall of massed items due to lowered attention as a word repeats itself in adjacent positions. As the word is shown successively it is as if the subjects say to themselves, "I am sick of seeing that word." Thus, attention is reduced, or attenuated, resulting in poorer recall than for the spaced items where attention is much less attenuated as a word is repeated. Heavy attenuation of attention for a massed item means that essentially the input was of little or no consequence for later recall. It will be remembered that Cooper and Pantle (1967) distinguished between nominal and effective study time when reviewing data relevant to the total-time hypothesis. Attention theory assumes that there is a marked discrepancy between nominal and effective study time for the massed items.

One might ask why a subject would attenuate attention to the massed words more than to the spaced words. Zechmeister and Shaughnessy (1980) may have obtained the answer to this question. They asked subjects to rate the probability of recall of each item immediately after it was shown. Subjects rated the massed items higher than the spaced items, implying that they thought they had better knowledge of the massed than the spaced words. This could lead to the attention differences for the two types of items.

One obvious problem with the attention theory is that the meanings of attention and attention changes are somewhat vague. Still, the intuitive meaning of attention can lead to particular experiments that appear to be germane to the theory. Some tests of the theory will be described.

1. If subjects are given a list to study such as one used in the illustrative experiment, and are then asked to estimate the number of times each word

was shown (or spoken), the results show that the subjects underestimate the number of times a massed item was shown relative to the number of times a spaced item was judged to have occurred (Underwood, 1969b). It is as if some of the occurrences of the massed item did not "register."

2. Zimmerman (1975) allowed his subjects to pace themselves through a long list. The subjects knew they were to have only a single study trial, but they could study each item as long as they chose. Zimmerman measured the amount of time the subject allowed each word to remain exposed. The idea was that if there is an attenuation of attention for a massed item, the length of exposure on successive occurrences of the item will decrease sharply. This is exactly what he found; the decrease in exposure time for massed words was appreciably sharper than the decrease for spaced items. It was just as if the subject did not want to see the massed item on its later occurrences. The results suggest that the spacing effect is due at least in part to differences in study time for the massed and spaced items.

3. It is possible to present two lists to learn simultaneously. The words in one list are clearly different from those in the other list. For example, one list might be made up of three-letter words, the other of six-letter words. On any given exposure on a study trial, one word from each list is shown. In learning lists simultaneously, the subjects are told that the object is to learn as many words from each list as possible. In testing, subjects are instructed to recall one of the lists first, followed by the other list.

Now, suppose that in a task where two lists are being learned simultaneously, the following sequence of four exposures is given:

List 1	List 2
rum	carpet
bin	carpet
cup	carpet
den	carpet

As may be seen, *carpet* is a massed item and it occurs four successive times, each time with a different item from List 1. According to attention theory, the subject should decrease attention to *carpet* across the four exposures and increase attention or time given to the study of the three-letter words. We should find, therefore, that the study time, hence the recall, of the three-letter words should increase with each exposure, i.e., the recall of the three-letter words presented along with repeated (massed) words should be greater than the recall of three-letter words which are not positioned opposite a massed word. Evidence in support of this expectation has been found (Underwood & Lund, unpublished).

4. Assume that the rate of presentation of a list containing massed and spaced items was quite fast, e.g., one second per item. Under such a circumstance, it might be expected that the subject would be less likely to attenuate attention to the massed item than if the rate were quite slow, e.g.,

five seconds per item. Therefore, the spacing effect should be less with a fast rate of presentation than with a slow rate. Some support has been found for this prediction (Wenger, 1979).

These illustrations should be sufficient to give the flavor of attention theory, and how it has been tested. Basically, the theory assumes that the total-time hypothesis is correct, and that the massed item is simply less well learned than the spaced item because the subject does not effectively use the study time for the massed item.

Contest Theory or Variable-Encoding Theory. This theory has a number of different versions if details are considered, but they have a common core in terms of a basic assumption. The theory assumes that the spacing effect results from a positive effect for the spaced items, not a negative effect for the massed items. The positive effect results from the fact that with two or more spaced occurrences, the item in question occurs in two different linguistic environments. Occurring in two different linguistic environments, or two different contexts, allows for two different associations to be formed, one between the first context and the item, and the other between the second context and the item (and a third and a fourth, if more than two occurrences are used). Given that two different or distinct memories are formed, the probabilities that one or the other of the contexts will produce recall is higher than if only a single context was involved, as is presumed to be the case for a massed item.

This is a very engaging or compelling theory, but the facts now indicate that it probably cannot account for the spacing effect with any degree of consistency. Some studies will be examined.

1. Maki and Hasher (1975) presented their items twice, in some cases with the context the same for both occurrences, and in some cases with the context different. All items were spaced. Let letters indicate words, with X being the target word. When X first occurred the context was ABXCD (two neutral context words on either side of the target word). On the second occurrence the context was either the same (ABXCD) or different (EFXGH). Context theory would predict better recall when the context was different on the two occurrences than when it was the same. Maki and Hasher report no differences as a function of the same or different contexts. A very similar study with comparable results was carried out by Maskarinec and Thompson (1976).

2. Schwartz (1975) used paired-associate lists in testing the context theory. One version of context theory holds that different contexts lead to different encodings of the word and that this increases probability of recall. Schwartz directly tested this notion. The paired-associate items were bigram pairs, e.g., AR-LE. The two letters in each bigram represented the first two letters in two words which are normatively associated. That is, in word-association tests ("give me the first word you think of to each of the following words"), these two words (*arm* and *leg*) were associated by

most subjects. In fact, Schwartz chose two pairs of associated words for each bigram pair. Thus, AR-LE are the first two letters of the associated pair *arm-leg* and also the first two letters of the associated pair *arrive-leave*. In the experiment, one variable was massing versus spacing, and another was constant versus variable learning aids. This variable will become clear shortly. The subjects were told that they were to learn to say the second bigram when the first was shown alone, and that they might be helped by the word pairs which were shown on the study trial along with the bigrams, as follows:

AR-LE

arm-leg

Each pair was shown twice for study. The same study aid occurred on both exposures (constant), or the aids differed (varied) on both occurrences of the bigram pair. Four conditions represented by four unmixed lists were necessary to accommodate both variables: spaced-varied, massed-varied, spaced-constant, massed-constant. Each of the sixteen pairs was, as noted above, presented twice, and if the item was massed it occurred twice in succession. If distributed, the list of sixteen different bigram pairs was presented once, and then a second time in the same order as the first. After completion of the study phase, the subjects were given a sheet on which the sixteen bigram stimulus terms occurred and they were requested to fill in the appropriate bigram response term for each stimulus term.

The results (mean number of correct bigrams recalled) are shown in Figure 5.4. It can be seen that a spacing effect was found for both constant and varied recall aids. In fact, the spacing effect was larger with constant than with varied aids, although this difference was not statistically reliable. Further, it can be seen from Figure 5.4 that overall performance with varied aids was poorer than with constant aids. This study would suggest that varied context is not responsible for the spacing effect.

3. Shaughnessy's procedure (1976, Experiment 3) demonstrates a further way of varying linguistic contexts. The subject made ratings of each word as it appeared. Three different ratings were used: frequency of usage of the word, ease of forming an image of the object symbolized by the word, and pleasantness-unpleasantness of the word. One group of subjects used the same rating scale every time a word appeared; another group rated on different scales for each presentation. No word was presented more than three times. The idea of the use of the rating scales is that with different scales, more different contexts will be established; hence recall might be better for the words having been rated on different scales than for words rated on the same scale several times. Shaughnessy found a large spacing effect, but it made no difference whether the ratings of a word differed with successive presentations of a word or whether the word was rated on the same scales. It should be mentioned that the subjects were not told that they were going to be asked to recall. Thus, the learning

Figure 5.4.
Paired-associate learning as determined by the interrelationships among constant and varied contexts and the spaced-massed variable. Data from Table 1 of Schwartz (1975).

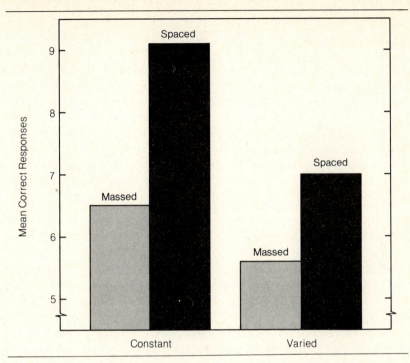

that occurred was said to be incidental learning, a topic which will be discussed more thoroughly later.

Some Summary Comments.   The studies described above would seem to conclude that the attention theory can more readily handle the spacing effect than can the context theory. Available studies would support this conclusion, yet it would be incorrect to leave the impression that theoretical matters are settled. There are data which do not coincide with attention theory (e.g., Maskarinec & Thompson, 1976), there are data which are interpreted as supporting context theory (e.g., McFarland, Rhodes, & Frey, 1979), and there are data which are troublesome for any theory (e.g., Underwood, Kapelak, & Malmi, 1976b). On balance, the attention theory has received more support than has the context theory. Perhaps, however, the spacing effect is far more complex than has normally been thought, and this complexity will sooner or later have to be reflected by more complex theories than have been described here. One investigator, originally in sympathy with context theory, now believes that the complexity is needed and he has given a tentative outline of such a theory (Glenberg, 1979), but we will not proceed further with the issue.

Let us be reminded of the generality of the spacing effect. It occurs under a great variety of conditions and with a great variety of materials. It occurs with children and with the aged. Hintzman (1974) may be consulted to gain the documentation for these statements of the ubiquity of the spacing effect. It may be evident that a phenomenon so pervasive and so large in magnitude is one that probably has applied value. Associative learning of almost any kind will take place more rapidly under spaced rehearsal than under massed rehearsal. For example, Landauer and Ross (1977) found that instructing college students to use spaced practice produced more rapid learning of telephone numbers than when the subjects practiced as they normally would. Attaining knowledge in any discipline requires the learning of the vocabulary of the discipline, and such learning will surely be facilitated by spacing of practice.

INCIDENTAL LEARNING

Accepting the position that time per se is not responsible for learning, we proceed with an examination of some activities that occur with time and do produce learning. The activities associated with incidental-learning situations are of central interest in this section. The basic difference between the instructions given for intentional learning and for incidental learning is that the former prepares the subjects for a test of learning over specified material, whereas the latter does not, although, of course, the subjects must be exposed to the material.

The research on incidental learning has a long history, a history that will not be reviewed here. A concise empirical summary of the earlier work may be found in Postman (1964a). Postman's view of the data available to him at that time led him to the following conclusion:

> There is little or no reason to maintain a conceptual distinction between intentional and incidental learning. What is learned depends on the responses elicited by the stimuli in the experimental situation. (p. 193)

Postman views intentional-learning instructions as an easy way to get the subjects to engage in activities which are appropriate for learning. If one can find ways to get the subjects to engage in these activities without informing them that they will be tested, the learning will occur nonetheless.

Some Sample Experiments

Postman and Adams (1960) presented their subjects a prose passage of 214 words, with thirty-five relatively important words deleted. The deletions were spaced rather equally throughout the passage. The subjects in two groups were asked to go through the passage filling in the thirty-five blanks with the words that they thought would best fit. One group was told that free recall of the thirty-five words would be requested; the other group was given no indication that a memory test would occur. By means that need not be detailed here, the subjects were paced through the task so that the total time required to fill in the blanks was essentially the same for both groups. In the recall, the incidental group produced a mean of 15.32 correct responses, those in the intentional group, 16.90. Although these two means do differ statistically, the difference is relatively minor in an absolute sense.

In a study by Plenderleith and Postman (1957), the subjects were shown one hundred common words, each for six seconds. The instructions called for the subject to write the first associate which came to mind upon reading each word. There were two groups of subjects, one group being told ahead of time that recall of the presented words would be requested, and the other not being warned. The mean number of words recalled by the intentional subjects was 36.62, and the mean for the incidental group was 34.96. The difference was not reliable statistically.

A further study used quite a different procedure for exposing the incidental subjects to the learning material (Postman, Adams, & Phillips, 1955). Two subjects worked together, one being arbitrarily designated as the examiner (E) by the investigator, the other being designated as the subject (S). Both E and S sat before the memory drum as nonsense syllables (CVCs) were exposed singly for four seconds each. As each syllable appeared, E spelled it aloud, letter by letter. The S repeated the syllable aloud as soon as it was spelled by E. The S was the "real" subject and had been instructed to learn the items in preparation for a free-recall test. Unexpectedly, the E was also asked to free recall the nonsense syllables and thus served as the incidental-learning subject.

In the Postman et al. study there were four levels of association value (0, 33, 67, and 100 percent), five syllables at each level. The purpose of the experiment, then, was to determine incidental learning as a function of the association value of nonsense syllables. The results show that the intentional and incidental subjects recalled an equivalent number of the syllables with the higher association values (67 and 100 percent), whereas the intentional subjects recalled more of the lower association-value syllables than did the subjects in the incidental group. Thus, intention to learn was of value when the materials were quite unfamiliar, but of little value when the materials were common.

A matter of method for incidental-learning experiments should be mentioned. It may have occurred to some readers that subjects in incidental learning groups may in fact have expected to be tested, and therefore they deliberately tried to learn the materials. They might have expected to be tested because of a general suspicion that a psychological experiment is never what it is purported to be. It has been common practice to identify subjects in the incidental groups who tried to learn. This may be done by a nonpunitive interview or by a questionnaire. The data of those subjects in the incidental groups who tried to learn are then eliminated.

As noted earlier, Postman concluded that if the subject makes particular kinds of responses, learning will be as good under incidental instructions as under intentional instructions. A Norwegian investigator (Björgen, 1964) arrived at essentially the same conclusion as a result of his experiments: "The subjects do not have to know that they are going to learn as long as the experimenter makes sure that they engage in the right kind of activity . . . " (p. 80) Of course, a critical question concerns just what are the right kinds of activity. For Björgen the proper activities were establishing relations between CVCs (the learning material) and common words, and then establishing connections between the pairings. If we accept the idea that conceptually there is no distinction between incidental and intentional learning, then whatever we decide is involved in intentional learning is also involved in incidental learning. This is not a matter we shall pursue further at this point. Rather, we will continue to examine some of the empirical studies.

We will look at one (Hyde & Jenkins, 1973) of a number of studies which were carried out at the University of Minnesota. The experiment is notable for the broad range of subject activities that were induced as a means of exploring their influence on incidental learning. The critical question concerned just what it is that an incidental-learning subject must do (what activities he must carry out) in order to recall as many items as the intentional subjects. The list used consisted of twenty-four unrelated words plus two fillers at the beginning and two at the end, these fillers not being included in the analyses. As usual, the test was free recall.

The words were presented aurally at a three-second rate for a single trial. There were eleven groups of subjects and five different orienting tasks designed to produce a wide range of responses or activities to the words. For each orienting task there were two groups, one intentional and one incidental. The subjects in the eleventh group were not given an orienting task; rather they were told to study the list in preparation for a recall test. Each of the five orienting tasks will now be described.

1. *Pleasant-unpleasant.* The subjects rated each word on a five-point scale labeled "pleasant" at one end and "unpleasant" at the other.

2. *Frequency of usage.* Each word was rated as to the frequency with which it is used in the English language. The five-point scale was labeled "very infrequent" at one end and "very frequent" at the other.

3. *Parts of speech.* The subjects were required to identify each word as a noun, verb, adjective, or "some other" part of speech.

4. *Sentence frame.* The subjects determined whether the word could or could not fit into either of two sentence frames. The two frames were: "It is _____" and "It is the _____."

5. *E-G checking.* The subjects determined whether a word contained an E or a G or both.

The mean recalls for the eleven groups are shown in Table 5.3. The first fact to be noted is that the recalls for the first five groups listed are roughly equal and are clearly better than the recall of the other six groups. For the first five groups, incidental learning is essentially as high as intentional learning. With the last three orienting tasks, performance is not as high as that in the first two groups, even when intentional learning is required. It is as if the rating task interferes with or takes away time from intentional learning. The authors conclude that if the orienting task requires the subjects to process the semantic features of words, the subjects will use these features to recall. They consider only the ratings of pleasantness and frequency to involve the processing of the semantic aspects of words. This conclusion is obviously a speculation since there was no independent evidence that semantic features were involved in recall.

Many studies have now shown that certain orienting tasks will produce incidental recall that is as high as intentional recall. A problem has been to identify in a clear-cut fashion just how the different orienting tasks produce the differences in recall. Still, in some ways of viewing the situation and the data, it is remarkable that there are techniques or orienting tasks that can produce recall under incidental conditions that equal that which occur intentionally. As we move ahead, we should keep two issues in mind. First, we have not yet said anything about how free recall occurs under any circumstances. We know that we can vary the amount of recall by varying the orienting tasks, but that does not tell us how recall occurs. Second, having observed that with certain orienting tasks recall is as high as under intentional learning, we might find it easy to conclude that the underlying processes are the same for both intentional and incidental recall. There are no empirical grounds and certainly no logical grounds for such a conclusion. The same outcome may occur for quite different reasons. It is hoped, of course, that the processes leading to recall are the same for both incidental and intentional learning, but we have seen no data that tell us that this is true.

Table 5.3. Mean Number of Words Recalled from a 24-Word Free-Recall List as a Function of Orienting Tasks and Intentional Versus Incidental Learning

	Mean Items Recalled	
Orienting Task	Incidental	Intentional
None	—	10.9
Pleasant-Unpleasant	11.2	12.7
Frequency of Usage	10.2	10.4
Parts of Speech	8.1	8.1
Sentence Frames	6.6	6.2
E-G Checking	6.6	8.2

Data from Hyde and Jenkins (1973)

Depth of Processing

Craik and Lockhart (1972), using the work on incidental learning as a prime inference base, proposed a way of viewing the encoding processes for words. They suggested that there are two stages in encoding (or, as they say, in the subject's analysis of a word). First, there is an analysis by the subject of sensory features or attributes of the word. This would include such characteristics as acoustic properties when pronounced, the length, the letter configuration, and so on. This sensory analysis is followed by a semantic analysis, and the greater the amount of semantic analysis, the greater the depth of processing or encoding. The probability of recall was said to be directly related to the depth of processing.

Given this orientation, it is quite apparent how the data involving different orienting tasks for incidental learning are absorbed. When a subject rates a word as being pleasant or unpleasant it is believed that the processing is semantic, and therefore it is deeper than when the subject is asked to determine whether a word included a G or E, or whether the word is printed in lowercase or uppercase. The conception of this depth framework can be criticized on the basis that there are no independent criteria of what is "deep" or what is semantic. It has sometimes seemed that if an orienting task produced incidental recall that was about as good as intentional learning, the orienting task was then judged to be making contact with the semantic aspects of the word. Postman and Kruesi (1977) and Nelson (1977) have made this criticism. Recently, however, experimenters have attempted to differentiate levels by having subjects rate various orienting tasks in terms of the difficulty or effort involved in carrying them out (e.g., Seamon & Virostek, 1978). In addition, Packman and Battig (1978) have shown that orienting tasks requiring the rating of various semantic characteristics do not produce equivalent amounts of learning. They found that better recall follows the rating of words on pleasantness-unpleasantness than follows the rating of meaningfulness, categorizability, imagery, concreteness, or familiarity.

Whether or not the systematic and logical aspects of depth of processing can be placed into a tidy state, the facts are clear that casting the incidental-intentional learning paradigm into a depth framework intrigued many investigators if the number of studies published may be taken as an index of that intrigue. In fact, a book (Cermak & Craik, 1979) summarizing the views of a number of investigators was published only seven years after Craik and Lockhart wrote their original paper. We will not go over this literature. For our purposes, it will be sufficient to examine a few of the findings. Because these findings deal with incidental learning, we are simply adding further empirical facts to those already described.

Further Findings

Craik and Tulving (1975) used somewhat different techniques for experimenting on incidental learning than we are acquainted with. Their sub-

Table 5.4. Reaction Times and Recognition Scores (Hits) for "Yes" and "No" Answers to Four Types of Questions

Questions	Reaction Time (in milliseconds)		Hits (proportions)	
	YES	NO	YES	NO
Is the word in caps?	614	625	18	14
Does the word rhyme with _____?	689	678	78	36
Is the word in the category _____?	711	716	93	63
Would the word fit in the sentences _____?	746	832	96	83

Data from Craik and Tulving (1975)

jects were told that the experiment dealt with perception and speed of reaction. Each word was exposed for two hundred milliseconds by a tachistoscope. Before the word was shown the subjects were asked a question about the word about to be exposed. The questions were such that the subjects could answer YES or NO, and the reaction time of the answer to the question was taken when the subjects pressed a button as they decided YES or NO. After a series of words were presented, an unexpected retention test was administered.

In their first experiment, Craik and Tulving asked the following questions: "Is the word in capital letters?" "Does the word rhyme with _____?" "Is the word in the category _____?" "Would the word fit in the sentence _____?" These questions were purportedly chosen to produce successively deeper and deeper analysis of the words. Each subject was shown forty words, and each question was used equally often. The retention was measured by a YES-NO recognition test in which the forty experimental words were mixed with forty new words.

The mean recognition scores (percent hits) and the reaction times are shown in Table 5.4 where the data are given separately for the "yes" and the "no" answers to the forty questions. The data indicate that the time to answer the questions increased as the answer required more and more semantic analysis, and recognition hits increased in a like manner. At the extreme, the differences in the recognition scores are very large. When the subjects had to decide whether the word was or was not printed in capital letters, the recognition performance was very poor; when the subject had to answer whether or not the word would fit into a sentence frame, recognition performance was very high.

When the subjects answer NO to a question, recognition hits were consistently less than if the answer was YES. Although Craik and Tulving (and others) have attempted to discover why this difference between yes and no questions occurs, no solutions of a satisfactory nature have been given. We must mark down the yes-no difference as one of the unsolved puzzles in the depth-of-processing literature. It is a puzzle because if a subject is asked whether or not a word will fit in a sentence, it would seem that the amount of semantic processing required for a NO response is equivalent to that for a YES response. At least the time involved to reach a YES or NO response is about the same. If the amount of processing is the same, why are the recognition scores not equivalent? Earlier, Schulman (1974b) had reported a similar finding. For example, if the subject was given the question "Is a dungeon a jail?" recall of the word *dungeon* was higher than if the question was "Is a *dungeon* a scholar?" Schulman speaks of the latter question as representing an incongrous query, but just what incongruity has to do with subsequent retention does not immediately follow.

A second issue which intrudes itself in the data given in Table 5.4 has to do with differences in reaction time in the responses to the various questions. Reaction time increased directly as the presumed depth increased. We have seen earlier that learning and exposure time are usually related. Therefore, it could be argued that the differences in recognition merely represent differences in exposure time of the words being presented and that the nature of the question is irrelevant. Craik and Tulving recognized this possibility and subsequently (Experiment 5) performed a study to assess the matter directly. Their idea was to use a shallow or nonsemantic orienting task that would take longer to perform than would a deep-processing question. For the shallow task the subjects were asked to determine if the word fit a given pattern of consonants and vowels, thus: "Does the word fit the pattern CCVVC?" As Craik and Tulving suspected, it took over twice as long to answer the pattern question than to answer the deep-processing question, which was the sentence-frame question used in the first experiment. Still, the results showed that the sentence task yielded consistently more recognition hits (76 percent) than did the question about the vowel and consonant pattern (54 percent).

The above outcome with regard to exposure time does not, of course, provide us with a license to ignore exposure time differences. If so-called deeper processing is to be refined by determining levels within the deep level, the exposure time must not be allowed to vary. This will not always be simple to accomplish when different questions result in appreciable differences in time to produce the appropriate responses.

One final finding reported by Craik and Tulving should be mentioned. In their last experiment they offered incentives for high recognition performance. Different groups were given different incentives (one, three, or six cents per word) for correct recognition. Thus, learning was intentional for all groups. The incentives had absolutely no effect on performance; words given shallow processing were recognized as poorly with incentives as they were without incentives. The recognition of words on which deep processing occurred was also uninfluenced by incentive magnitude.

Much earlier we examined data which indicated that incidental learning of nonwords, such as low-meaning CVCs, was very poor. More recently we have seen that depth of processing has a major effect when words are used. What happens if nonwords are used and the depth questions are asked? A study by Jacoby, Bartz, and Evans (1978) provides an answer. They used CVCs of 90–100 percent association value and 40–50 percent association value. The lists were unmixed. There were two orienting tasks. In one, the subjects were shown pairs of CVCs; and they were to pick the one in each pair that brought the larger number of associations to mind. In the second task the subjects were to identify the most pronounceable word in each pair. It was presumed, of course, that the first orienting task produced deeper processing than did the second. The subjects were all under incidental conditions.

The results showed that for the CVCs of 40–50 percent, association value the recall was very low and did not differ for the two orienting tasks. For the syllables with meaningfulness ratings of 90–100 percent, recall following the semantic orienting task was substantially better than that following the pronounceability judgments. The data indicate that it is not possible to process deeply the low-meaningful verbal units. These data, taken in conjunction with those reported earlier by Postman and Adams (1960), indicate that intentional learning is of importance for the learning of difficult verbal units.

Finally, it should be pointed out that the results obtained for levels-of-processing approach for individual words can be reasonably well matched when prose material is used. In a study by Arkes, Schumacher, and Gardner (1976), the orienting task involved at one extreme that of circling each *e* in the words in a paragraph, and, at the other extreme, copying the paragraph. The retention performance differed markedly for these two operations.

As we complete this section on incidental learning, some reminders may be necessary. First, because certain orienting tasks will produce incidental learning that is as high as that produced under intentional learning without the orienting task, we must not conclude that performance in both cases is mediated by the same processes or encodings. One may choose to hypothesize that this is true, but the data do not demand that it be true. Second, we tend to emphasize the fine recall produced by the so-called deep processing orienting tasks. We must not forget, though, that shallow processing results in some items being recalled or recognized. How are we to view this? Does this mean that shallow processing is as good as deep processing for some of the words? If so, what particular type of words? But, if we assume that deep processing is necessary for a word to be recalled, are we to conlude that even the shallow processing has a deep or semantic component which is really responsible for the recall? Postman, Thompkins, and Gray (1978); Hunt, Elliott, and Spence (1979); and Baddeley (1978) should be consulted for a thorough discussion of such issues.

Third, we have discovered no reason why a subject is able to recall even one word. Learning per se has been taken for granted; the levels-of-processing operations provide a means whereby different amounts of learning can be induced, but we have not learned how it is that a subject is able to recall or recognize any word. There is a detail we should mention as a part of this larger problem. It may have been noted that all of the experiments we discussed involved free recall or recognition. Experiments involving incidental learning in which associative learning is clearly required (as in the paired-associate task) have not been fitted into the deep-processing orientation.

SUMMARY

The total-time hypothesis holds that the amount learned is a direct function of the amount of study time regardless of how the time is divided. There is much evidence to support this hypothesis, but one clear exception is known as the spacing effect. When there are multiple occurrences of items in a study list, and when these multiple occurrences are separated by the occurrence of other items, recall is higher than if the multiple occurrences occupy adjacent positions in the study list. Thus, study time is equivalent but amount learned differs. Two theories were described which have been used to account for the spacing effect, namely, the attenuation-of-attention theory, and the variable-encoding theory. The evidence was judged to support the first theory more than the second.

Some of the methods used to study incidental versus intentional learning were reviewed. The evidence supports the idea that if the subjects in incidental-learning situations are induced to make the appropriate coding responses, learning occurs as rapidly as under intentional conditions. Recent studies of incidental learning have been done under an orientation called depth-of-processing. Semantic or meaning encoding is presumed to be "deeper" or "broader" then encoding of superficial attributes of the words (e.g., orthography) and therefore leads to better learning.

6

Recognition

We have already examined recognition when viewed merely as a task. Now we will examine recognition as a process. In making this examination we will use as context a simple theory which does quite well in handling the basic facts of recognition. Initially the theory will be given in very abbreviated form. Elaborations will be needed later in the chapter when we get to recognition as it occurs in tasks involving arbitrary event classes. The theory is spoken of (sometimes kindly) as frequency theory, and it had its beginnings in the writer's laboratory (Ekstrand, Wallace, & Underwood, 1966). To understand the theory requires first that we understand what is meant by frequency information.

FREQUENCY INFORMATION

Here are three words: *cab, car,* and *cad.* If you were asked to indicate which of these words occurs most frequently in printed English you would almost certainly reply "car." Then, if you were asked which one of the remaining two words occurs least frequently in printed English, it is almost a sure thing that you would reply "cad." That you can make such decisions quickly and accurately does not depend upon your having gone through various printed texts tallying on a sheet of paper the number of times each word occurred. But that you have, without intention, been tallying the number of times you have seen words seems beyond doubt. We may look at some data with respect to this matter. Subjects were given a single sheet of paper on which eight four-letter words were listed. The following instructions preceded the eight words:

> Below are eight four-letter words. We want you to think about how frequently each of these words appears in print. That is, think about how frequently each word appears in books, magazines, newspapers, and so on. We are *not* interested in the frequency with which the words are spoken by you or others; we are interested in how frequently you have seen each word in print.

We want you to rank order the words in terms of their printed frequency. Find the word among the eight that you think occurs most frequently and assign it a value of one. Then, find the word that you think occurs second most frequently, and assign it a rank of 2. Continue along this line until the least frequent word is assigned a rank of 8. You must assign a different number for each word; if you think two words have the same frequency, flip a coin (mentally) to decide which gets the higher rank.

news _____ amir _____ clog _____ oboe _____
sang _____ idol _____ moss _____ lamp _____

Actually, ten different sets of eight words each were used, each being given to seven subjects to rank. Thus, there were seventy subjects. The true frequency of the words varied from less than one per million words of printed discourse to over one hundred words per million. For the eight words given above, the rank order from most to least frequent is: *news, lamp, sang, moss, idol, clog, oboe, amir.*

Combining the results for the ten sets produced the results shown in Figure 6.1, where the mean judged rank order is plotted against true rank order. As is apparent, the relationship is quite strong; we are able to assign relative frequency ranks with high validity.

Figure 6.1.
Judgments of the frequency with which words occur in printed discourse. The subjects rank-ordered eight words from high to low frequency of occurrence, and the graph relates true ratios to mean judged ratios.

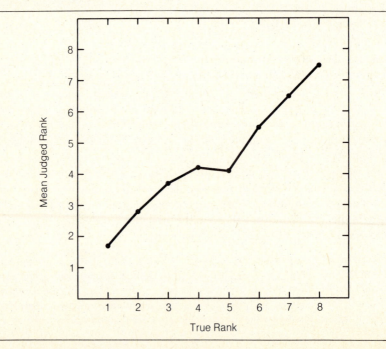

Our memories, it seems, include an enormous amount of information about the relative frequency with which various events have occurred. The information concerns not only word frequency, but other events as well. For example, it seems that if we were asked whether there are more delicatessens than gas stations in our country, we would say "no" quickly. If we were asked whether more potatoes or artichokes are eaten in this country, we would undoubtedly say "potatoes," and it is likely that these answers are the correct ones. Just as we have frequency information about verbal units, we also have vast amounts of information about the frequency of other, nonverbal events which repeat themselves. A number of studies have shown that the judgments on the frequency with which words occur in print do in fact coincide quite closely to true relative frequency as given in the Thorndike & Lorge (1944) book or in the Kucera-Francis (1967) lists. Both of these volumes give counts of the numbers of times words occur in printed English. We refer to this information as *background frequency*—the frequency information about words we carry around with us.

It will later be seen that certain memory phenomena result from differences in background frequency of words used in lists. However, as might be anticipated, if we want to study most precisely the effects of frequency we must manipulate it in the laboratory. That is, we study the effects of *situational* frequency by "inserting" the desired frequencies into the memory system.

There are two methods for studying factors influencing the assimilation of situational frequency. First, absolute judgments may be requested. The subjects are presented a list of items, one at a time, with some occurring once, some twice, some three times, and so on. On the test the subjects are presented each word and are asked to judge the number of times the word had been shown in the study list. The experimenter may include items on the test that were not on the study list and for which, of course, the correct response is zero. Results of such studies are quite consistent. When the mean judged (apparent) frequency is plotted against true frequency, two characteristics are evident. First, the relationship is linear. Second, the judgments on the low-frequency items are overestimated, and those on the high-frequency items are underestimated. Thus, the normal expectations are shown in Figure 6.2, in which we have assumed that frequencies of from zero through six were judged by the subjects.

The second technique used to study factors influencing frequency assimilation is a forced-choice procedure that corresponds closely to the method used to study forced-choice recognition. We will illustrate the method by reporting briefly on an experiment in which four-letter words were used, and in which the frequencies were 0, 1, 2, 3, and 4 on the test form. The thirty-four subjects were instructed as follows before the study list was presented:

I will show a rather long list of words on slides, each word being shown for two seconds. Some of the words will be shown once, some twice, some three times, and some four times. After the list is presented, I am going to test your memory for the relative frequency with which the words were shown. More specifically, you will be shown pairs of words on the test, and for each pair you must identify the word that occurred most frequently—occurred most often—in the study list.

There are far too many words in the study list to try to count on your fingers and toes; rather, you should observe each word carefully as it is shown and try to get the "feel" for words that occur once, for those that occur twice, and so on. Questions?

The study list contained forty words presented once, twenty presented twice, ten presented three times, and five words presented four times. On the unpaced, forced-choice test there were four types of pairs. Two were 0–1, in which a new word was paired with an old word that had been presented once, and 1–2, in which one word in the pair had been presented once, the other twice. The other pairings were 3–4 and 0–3. There were twenty pairs of the first two types and five of the second two types. However, because the subjects had two successive lists of exactly the same structure, we have combined the data for the two. The errors for each type

Figure 6.2.
The expected relationship between true situational frequency and judged frequency.

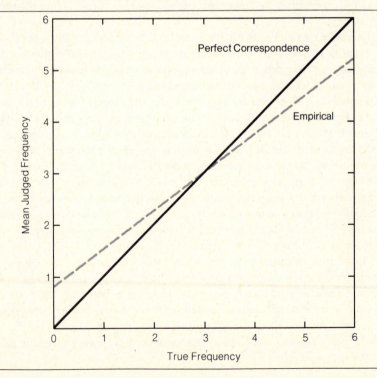

were as follows: 0–1, 21.6 percent; 1–2, 29.9 percent; 3–4, 38.8 percent; and 0–3, 4.4 percent.

It should be noted that the first three types all have a common feature, namely, that the difference in the frequencies of the two words is one. This similarity might suggest that the discrimination among the three types would be equivalent. This is obviously not the case; the percentage of errors increased as the lowest frequency in the pairs increased. These results illustrate the principal underlying the classical psychophysical function known as Weber's Law, and various derivations from it. This law holds roughly for many of our sensory discriminations. The function shows that the amount of change necessary to produce a just noticeable difference (also called a difference threshold) is a constant proportion of the base magnitude (in our case, the lowest frequency member of the pair). Thus, the larger the base magnitude, the greater the number of errors to be expected if the difference between the two frequencies in the pairs remain constant. Our data demonstrate exactly this outcome for the frequency judgments; errors increase in number from 0–1, to 1–2, to 3–4. In fact, when the two frequencies were 3 and 4, some of the subjects performed at a chance level. As would be expected, when the two words in a pair were 0 and 3, performance was almost perfect.

Two points will be made about frequency judgments as a means of putting them in perspective. First, the study of frequency assimilation and frequency discrimination has become an area of study in its own right. We will not attempt to summarize this literature. Howell (1973) may be consulted for a summary of the earlier literature. It is sufficient for the moment for us to recognize that we are able to assimilate frequency validly and to discriminate among frequency differences.

Secondly, almost without exception, studies have shown that the precision of frequency judgments is as fine when the test of frequency judgment is unexpected as when it is expected. Or, to say this in the lingo with which we are already acquainted, the incidental acquisition of frequency information is as good as its intentional acquisition. Apparently, if the subject perceives an event it enters on to a frequency "counter," and nothing will change that process. Frequency assimilation is sometimes spoken of as being automatic or obligatory. It further follows that instructions to the subject need not be as elaborate as those quoted earlier. Indeed, many experimenters simply tell the subject that there will be a memory test without specifying in any way the nature of the test.

FREQUENCY THEORY

The history of psychology has not shown that apparent frequency of events has entered seriously or basically into theoretical formulations. Viewing frequency discrimination as a skill, it did not seem to us that nature would give us this skill without there being some particular function it would fill. Or, to say this another way, it did not seem that a skill so finely honed would be like a vermiform appendix, a structure which apparently has long since outlived its usefulness. However this may be, frequency theory holds that the discrimination between old and new items on a recognition test is based on a frequency discrimination. This may be most clearly seen in the forced-choice test with two alternatives—old and new. The new item has a situational frequency of zero, the old item a situational frequency of at least one. If the subject chooses the item in a pair which has the highest frequency, it is called a correct choice. We will return to this momentarily.

It may be noted that we have specified *situational* frequency in the above description. How can there be a frequency of one for a common word when that word has been seen many times before? The fact is that when subjects make situational frequency judgments, background frequency does not appear to intrude at all into situational frequency. It is as if words with varying background frequency start at the same level in the situation in which situational frequency is manipulated. A matter for later concern is the fact that in some recognition experiments it does appear that background frequency and situational frequency do tend to get confused. For the time being let us assume that subjects keep the two sources of frequency quite separate.

The theoretical situation may be depicted in somewhat more quantitative, but schematic terms in Figure 6.3. There are two distributions. The one to the left, which appears merely as a descending line, represents the tail of a distribution of items with zero situational frequency. The apparent frequency of the words presented once in the study list is depicted in the distribution to the right. The two distributions overlap. For whatever reasons, some items with a true frequency of zero are judged by some to have an apparent frequency greater than zero. Too, some items with a situational frequency of one are judged to have an apparent frequency of less than one. These statements may not seem completely accurate. A given subject will always judge an item to have zero frequency or a whole number frequency; a subject does not judge an item to have occurred .5 times or .2 times. However, when a large number of items are judged and the measure is the mean judged frequency, a continuous scale results.

With the overlap between the two distributions as depicted in Figure 6.3, one expects that there will be times when in the forced-choice test with a 0–1 difference, the zero item will have a higher apparent frequency than will the item with a true frequency of one. The result will be an error in recognition. If the forced-choice test is between an item with zero frequency and one with a frequency of two, the likelihood of an error is sharply reduced because only a very small bit of the two distributions will overlap. In Figure 6.3 the right distribution will move further to the right if the frequency is two, whereas the distribution for zero frequency will remain fixed.

Figure 6.3.
The situation expected with respect to apparent frequency when large numbers of words are judged for frequency following a situational frequency of one, and when a large number of words is judged for frequency when the situational frequency is zero.

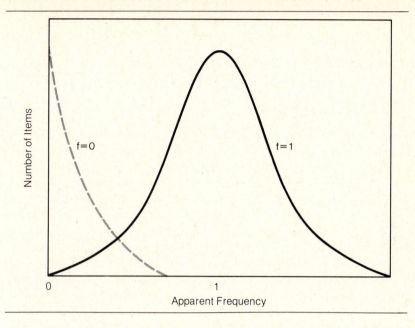

The application of the theory when dealing with a YES-NO test is very much the same as with the forced-choice test, although it may be complicated by the presence of response-criterion differences for different conditions. Basically, however, the subjects will respond YES to all items with an apparent frequency at and above a given level. To repeat, the theory simply asserts that the recognition decisions are made on the basis of apparent frequency. However, it has been found necessary to accept the idea that under certain circumstances the subjects may use information of types other than frequency in reaching decisions. For example, if an old and new word appear to have equal subjective frequencies (a situation which must necessarily occur once in a while), the subjects must obviously turn to other information (attributes) in an effort to reach a decision. This other information might include meaning (the subject remembers that a word with that particular meaning was in the study list), orthographic characteristics, acoustic aspects, and so on. This may seem to indicate that the theory has escape hatches. However, the theory clearly must predict that cases will arise in which frequency differences cannot mediate recognition decisions because there is no discernible frequency difference. Under these circumstances the subject (who has been instructed to make a decision on all items) must either guess or turn to other types of information. We presume that both events do in fact occur. Frequency theory assumes that frequency differences will be the major, but not exclusive, vehicle for providing recognition decisions.

We will turn now to some tests of frequency theory as applied to old-new recognition decisions.

SOME TESTS OF FREQUENCY THEORY AS APPLIED TO OLD-NEW RECOGNITION

Individual Differences

Frequency theory assumes that the discriminations involved in making frequency judgments are the same discriminations made in reaching recognition decisions. It must follow from this assumption that individuals who can make fine frequency discriminations will be good "recognizers" and individuals who have trouble making fine frequency discriminations will be poor recognizers. This supposed relationship may be evaluated by calculating a correlation between scores on a frequency-judgment task and those on a recognition task. A positive correlation indicates that the theory is tenable, but it cannot be taken as a form of proof. The performance on the two may be correlated, but that does not mean that a single process underlies the performance on both tests. On the other hand, a zero correlation (statistically speaking) between the two tasks would indicate that the theory is probably wrong and should be discarded. There are ways to interpret a zero correlation that do not imply the above conclusion. As a general rule, though, one would follow a hazardous theoretical route if a theory such as frequency theory were maintained following the discovery of a zero correlation between two tasks as indicated above.

The facts in the case support the theory. A study in the Northwestern laboratory (Underwood, Boruch, & Malmi, 1978) showed a correlation of .55 between performance on a frequency-judgment test and a recognition task. Further, this study included a number of other memory tasks. The factor analysis of all of the tasks showed that frequency judgments and recognition scores had the highest factor loading of any tasks on one of the five factors which emerged. This indicates that there may be commonality in the processes underlying the two tasks.

Parallel Manipulations

Another approach for testing frequency theory involves the use of parallel manipulations. By parallel manipulations is meant the determination of the effects of a given independent variable on two different dependent measures. In the present case the two different dependent measures are frequency judgments and recognition decisions. In one such study (Underwood, 1972b) the independent variable was the number of alternatives on the forced-choice test, ranging from two to five. The number of alternatives was a within-subject manipulation. Two groups of subjects were presented exactly the same list, but with different instructions concerning the testing. That is, one group was told they should learn the words so that they could identify them on a subsequent multiple-choice test. The other group was told that they would be asked to choose the most frequent word in the multiple-choice sets. Words were actually presented one or two times on the study trial, but on the tests only one item in each multiple-choice set had in fact been presented for study. All of the other items were new.

The results showed that the number of errors made was statistically equivalent for the two groups and that for both groups, the number of errors increased in a comparable manner as the number of alternatives increased. To a thoughtful skeptic, such evidence is not strongly compelling with regard to support for frequency theory. It could be argued that the same results for the two types of tests could be produced by two quite different underlying mechanisms. However, it is possible to at least blunt such an argument by looking at another type of data. Any recognition study will show evidence that all items do not have equal probabilities of producing errors. Some items will produce many errors; some will produce none. These differences are reliable in the sense that if the two different groups are tested and the number of errors made on each item are determined for each group, the correlation between the two distributions of errors will indicate a strong relationship. This means that item difficulty is consistent.

Given that item difficulty is reliable, the theory must predict that errors made in judging frequency differences will fall on the same items as will the errors made in recognition decisions. This prediction was fully confirmed in the present study, in which the correlation was shown to be .74. This relationship strongly suggests that common processes underlie both recognition decisions and frequency judgments. Other studies have produced the same finding (e.g., Underwood, 1974).

It is proper to note here that Proctor (1977) objected to the above experiment on the grounds that the forced-choice test essentially makes the two types of judgments equivalent because in both cases the subject identifies the word that was in the study list. Proctor used a YES-NO test in his experiment, and he found that performance under recognition instructions was poorer than that under frequency instructions. It can be seen that any frequency test that requires absolute judgments can be scored as a recognition test. Assigning a word a frequency value of one or more indicates that the subject thought the word was in the list; assigning a zero indicates that the subject thought the word was not in the study list.

It is not evident why Proctor's results do not coincide with those of the author's, or vice-versa. The differences in results are not due to a YES-NO test versus a forced-choice test because a correspondence between frequency judgments and recognition decision has been found with the YES-NO procedure (Underwood, 1974). Proctor does not give data on the reliability of item difficulty and the correlation of errors made under the two different sets of instructions. Consequently, we cannot tell whether or not the studies deviate on this important measure. Of course, it is not a rare thing to find discrepant results in the literature; such results usually indicate that some variable of importance was set at a different level for the two experiments. Sooner or later the discrepancies will be rationalized. For the time being, we will simply note that Proctor interprets his results as being at odds with the notion that frequency information underlies recognition decisions. Obviously, in the overall picture, we do not believe that Proctor's results should cause us to abandon the theory. And, Harris, Begg, and Mittener (1980) were unable to replicate Proctor's results, and they interpret their findings as being consonant with frequency theory.

In the above experiment the number of alternatives functioned as the independent variable in the parallel manipulations. Presumably one could take any independent variable and test its effect on recognition and on frequency assimilation. For example, we could ask about exposure duration, or about the length of the study list. Such experiments simply have not as yet been conducted using the parallel-manipulation logic.

Deductive Consequences

Repeated Items in Testing.   Two studies will be used to illustrate how deductions from the frequency theory may be evaluated. The first deals with the use of repeated words during testing (Underwood & Freund, 1970a). A group of subjects was presented a long list of words as the study list for a forced-choice test of recognition. Two independent variables were introduced during the testing. One was the number of times a particular wrong (new) word was used in the forced choice tests, and the other was the number of times a correct (old) word was tested, each time with a different new word. Assume that the letters A, B, C, D, E represent the five old words and that the letter V represents the new word. To symbolize the first manipulation, the five test pairs are listed along with the situational frequencies that would correspond to each test.

Successive Test Pairs	Frequency Inputs
A–V	1–0
B–V	1–1
C–V	1–2
D–V	1–3
E–V	1–4

The first test, A–V, took place at a time when the new word had a frequency of zero and the old word a frequency of one, since it had been presented once during the study trial. At a later point, the pair B–V is tested. As a result of the first test (A–V), the wrong word gained a frequency unit (the subject looked at it on the test) and so both B and V should have frequencies of one. In the actual experiment a minimum of twenty pairs fell between the successive tests in which the same word appeared.

If the frequency accrues as above, it becomes quite evident that by the third or fourth test, the subject should be choosing the wrong item (V). Clearly, frequency theory would predict that the choice of the correct item would decrease across tests. Indeed, if we attend only to the numerical representations, we would have to predict that by the fifth test (E–V), selection of the correct choice should be reduced to near zero.

The results showed that performance fell across the five tests, with successive scores of 83, 66, 58, 59, and 57 percent. Although scores decreased by twenty-six percentage points from the first to the fifth test, it is apparent that performance did not fall to the zero level as would be expected from a strict application of frequency theory. Two factors could modify the expectations. First, even though twenty or more other pairs separated successive occurrences of the V item, some subjects would surely remember that the wrong word had occurred in an earlier pair. Furthermore, they might remember that it had been judged wrong (zero frequency) and this would lead them to continue calling it wrong. Thus, the memory for what was wrong supercedes frequency information in making the decisions. Second, college-student subjects are far from being idiots when it comes to evaluating the validity of their information. They may conclude that frequency information is invalid and therefore turn to other types of information. Either or both of these factors may be involved in the experiment and would prevent the extreme expectations of frequency theory from being supported.

The second variable was the frequency of repetition of the correct word, and this manipulation may be schematized as follows:

Successive Test Pairs	Frequency Inputs
A-V	1–0
A-W	2–0
A-X	3–0
A-Y	4–0
A-Z	5–0

The letters V through Z represent successive wrong words, whereas A is the correct word tested five times. Obviously, the frequency data lead to the prediction that performance on the A item should increase across the five tests. The five values were 83, 91, 92, 93, and 92 percent. Strictly speaking the performance should not have leveled off at 92 percent; that it did is not predicted by the theory. Still, overall, the fact that a ten percentage point increase does occur during the act of testing is viewed as substantial support for frequency theory.

Syllable as a Unit.   That we can accurately judge the relative frequencies with which the twenty-six letters occur in words means that we have abstracted the letter-frequency knowledge from larger units, namely words. That we can rather accurately estimate the frequency with which words occur in printed discourse means that we have abstracted and assimilated the word frequency from larger units or contexts (sentences). All of the above refers to background frequency. The present experiment (Underwood & Zimmerman, 1973) is based on the idea that situational frequency assimilation may also be abstracted from larger units. More particularly, it is assumed that each syllable of a multisyllable word has a frequency representation in the memory, and that this information is dissociated from the word per se.

With this description of frequency assimilation as background, the purpose of the study may be understood. Suppose that in the study list the words *consult* and *inbred* appear. And, assume that each syllable in each word has a frequency representation in memory that is in some degree independent of the word. If, then, on a test we present a new word such as *insult*, it would show a higher level of false alarm than would appropriate controls. The word *insult*, it can be seen, has one syllable from each of the two words (*consult* and *inbred*) that appeared in the study list. The subject might be expected to view the word as old because each of its two components has a frequency of one. The details of the experiment may now be described.

Subjects were presented forty-eight two-syllable words as the study list. These words were presented singly, but they may be thought of as twenty-four pairs. From each pair a new word could be formed or derived by using one syllable from each of the two words. We will speak of these new words as D Words. In the study list the forty-eight words were randomized subject only to the restriction that the two words from which a D Word would come did not occupy adjacent positions. For the test, the twenty-four D Words were used as "new" words in the two-alternative forced-choice tests, along with twenty-four true new words (C Words). The twenty-four D Words and twenty-four C Words were paired with the forty-eight words from the study list. A D Word was never paired with one of the two words from which it was derived. The expectation from frequency theory was that subjects would make more errors on the test pairs having the D Words than on the test pairs having the C Words.

The experiment carried a further test of frequency based on the same reasoning that was used to construct the tests in which words were repeated (as described earlier). The test can be best explained by using an illustration. *Consult* and *inbred* were two study-list words used to derive the word *insult*. Assume that in the test series the test pairs containing the words *consult* and *inbred* were presented before the test pair that included *insult*. When the subject is tested on *consult* and *inbred*, the syllables *in* and *sult* should gain an additional frequency unit. Thus, when *insult* is tested, more errors would be expected. If, on the other hand, the test pair involving *insult* were tested before the pairs including *inbred* and *consult*, the likelihood of an error rests only on the single unit of frequency induced for each syllable during the study trial. The order of the pairs on the test was set up so that half the D Words were tested before their inducing words were tested, and half were tested after the inducing words were tested. The difference in the errors on the D and C Words should be greater in the first case than in the second. To say this another way, the type of test word was expected to interact with the test stage, which is identified as first half (D Words tested before the inducing words) and second half (D Words tested after the inducing words).

The results are shown in Figure 6.4 and support both expectations. The number of errors made on test pairs in which the D Words occurred was greater than the number of errors on the pairs in which the C Words occurred. And, the difference is greater in the second half than in the first half. It is as if the inducing words put two familiar syllables in the D Words. In short, by assuming that syllables of words gain situational frequency as a result of occurring on study and test trials, certain predictions follow about errors made on "new" words constructed from those syllables. Other studies, based on the same idea but using different subunits have also supported the expectations from frequency theory (Underwood, Kapelak, & Malmi, 1976a).

The tests of frequency theory as presented ought to be sufficient to get the flavor of the theory as applied to old-new recognition. Other theories of recognition will not be given equal time here. A broad discussion of various types of theories of recognition may be found in Mandler (1980) along with a sketch of Mandler's own theory which assigns a role to frequency but which emphasizes retrieval aspects of the recognition process. Later in the chapter we will examine frequency theory as applied to recognition tasks which require discrimination between arbitrary event classes. Before doing so, however, we should not let devotion to theory mask the basic facts a theory must accommodate. Therefore, further facts discovered in the old-new recognition paradigms will be listed with a minimum of theoretical elaboration.

FURTHER FACTS AND THOUGHTS
ABOUT OLD-NEW RECOGNITION

Exposure Duration

Old-new recognition of words is influenced positively by exposure duration (e.g., Schulman & Lovelace, 1970; Lutz & Scheirer, 1974). However,

Figure 6.4.
Forced-choice recognition errors when a test word (D Word) consisted of two syllables which had occurred independently in other words in the study list, and when they had not (C Word). Data from Underwood and Zimmerman (1973).

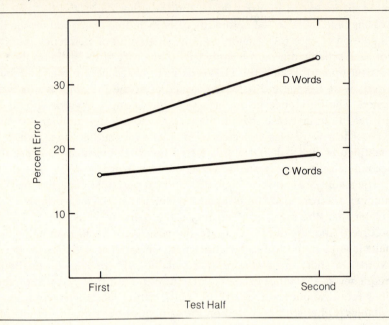

this effect is not great. For example, in one study using a forced-choice technique, in which the study time varied between two and six seconds per item, the number of errors decreased by 2 percent for each additional second of study (Underwood, 1972b).

Hintzman (1970) showed that frequency judgments did not change for study durations between two seconds and six seconds. It takes no great perception to see that Hintzman's finding, viewed in conjunction with the findings relating old-new recognition and study time, conflicts with frequency theory. The theory assumes that a given variable will have parallel effects on recognition scores and on frequency judgments. Still, increases in study time beyond a certain point do not facilitate old-new recognition. In one study the exposure interval was either five, ten, fifteen, or twenty seconds, and no difference was observed in the recognition scores (Underwood & Malmi, 1978b).

Recognition Errors

Recognition errors increase directly as the number of alternatives in a forced-choice test increases (Underwood, 1972b). The same law holds for miniaturized tasks (Kintsch, 1968). This would be expected from frequency theory but would also be expected with any thoughtful analysis of the situation. To do this experiment properly (an experiment in which number of alternatives is varied) requires a mixed test list—mixed in the sense that tests on items with different numbers of alternatives must be included in the test list. To use unmixed lists (in which one group is tested with two alternatives, another group with three alternatives, and so on) confounds the number of alternatives with both the length of retention interval and the number of words seen during the test.

Similarity Between Old and New Items

The similarity between the old and new items is a variable influencing recognition. The higher the similarity between old and new items, the greater the number of errors. The more critical issue concerns the nature of the similarity. That is, which characteristics must be similar in order to effect performance? The answer is, almost any characteristic. Small effects are produced by similarity of meaning, such as with synonyms; small effects may also be produced by orthographic or formal similarity, by acoustic similarity, and so on. The point that must be emphasized is that the effects are relatively small for any one of these characteristics, but many different characteristics have been shown to have an influence under certain circumstances.

Context Manipulations

Context manipulations may take several forms. If subjects study in one physical environment and are tested in a quite different physical environment, recognition is not influenced to any appreciable amount (Smith, Glenberg, & Bjork, 1978). There are a number of ways of manipulating what is called verbal context, and these fall into the general categories of specific and nonspecific verbal context changes. Three different nonspecific context changes may be identified.

Context Addition.   In this procedure a subject studies single units, but on the YES-NO test the old item has a new item in close proximity. The subjects are told that they have only to make a decision on the one item and that the other may help make the decision. The target item might be printed in capital letters, the context item in lower case. The experiments indicate that context addition does not have any consistent effect on performance (Underwood & Humphreys, 1979).

Context Change.   Context change is implemented by having one or more items (in addition to the target item) present at the time of study. The subjects are told that they will be tested on only one of the words (and this word is identified, perhaps by being printed in caps while the others are in lower case), but these additional words might help remember the critical or target word. Then, on the test, the old context words are replaced with new ones. Thus, on the study trial, one item might be *desk HORSE sky*, and on the test the item might be *HORSE pen water*. There would, of course, be control items or conditions in which the context remains the same on study and test. Context change has been shown in a number of studies to produce a decrease in performance (e.g., DaPolito, Barker, & Wiant, 1972).

Context Deletion.   This manipulation is the opposite of addition; context is deleted between study and test. For example, the subjects may be presented a series of pairs of words for study and then be tested on single words extracted from the pairs. Recognition of the single word is found to be poorer than the recognition of the study pairs (e.g., Underwood, 1974).

The reasons for poor performance as a result of context change and context deletion are obscure. Empirically we can generalize that if the verbal context present at study is not present at the test, a decrement will be noted, but this generalization is no substitute for a theoretical rationale for the observed losses. Frequency theory, as thus far developed, has no ready accounting of the effects of these context manipulations.

The above three types of context operations refer to nonspecific context changes. They are nonspecific in the sense that there is no particular relationship between the target word and the context words. Usually, they are chosen randomly. Specific context manipulations, on the other hand, refer to the introduction of words which have specific relationships to the target words. Perhaps the most widely used procedure of this nature is the one using homographs. An illustration will be given. On the study list the subject is shown *savings BANK* and is instructed to remember *BANK*, with the other word serving as a memory aid. On the test the item will be changed to *river BANK*. The subject's recognition decision is whether or not *BANK* was in the study list.

The above operations obviously deal with the role of word meaning in recognition. The earliest study using homographs was conducted by Light and Carter-Sobell (1970), and their results certainly indicated an appreciable loss in recognition when the meaning was changed by a change in the prefix word. However, the accumulative work since that time suggests that at best the homographic manipulation produces only a very small effect. This literature is summarized by Underwood and Humphreys (1979). Hunt and Ellis (1974) describe the various conditions which must be used if unambiguous decisions about the homographic manipulation are to be drawn.

Association Values

Association values (meaningfulness) of both consonant syllables (CCCs) and nonsense syllables (CVCs) have been shown to be inversely related to the number of errors in the running-recognition paradigm (Martin &

Melton, 1970). McNulty (1965), on the other hand, found just the opposite; low-meaningful units (e.g., *neglan, volvap*) were a little better recognized than were high-meaningful units (e.g., *garment, insect*). This contradiction needs to be discussed from two perspectives.

First, how can such a direct contradiction be rationalized? McNulty believed that his finding represented a manifestation of a phenomenon called the von Restorff phenomenon— also called the von Restorff effect or the isolation effect. This phenomenon was discussed in Chapter 5 and refers to the fact that if a word in a free-recall list differs in some obvious way from all other words in the list (such as being printed in red ink), it will be better recalled than if it does not differ from the other words. McNulty believed his results represented a von Restorff effect because the low-meaningful items (of which there were only five) "stood out" in the list like an item in red ink. This may represent a possible rationalization, but there is still another explanation, which represents the second perspective on the issue. The manipulation of meaningfulness by McNulty was handled by using a mixed list; there were five items from each of three levels of meaningfulness randomized in the fifteen-item list. The use of mixed lists for manipulating characteristics of tasks is now believed to be unsatisfactory. Subjects may distribute their study times unequally over the items by displacing rehearsal. Thus, in the present case, the subjects may rehearse a low-meaningful item while one of high meaningfulness is being displayed. The total-time law predicts that performance on the low-meaningful items could be better than that on the high if a sufficient number of subjects displace rehearsal. Whatever the case, McNulty's results probably do not represent the true relationship between meaningfulness and recognition. It is likely that the Martin-Melton study, in which unmixed lists were employed, represents the true relationship.

Background Frequency

The background frequency of words influences recognition in a way that is, to most people, quite unexpected: Low-frequency words give better recognition scores than do high-frequency words (e.g., Wallace, Sawyer, & Robertson, 1978). A theoretical position regarding this finding will be described in the next chapter.

Concrete Versus Abstract Words

Concrete words give better recognition scores than do abstract words. Pictures yield better performance than do words which name the pictures. If concrete words are used, performance is likely to be better if the subjects are instructed to imagine the objects named by the words. These and related facts were obtained in experiments reported by Paivio (1971) in his book dealing with imaginal processes.

Length of List

The greater the number of items in the study list, the poorer the recognition scores (Underwood, 1978).

Orthography

Words may be reliably rated on distinctiveness of the orthography. Words such as *xylem, sylph,* and *phlox* are rated as highly distinctive, with words such as *parse, scone,* and *poser* rated as having low distinctiveness. Zechmeister (1972) has shown that words of high distinctiveness produce higher recognition scores than do words of low distinctiveness.

Instructional Procedures

Various instructional procedures may influence recognition scores. It was noted above that subjects will do better if they are told to imagine the objects symbolized by concrete words than if they are not so told. A number of other instructions have been shown to influence performance. For example, Hall and Pierce (1974) asked one group of subjects to think of words which the study word reminded them of. Recognition on a YES-NO test was superior to that shown by a group left to their own devices. Light and Schurr (1973) gave their subjects ninety-six words in a study list. In one case the subjects saw successive blocks of eight items, and they were asked to make up a story using the eight words in order. Another group saw the same blocks but was given no special instructions. The first group had better recognition scores than did the second. In spite of these positive manipulations, very comparable ones may not produce positive effects (e.g., Raye, 1976). It is therefore difficult to reach generalized statements about the kind of instructions that will influence recognition and the kind which will not. Further, we must remember that positive outcomes are more likely to be published than negative outcomes.

FREQUENCY THEORY AND VERBAL-DISCRIMINATION LEARNING

Frequency theory was originally formulated to account for verbal-discrimination learning (Ekstrand, Wallace, & Underwood, 1966). Remember that in the verbal-discrimination task, the subjects are presented pairs of words, and one of the words in each pair has been designated arbitrarily as the correct word in the pair, the other being incorrect. The subjects' task is to learn which one has been called correct. In presenting the words for study, positions are changed randomly to avoid presenting obvious cues to distinguish between the correct and incorrect words.

The frequency theory as applied to this task assumes that subjects use a rule with which to base their decisions, namely, that the item in each pair with the highest frequency is the correct item. Let A–B symbolize the pair in which A is correct and B is incorrect. Assume the anticipation method is used in learning. The pair is presented, followed by the correct word (A) alone, thus:

A B

A

Assuming that the subjects respond to each word as shown, the frequency for A is two, and for B it is one. If the subjects can discriminate between frequencies of one and two, and if they choose the most frequent item the next time A and B are presented, they will be correct. Incidentally, data presented earlier in the chapter indicated that when subjects make forced-choice frequency judgments they are correct about 70 percent of the time when choosing from a pair in which the frequencies are two and one. The moment subjects correctly anticipate the correct word, the apparent frequency of it is probably increased. In addition, they may rehearse the correct word, thereby adding further to its frequency. Over trials, therefore, the phenomenal frequency difference between the correct and incorrect words is expected to increase. Work by Kausler, Wright, and Bradshaw (1979) shows that this does happen.

When the study-test method is used, the frequency inputs are again identified as being a minimum of two for the correct word, and one for the incorrect word. On the study trial under this method, A is underlined (A-B) to indicate that it is the correct word. It is assumed that A is perceived twice, B once. Actually, there is some reason to believe that a skilled subject will look only at A and not at B at all, a practice which would increase the discriminability of the frequency difference between the two words.

Processing Model of Frequency Theory

Frequency theory postulates that subjects apply a single rule across all pairs. Perceiving frequency differences between the incorrect and correct words, in favor of the correct words, is said to be the only rule that applies in the usual verbal-discrimination list. Just how or why the subject hits upon the frequency rule is not known. The theory can be somewhat formalized into a processing model as shown in Figure 6.5. Correct and incorrect items, identified by a plus and minus, respectively, are said to assimilate frequency as a part of the memory for them. The subjects, seeking a rule to handle the responding in the task, scan the frequency and frequency differences and use this information in making a decision for each pair. Frequency theory in its pure form would say that only fre-

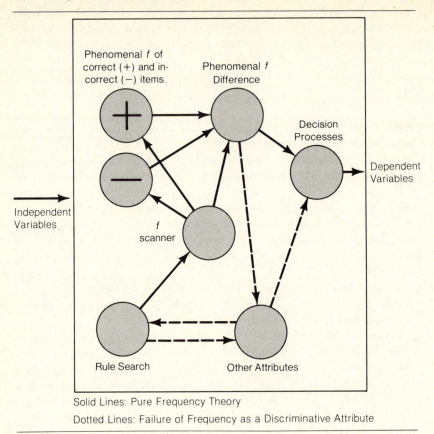

Figure 6.5.
A processing model of frequency theory.

Phenomenal *f* of correct (+) and incorrect (−) items.

Phenomenal *f* Difference

Decision Processes

Dependent Variables

Independent Variables

f scanner

Rule Search

Other Attributes

Solid Lines: Pure Frequency Theory
Dotted Lines: Failure of Frequency as a Discriminative Attribute

quency is used in making the decisions. It is quite reasonable for the subjects to choose the word with the highest frequency as the correct word because they can easily remember that it was in fact presented twice (in the anticipation method), whereas the incorrect word was presented only once.

The system with dotted lines indicates the "search" subjects make if they do not use the frequency attribute as a discriminative cue, or if they are forced to give it up because of the conditions of the experiment (which will be illustrated later). It is assumed that the subject will search for some rule that will allow correct responding. Even if frequency discrimination is believed to be preeminent, it is not the only possibility for the acquisition of the verbal-discrimination task. The three possibilities are:

1. Frequency rule;
2. Some other rule;
3. Some unknown way of learning of a nonrule nature.

At a later point more will be said about this third possibility. At the moment the intent is to show how rule detection and utilization comes very quickly in verbal-discrimination learning when the rule may seem easier to apply than the frequency rule. Several experiments have yielded data that are germane to the matter.

Kausler and Farzanegan (1969) used background frequency of words to establish a rule. In one condition, LH, the incorrect words were all low-frequency words, with the correct words being all high-frequency words. In a second condition, HL, these were reversed. The third condition served as a control in that for half the pairs the correct word was a high-frequency word, and for the other half the correct word was a low-frequency word. Thus, the subject could not form a rule based on background frequency. There were thirty subjects in each of the three conditions, and the learning of the twelve-pair lists was carried on until each subject achieved two successive perfect trials. The mean numbers of trials needed to reach this goal were 4.77 for LH, 5.03 for HL, and 9.83 for the control. A background-frequency rule cut the time to learn about in half. Frequency theory assumes, of course, that the control list was acquired by using situational-frequency discriminations.

Deichmann, Minnigerode, and Kausler (1970) showed again that background frequency could be used as a rule, but in addition, they demonstrated that subjects detected and used word-length differences. Thus, when all correct words had seven letters and all incorrect words had four letters, learning was more rapid than if word length was inconsistently related to correctness. In still further work, Kausler and his students (Kausler, Erber, & Olson, 1970) constructed lists in which all of the correct words belonged to one conceptual category (e.g., animals), and all the incorrect words belonged to a different category (e.g., vegetables). Learning was more rapid for those lists than for the control, in which the two categories were distributed equally across correct and incorrect words.

As a final illustration, a study by Green and Schwartz (1976) will be examined. The lists contained twenty-four pairs. In one condition all of the correct words began with the vowels A, E, O, or U, and all of the incorrect words began with the consonants C, F, G, and S. In the control condition there were no consistent relationships between correctness and nature of the first letters. The subjects were given four anticipation trials, and the mean number of correct responses was 71.04 for the rule group and 62.75 for the control, the difference being reliable statistically.

The above studies tell that subjects may choose rules other than frequency when such is available. At the same time, though, they allow for the possibility that a frequency rule could evolve and perhaps evolve quickly. To repeat, frequency theory assumes that in the usual verbal-discrimination task, a frequency rule is the only one available to the subjects.

The theory as described thus far presumes that the subject, when applying a frequency rule, chooses the most frequent. Under certain circumstances the subjects will choose the least frequent member of the pairs. The "certain circumstances" usually involve some kind of a transfer situation. For example, assume that subjects are initially given several study-test trials on a free-recall list. Then, each word in the free-recall list is paired with a new word to form a verbal-discrimination list. For this list, all new items are designated the correct words. Faced with this situation, subjects will, according to the theory, choose the least frequent members of the pairs. On the other hand, if the words from the free-recall list become the correct words in verbal discrimination the subject will follow the usual rule of choosing the most frequent word in each of the pairs. In either case, however, performance initially will be high because either the least frequent or the most frequent items in the pairs are clearly discernible.

We will shortly describe various tests of the frequency theory. At that time it will be seen that the number of different types of tests mediated by the theory is quite large in contrast to the number of tests generated when old-new recognition was involved. The difference appears to be that there are two different critical events—correct and incorrect items presented during learning—and that these two events may have the frequencies manipulated in a variety of ways. Because so many different tests have been conducted, the treatment will be selective. Later there will be a listing of studies dealing with variables not always considered critical for frequency theory. Eckert and Kanak (1974) have prepared a well-organized summary of the literature through 1972.

Tests of Frequency Theory

Individual Differences. It was shown earlier that old-new recognition scores correspond to the precision of frequency judgments. It would be expected that precision of frequency judgments and verbal-discrimination scores would also be correlated, but the facts in the case are quite confusing and inconsistent. A positive correlation that makes frequency theory tenable can be found in the usual experimental situation (e.g., Underwood, Shaughnessy, & Zimmerman, 1972a). Yet, a factor analysis study (Underwood, Boruch, & Malmi, 1978) found that performance on verbal-discrimination lists was only weakly correlated with frequency judgments and with old-new recognition; the scores on the verbal-discrimination lists actually formed a separate factor. Furthermore, Ghatala, Levin, and Subkoviak (1975) have demonstrated that although subjects normally use frequency information to learn the verbal-discrimination task, certain other characteristics dominate the discrimination under special instructional procedures. These procedures essentially transform the verbal-discrimination task into a two-category classification task.

It will be necessary to return to these matters later in the chapter. For the time being it will be concluded that the individual-difference approach to testing frequency theory has cast some doubt on at least the generality of the theory. That the theory might shrug off this reservation comes from the many positive results in testing the theory by the traditional method of manipulating independent variables.

Methods Variables. Many small variations in method can be made in presenting verbal-discrimination lists, and almost all of these could involve a prediction from frequency theory. They involve such predictions because the variations will always increase or decrease the frequency of the items. Two studies will be reviewed as illustrations.

The anticipation method makes it easy to manipulate the type of feedback. Wike (1970), in one condition, presented only the correct item on the feedback, and in another presented only the incorrect item on feedback. Presenting only the incorrect item provides information that is equivalent to the information provided when the correct item is given as feedback. In both cases the subject can identify the correct and incorrect items. However, according to frequency theory, presenting the incorrect item alone on feedback will be detrimental to learning because it adds a frequency unit to the incorrect item. Consequently, the subsequent discrimination between the two based on frequency difference is more difficult than if the correct item is given on feedback. Wike used a sixteen-pair list and found that over ten trials, feedback of the correct item resulted in a mean of 8.95 errors, whereas the feedback of the incorrect item produced a mean of 20.52 errors.

Hopkins and Epling (1971) used the study-test method. On the study trials the correct word was underlined. One group (Group P) was required to pronounce both the correct and incorrect words aloud once on the study trials. Group C was a control group in which the subjects were left to their own devices. Performance of Group C was superior to that of Group P. This study and others suggest a reason as to why the study-test procedure usually produces faster learning than the anticipation method. In the study-test method the subject might "ignore" the nonunderlined word, particularly if it is the second word in the pair. Thus, the incorrect word would not receive a frequency unit, thereby making the discrimination between the correct and incorrect items easier. In the anticipation method the subject has no basis (initially, at least) to ignore either word and each, therefore, probably gets a frequency input.

Frequency Induced Before Verbal-Discrimination Learning. Consider again a case in which the subjects are given a free-recall list for several study-test trials. Then, the words from the list are paired with new words to form a verbal-discrimination list. If the words from the free-recall list become the correct words, performance ought to be essentially perfect on the first trial and should remain so over trials. In effect, in carrying out these procedures we are presenting the subject with a frequency discrimination in which the two items may differ as much as ten to one (depending upon the number of free-recall trials given). If the items from the preliminary free-recall task become the incorrect words in the verbal-discrimination task, performance again should be very nearly perfect on the initial trial because the subjects will choose the least frequent members of the pairs. However, over trials the subjects may have trouble reaching or maintaining perfect performance because the frequencies of the two items in a pair become more and more equal with each trial.

One need not give free-recall learning to produce these effects. One could simply expose the subject to the items before they become part of the verbal-discrimination list. The procedures are a little cleaner perhaps if the subjects are required to pronounce each word as it appears in the preliminary exposures. But given that the subject responds to each word (indicating that they had perceived it, or as is sometimes said, had made a representational response to it), the expectation for verbal-discrimination learning would be the same as giving preliminary free-recall learning, and results meet expectations (e.g., Smith & Jensen, 1971).

Transferring from an initial task to a verbal-discrimination list has been done by Zechmeister, McKillip, and Pasko (1973) in an unusual way. They had their subjects read a 2000-word story into which they had inserted words with specified frequencies of occurrence. After the subjects read the story, they were given a verbal-discrimination task in which words from the story, hence, words with known situational frequencies, were used. These investigators found that expectations from frequency theory were supported. Thus, a word that occurred six times in the story and that became a correct word in the verbal-discrimination list was given correctly far more frequently than if it was a new word (had not been in the story) and hence had a zero frequency at the start of learning the verbal-discrimination lists.

Finally, we will examine a study by Berkowitz (1968). As the first step in his experiment, Berkowitz had the subjects learn a verbal discrimination list of sixteen pairs. The learning was carried to a fairly high level in that the practice continued until fifteen of the sixteen pairs were correctly responded to on a single trial, and then five more trials were given beyond this. The second list consisted of twenty-four pairs, eight of each of three classes. There were sixteen correct words in the first list learned. These sixteen words were paired randomly and will be called C–C pairs, since all were correct items in the first list. There were sixteen incorrect items in the first list, and these were also paired randomly to produce eight I-I pairs. To complete the list, Berkowitz added eight pairs of new words (N-N). The twenty-four pairs were randomized within the list, and eight learning trials on the second verbal-discrimination list were given.

What would frequency theory predict about the relative rate of learning the three types of pairs in the second list? Berkowitz concluded that the

N–N pairs would be the easiest to learn, the C–C pairs the most difficult, with the I–I pairs falling in between. The reason for these predictions, predictions which were confirmed, lies in Weber's Law. Remember that Weber's Law states that the higher the situational frequency (base frequency) the larger the frequency difference necessary to produce a discriminable difference between two frequencies. The pairs based on the new words would have zero situational frequency at the start of learning, so that a frequency discrimination could be developed more rapidly for these pairs than for either the C–C and I–I pairs. The I–I pairs have a lower base frequency than the C–C pairs because the incorrect words in a verbal-discrimination task accrue less situational frequency than do the correct items. Incidentally, several investigations have shown that if frequency judgments are required following the learning of a verbal-discrimination task, the correct items are judged to have higher frequency than the incorrect items, just as the theory assumes. The results Berkowitz found are quite in line with theoretical expectations.

Repetitions Within a List. In the usual verbal-discrimination list, each word occurs once. What are the consequences, as viewed by frequency theory, when certain words occur more than once in a list? Frequency theory leads to some rather unusual predictions for some of the manipulations. A study by Underwood and Freund (1969b) explored the full range of item repetition for twelve-pair lists. The study can be most readily understood by examining the lists used. There were eight lists, the structures of which are shown in Table 6.1, where letters are used to symbolize

Table 6.1. Structure of Repetition for the Eight Lists Used by Underwood and Freund (1969)

Lists C2 and I2	Lists C4 and I4	Lists C6 and I6	Lists C12 and I12
A-C	A-E	A-G	A-B
A-D	A-F	A-H	C-D
A-E	A-G	B-I	E-F
A-F	B-H	B-J	G-H
A-G	B-I	C-K	I-J
A-H	B-J	C-L	K-L
B-I	C-K	D-M	M-N
B-J	C-L	D-N	O-P
B-K	C-M	E-O	Q-R
B-L	D-N	E-P	S-T
B-M	D-O	F-Q	U-V
B-N	D-P	F-R	W-X

	Assumed Frequency of C and I Items in Each List			
C Lists	12:1	6:1	4:1	2:1
I Lists	2:6	2:3	2:2	2:1

the words. Each of the lists will be examined in turn. This examination leads to the predictions of learning based on frequency theory.

The first lists, C2 and I2, have only two different words in the left column. Each of these words, A and B, occurred six times. When these two words were correct words, the list was designated C2; when the two words were incorrect words in the verbal-discrimination list, the list was designated I2. Lists C4 and I4 have four words, each occurring three times, and in Lists C6 and I6, each of six words occurs twice. Finally, Lists C12 and I12 are normal lists with no words repeated. They differ only in that in the experiment, the left members of the pairs were called correct for List C12, and the right members were called correct for List I12.

Attention is called to Lists C2 and I2. The frequencies for the C and I items can be calculated as they should exist following the first trial, in which the anticipation method is used. A conservative frequency counting procedure was used in which on a given trial the C items have two frequency units in memory, the I items one unit. For List C2, where A and B are correct items, there should be a total of twelve units accrued to A and twelve to B (each occurs six times). Therefore, in relation to the incorrect items (C, D, E, etc.), the ratio is 12:1 for each pair as indicated in the table. On the other hand, for List I2, in which A and B are incorrect words, the frequency ratio becomes 2:6 for each pair.

Still concerned only with Lists C2 and I2, it is clear that frequency theory predicts that the two lists will not be equivalent in difficulty. The theory predicts that List I2 will be more difficult to learn than List C2. With I2, the subject may respond with the least frequent word if a difference of 2:6 frequency units is discriminable, which will surely be true for some subjects. However, for C2, the ratio is 12:1, and performance should be essentially perfect on the first trial. Across trials the frequency difference between the two items will continue to grow for C2, but will quickly diminish for I2.

The predictions of frequency theory should be contrasted with that of a different rule, one that seems to be intuitively appealing or appealing to common sense. For List C2 this rule would be about as follows: "Words A and B are always correct words; respond only with these two words." For List I2 the rule might be: "Words A and B are always the incorrect words; never respond with them; always respond with the words with which A and B are paired." This line of thinking could well lead to the conclusion that the two lists will be of equal difficulty.

Proceeding with an examination of the expected frequency ratios for the lists, it can be seen that for the C lists, performance should decrease consistently from C2 through C12 because the corresponding frequency ratios are 12:1, 6:1, 4:1, and 2:1. For the I lists, on the other hand, Lists I4 and I6 should be very difficult to learn because the frequency inputs produce near equality in the frequencies for the correct and incorrect items. Strictly speaking, the theory would predict that List I6 could not be learned. However, it is necessary and realistic to presume that rehearsal mechanisms will increase the frequency of the correct words over the incorrect ones so that learning will occur, albeit quite slowly. The theory clearly predicts that I6 will be more difficult to learn than I12 and C12, the control lists.

The discussion of the expectations from frequency theory necessarily revealed some of the methods used in the experiment. However, some additional procedural details need to be outlined. The eight different lists were learned by eight different groups of twenty subjects each. The first trial was strictly a study trial; the subjects did not respond until the second trial when, as is customary, they were asked to respond to each pair, guessing if necessary. There were four anticipation trials beyond the initial study trial. It should be clear that the pairs were randomized from trial to trial; they were not blocked by repeated words as in Table 6.1.

The results are shown in Figure 6.6, where the mean total errors are plotted for the first trial. The base line is the number of different C and I words. Attention is called first to the finding for List C2; performance was

Figure 6.6.
Errors in verbal-discrimination learning as a function of the number of different correct (C) and incorrect (I) words used in the lists. See Table 6.1 for the nature of these lists. Data from Underwood and Freund (1969).

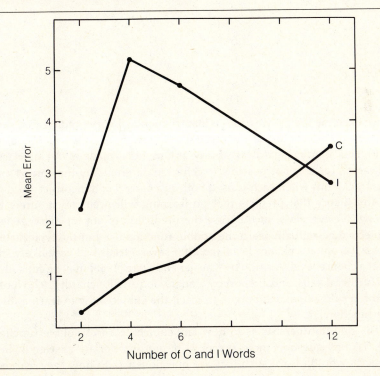

almost perfect on the first trial. (Those who have not done much research must understand that there are always a few subjects who seem to have it in their minds to not conform to the theory being tested in the experiment.) As expected by frequency theory, the performance on I2 is considerably worse than that on C2. The performance on Lists I4 and I6 were not greatly better than chance (six errors). Generally speaking, the results provide very firm support for frequency theory.

Double-Function Lists. As discussed just above, when each incorrect word is used twice in a list, with each correct word used once, performance is poorer than for the usual list in which no word is repeated. It was noted that using a conservative counting procedure, the subjects should not be able to learn a list in which each incorrect word occurs twice. Researchers have presumed that because subjects do learn such lists, rehearsal mechanisms do in fact produce discriminable frequency differences. The originators of frequency theory have never been happy with this state of affairs. However, work on the double-function list may support the idea that the rehearsal mechanisms assumed for the usual verbal-discrimination list do in fact exist.

In the double-function list, each word occurs once as a correct item and once as an incorrect item. Thus, a four-pair list may be symbolized as follows:

Correct	*Incorrect*
A	B
B	C
C	D
D	A

If we examine the list we can see that frequency theory predicts that such a list is impossible to learn because the frequency of all words is equivalent. This is true regardless of any assumptions made about displaced rehearsal, for it is not possible to rehearse differentially the correct and incorrect items when each is used both as a correct and incorrect word.

Any theory that predicts that no learning will occur must surely be wrong. Nevertheless, in this case the prediction is not far awry. A few subjects do eventually learn the double-function list, but the typical subject starts out at a chance level and after several trials will very likely still be at a chance level. A study by Kausler and Boka (1968) may be consulted for further details, and a report by Underwood and Reichardt (1975) looks at the results of some attempts to teach the subject how to learn a double-function list.

The question persists as to how any subject learns a double-function list. To this question there seems to be no appropriate answer. When subjects who do learn such lists are questioned as to how they learned, they are usually not able to provide a coherent answer, or they produce stories about their learning which cannot possibly account for the learning. Notwithstanding, the extreme difficulty of learning of the double-function list is taken as very strong support for frequency theory. It is a side issue, although a curiously fascinating issue, as to how any increase in performance arises when a double-function list is given to the college student.

The double-function list can be simulated in the laboratory (Boulay & Underwood, 1976). The subjects in the critical condition of the experiment were given a sixteen-pair list. One item in each pair was underlined, and a study-test procedure was used for learning. The instructions were unusual. First, the subjects were given instructions for bidirectional paired-associate learning. Thus, on some study trials the pair was in the order A–B, and on other trials the order was B–A. On some test trials A was shown and B was to be recalled; on other trials B was shown and A was to be recalled. The purpose of the bidirectional learning was to keep the frequency of A and B roughly constant, as in the double-function list. The second part of the instructions informed the subjects that on the test trials they would be tested for verbal-discrimination learning as well as for associative learning via the paired-associate task. On the test trials half the pairs were used for verbal-discrimination testing. The pairs were presented with the underlining removed, and the subjects were to identify the correct (underlined) word as it appeared on the study trial. The other half of the pairs were tested for paired-associate learning as described earlier. Across the twelve trials each pair was tested six times for verbal-discrimination learning and six times for paired-associate learning.

The results showed that paired-associate learning increased steadily across the twelve trials. On the other hand, performance on the verbal-discrimination task did not show a statistically significant increase, although performance was above chance on the first trial (about 60 percent) and increased a small amount beyond that value. These results also offer support for frequency theory because the equalization of frequency via the paired-associate learning apparently removed the frequency differential normally used to discriminate between the two words in each pair.

Further Facts Briefly Noted

Background Frequency. Situational frequency judgments of words are made without intrusion from background frequency. It is as if all words start out with a frequency of zero when situational frequency inputs are made. Given this, it might be expected that verbal-discrimination learning would not be influenced by differences in background frequency of the words used in the lists; a list of high-frequency word pairs might be expected to produce about the same rate of learning as a comparable list of low-frequency word pairs. Experimental tests of this proposition have been mixed in outcome. According to frequency theory, if background frequency intrudes upon situational frequency, a verbal-discrimination list of high-frequency pairs would be more difficult to learn than a list of low-frequency pairs. This is because of Weber's Law; the higher the background frequency the greater the frequency change necessary to produce a noticeable difference.

There have been a number of studies, but the results are contradictory. For example, Ingison and Ekstrand (1970) and Schulz and Hopkins (1968) failed to find an influence of background frequency, whereas Lovelace and Pulley (1972) and Rowe and Paivio (1971) did find the effect expected if background frequency and situational frequency merge. No satisfactory resolution of these conflicting results has been put forward.

Concrete Versus Abstract Words. Many studies have shown that concrete word pairs give more rapid learning of verbal-discrimination lists than do abstract pairs (e.g., Rowe & Paivio, 1972). Such a finding is troublesome for frequency theory unless additional assumptions are made. However, further research has led to the possibility that the critical variable is not concrete versus abstract. For unknown reasons, abstract words are judged to have higher background frequency than are concrete words when the objective frequency is equivalent (Galbraith & Underwood, 1973). Ghatala and Levin (1976) recognized that phenomenal (subjective) background frequency was probably not equivalent for concrete and abstract pairs in the studies showing that concrete pairs produced an easier verbal-discrimination task than did the abstract pairs. Therefore, these investigators constructed lists of concrete and abstract pairs in which in one case the phenomenal background frequency was equivalent for the two kinds of pairs, and in another case in which the abstract pairs had higher phenomenal frequency than the concrete pairs. In both cases objective background fequency was equated.

The results showed that when phenomenal background frequency was equivalent, the learning of the two types of pairs did not differ. The mean number of correct responses across four trials was 29.58 for the nine abstract pairs and 30.25 for the nine concrete pairs. When the concrete and abstract pairs differed on background frequency the mean value for the abstract pairs was 27.46 and 30.50 for the concrete pairs (a highly significant difference statistically). Thus, according to Ghatala and Levin, it is not the concrete-abstract variable that has produced the difference in verbal-discrimination learning, but the correlated difference in phenomenal background frequency. It may seem that the matter was cleared up and that the data in the past represented a confounding of the concrete-abstract variable and background frequency. However, this tidy state of affairs did not last long. A more recent study by Goedel and Englert (1978) failed to replicate the Ghatala-Levin finding. Indeed, the results obtained by these investigators led them to conclude that there is a large effect of the concrete-abstract variable and no effect of phenomenal background frequency. Once again, the outcome of experiments proves that to obtain firm and analytical conclusions about the basic factors underlying the influence of task variables is very difficult.

Length of List. Frequency theory indicates that list length should be of no consequence. Experiments show that it is of consequence (e.g., Savage & Kanak, 1973). Such results are normally not considered a serious problem for frequency theory. As the number of pairs in a list increases, the number of possible overlapping elements across pairs, e.g., syllables, increase. These overlapping elements may produce interference because the frequency accrual would not be limited to a given item in a single pair.

Number of Alternatives. All of the studies reviewed thus far involved pairs of words. As with old-new recognition tests using forced choice, one need not be restricted to the two-choice format. In old-new recognition performance decreases as the number of alternatives increases. Strangely enough, in verbal-discrimination learning, performance improves as the number of alternatives increases (Radtke & Jacoby, 1971). These investigators used a sixteen-item list, eight of which had two alternatives and eight which had four alternatives. Each item was presented for three seconds on the study trial; then the correct alternative was shown for one second. On the tests the items were presented for four seconds, and the subjects were asked to call out their choices. Learning was carried to three consecutive errorless trials.

The results showed that two alternatives produced a mean total of 6.31 errors, whereas with four alternatives the mean was 4.12 errors. These values were not corrected for potential differences in guessing. As is obvious, guessing would be less likely to produce correct responses when there were four alternatives than when there were two. So, the difference between the two conditions is in fact greater than what the means given imply. The investigators interpret their results as supporting frequency theory. This may be thought of in terms of amount of time which could be allotted each alternative on the study trial; the greater the number of alternatives, the less the amount of time allotted to each alternative which could be translated as being less phenomenal frequency for four alternatives than for two. This is not a clear predictive case because the correct item will receive less input for the four-alternative case than for the two on the study phase. However, Weber's Law again applies; adding a full unit to the correct response (by the feedback procedure) will increase the difference between correct and incorrect items for the four-alternative case more than for the two-alternative case.

Formal Similarity. Using homophones in a verbal discrimination list retards performance (e.g., Kausler & Olson, 1969). So also does the use of words with high formal similarity, words such as *sword* and *swore* (e.g., Schulz & Lovelace, 1972). In these studies one member of the homophone pair (or the formally similar pair) was a correct word, one an incorrect word. It must be presumed that the frequency information for words is associated with the acoustic properties (although not necessarily that alone) and that a form of interference results because an increment in frequency of one member of the pair results in an increase in the frequency of the other. However, the role of the acoustic attribute of the representational response must not be overemphasized, nor should it be considered as a critical component in verbal-discrimination learning. For example, profoundly deaf children learn a verbal-discrimination list without serious difficulty (Putnam, Iscoe, & Young, 1962).

Implicit Associative Responses. The original formulation of frequency theory assumed a role for implicit associative responses. A word was assumed to produce an associate implicitly (*cup* produces *saucer*). This implicit response had to be considered to have a frequency in the same sense that a word actually shown on the study list has a frequency. This assumption opened up many predictive possibilities. For example, if *king* and *queen* were paired in a list, the correct response would be difficult to learn because *king* elicits *queen* and *queen* elicits *king*; the frequency of the two words would then be roughly equivalent, making learning difficult. Another prediction would be that if the two words (such as *king* and *queen*) were both correct items in a list, learning would be facilitated because the frequency of each word would be augmented. On the other hand, if both of the words were incorrect words, learning would be retarded because the incorrect words would be augmented in frequency. Many, many studies have been conducted to test the role of the implicit responses. It is proper to say that in very few cases has the theory been supported. This adjunct of frequency theory apparently should be discarded.

SOME FURTHER THOUGHTS ABOUT THEORY

An experiment was reported earlier in the chapter in which a single incorrect word was used with two correct words. A frequency interpretation indicated that the frequency input for the correct and incorrect items would be sufficiently equivalent so that the discriminations could not be learned. Learning, nonetheless, did occur. Such a list is more difficult than the conventional list, but it is learned without a serious problem. Keeping this fact in mind, we turn to another situation.

A number of studies have examined transfer effects. For example, a group is given a standard list to learn. Then, as a transfer phase, the same list is presented again, but with the correct and incorrect words reversed. Thus, if A was correct and B incorrect in the initial list, B will be correct and A incorrect in the transfer list. What happens during the learning of the second list? First, providing the subjects are told about the reversal before being given the second list, performance will be very high on the initial trials because the subjects will choose the least frequent member of each pair. As trials continue, performance improves but little as the frequencies of correct and incorrect items become equivalent. Frequency theory would predict a drop in performance to a chance level, but this does not happen; there may be very little gain on several trials, but it is a rare case when performance actually gets worse.

It will be recalled that if subjects are given a free-recall list to learn, and these words are then used as wrong words in a verbal-discrimination list, performance is much like the case discussed above. So, we have several cases in which frequency of correct and incorrect items becomes equivalent and (according to frequency theory) performance should fall apart, but in fact it does not. This is a fundamental issue facing frequency theory. How is it to be handled?

Earlier it was pointed out that learning of the verbal-discrimination list might occur in one or more of three ways: (1) applying frequency rule; (2) applying some other rule; (3) nonrule learning of unknown properties. For the case before us, where frequency theory does not handle the results adequately, which of the two remaining alternatives is to be accepted? The fact is, no one has suggested any other discriminative rule that might be applied; thus it appears that the third alternative must be considered seriously.

What other form of learning could be involved? An analysis of the verbal-discrimination task shows that it could be viewed as a two-category classification task; correct responses are assigned or placed in one category, incorrect responses are placed in another. The learning of such tasks takes place at a surprisingly rapid rate (Ghatala, Levin, & Subkoviak, 1975). It would not be out of line, then, to suggest that verbal-discrimination learning is really a two-category classification task and that when that task is understood, so too will the verbal-discrimination task. The problem with this approach is that it simply cannot handle the very fact that also threatens frequency theory: subjects do not fall apart when the frequencies of correct and incorrect words become equivalent. In a reversal situation, for example, if a two-category classification learning has occurred, when the correct and incorrect items are reversed there should be absolutely no change in the subjects' behavior. Performance should be perfect on the reversal trial and remain so with further trials. Furthermore, in the experiment described earlier in which the variable was the number of times a correct or incorrect word was used, there should be no difference between the C lists and the I lists if a two-category classification was involved. A further fact should be mentioned relative to this issue. If a subject is given a free-recall task to learn first, followed by a verbal-discrimination task in which the items learned in free recall become incorrect items, performance should be markedly facilitated if only a classification is involved. Finally, it is difficult to see how Weber's Law would apply in the learning of the two-category classification task. Such facts lead to the conclusion that it is highly doubtful that verbal-discrimination learning is simply a two-category classification task.

Theories come and theories go. At the present time frequency theory does a rather artful job in organizing the facts of old-new recognition and verbal-discrimination learning. It is simply necessary to realize that the theory has trouble with some of the findings, particularly the transfer findings.

SUMMARY

The data on recognition memory were viewed initially in terms of what has come to be known as frequency theory. This theory assumes that in the usual experiment, recognition decisions are primarily mediated by frequency discriminations between old and new items in classical recognition, and between right and wrong items in verbal-discrimination learning. A distinction was drawn between background frequency (frequency information accumulated throughout life) and situational frequency (frequency induced in the laboratory). Frequency theory is stated in terms of situational frequency. The theory assumes that the frequency attribute will mediate recognition decisions unless frequency becomes equivalent for old and new, or right and wrong, at which point other attributes may be used to reach decisions. Several tests of the theory were given, followed by a brief description of the effects of a number of independent variables without special regard to the theoretical implications of the relationships.

Verbal-discrimination learning is viewed as a form of rule learning, with the subjects' decisions being made on the basis of a frequency rule ("choose the word with the highest frequency"). A processing model was described and several tests of the theory were given. The effects of a number of additional independent variables were examined briefly. Overall, frequency theory accounts for a large body of data in verbal-discrimination learning. There are a few findings, however, in which the adequacy of the theory is in doubt.

7

Implicit Associative Responses

In the normal course of our living, words become associated with each other, and these associative relationships become a part of the memory systems with which we must deal. Furthermore, word-association tests show that the particular words which become associated to one another have considerable communality across subjects. To the stimulus word *cup*, we can be reasonably confident that many subjects will respond with the word *saucer*. This consistency across subjects must lead to the conclusion that there is considerable underlying similarity in the linguistic environment whether people reside in Asheville, Center Point, or Spokane. Facts and theories about word associations per se may be found in Cramer's book (1968).

Just how words become associated, within the laboratory and without, is a matter that will continue to be skirted. We are going to assume that we develop an associative repertoire that consists (among other things) of associations between words, and we will not now inquire as to how the associations got there. The intent is to show that certain phenomena in recall and recognition may be understood if the implications of associative responses are traced out. We will speak of implicit associational responses (IARs), and the plan is to show how such responses can be used theoretically.

When a word is presented in a learning task, we must assume that the subjects perceive it in the sense that they could pronounce or spell it immediately after it was shown. Earlier we used the term representational response (RR) to identify the act of perceiving a word. Beyond this, it is assumed that subjects may produce IARs to the perceived words, and that these IARs are those that would occur if the subjects were given word-association tests in which the associated responses are overt. The theoretical question is: Assuming that a particular IAR is produced to a word in the list, what implication does this have for performance (recall, recognition, retention, and so on)?

To assume that IARs occur in a typical learning situation in which common words appear is not a very daring assumption. As will be seen later, various transfer paradigms that produce either positive or negative transfer must assume that associations acquired in the laboratory do occur as IARs. A number of years ago a favorite area of research dealt with so-called mediation paradigms. Perhaps the one studied most frequently was identified as A-B, B-C, A-C. Subjects learned three successive paired-associate lists with the relationships between lists being as indicated. If positive transfer was found in learning the third list (A-C), researchers concluded that in learning each item in this list, two associations occurred implicitly, namely, A-B and B-C. In effect, the subjects did not learn new associations in performing the third list; rather, the two old associations (A-B, B-C) were used as implicit mediators between A and C. To give theoretical status to implicit responses, therefore, is merely to continue a practice initiated long ago.

We will turn to various areas of research in which it appears that IARs provide useful theoretical devices. Sometimes the inferences as to the operation of IARs are rather remote; at other times they are more direct.

PAIRED-ASSOCIATE LEARNING

Conceptual IARs

Two sixteen-item, paired-associate lists are shown in Table 7.1, one having low conceptual similarity among the items, the other having high conceptual similarity. The high-similarity list consists of four instances each of four concepts as stimulus terms, and four instances of four additional concepts as response terms. Furthermore, the four instances of a concept on the response side are paired with the four instances of a concept on the stimulus side. For example, the names of four countries are paired with the names of four animals. Of course, in presenting the list for learning, the pairs were randomized.

The two lists were used in a study in which the subjects were given fifteen anticipation trials following an initial study trial (Underwood & Schulz, 1961). The mean numbers of correct responses on each trial for each list are shown in Figure 7.1. These acquisition curves clearly indicate that the high-similarity list presented a more difficult task for the subjects than did the low-similarity list. Why should this be? According to IAR theory, the answer would seem quite evident. On the first trial, and if not on this trial, certainly on the second or third, the subjects produce category names primarily as IARs. In addition, they acquire four associations between unrelated concepts (countries-animals; elements-dances, and so on). Note that the concept or category names were not in the list; they must have occurred as IARs. That associations between the conceptual IARs did in fact develop was indicated by an analysis of the overt errors. It was found that 97 percent of the misplaced response errors were appropriate

Table 7.1. Sixteen-Pair Lists Used to Study the Influence of Intralist Conceptual Similarity on Paired-Associate Learning

Low Similarity	High Similarity
cruiser-head	Bob-measles
emerald-wall	Bill-mumps
blue-cotton	Joe-polio
theft-bee	John-cancer
doctor-bus	cow-Russia
copper-table	dog-France
dog-France	cat-England
gasoline-maple	horse-Germany
waltz-oxygen	rabbi-bluejay
wine-geology	bishop-canary
trumpet-knife	minister-sparrow
apple-trout	priest-robin
hat-second	rhumba-nitrogen
John-cancer	foxtrot-hydrogen
football-daisy	waltz-oxygen
priest-robin	tango-sulphur

Underwood and Schultz (1961).

for the pairings. For example, when a subject committed an overt error to the stimulus term BOB, it was by giving one of the three diseases (mumps, polio, cancer) that were paired with other names.

If, as assumed, the subjects learn associations between category names initially, this should produce a positive effect on learning, a positive effect which is not present in the low-similarity list. This effect is implied by the overt-error analysis. The number of possible response terms for a given stimulus term is sixteen if category learning does not occur. But, if category learning does occur—if the subject learns that the four countries are paired with the four animals—then the number of possible response terms for a given stimulus term is four. Nevertheless, while such knowledge should provide a facilitating factor, the subjects consequently have to face a severe negative factor as well. The associations between concepts are completely nondiscriminating for the specific pairings of instances within the concepts. In effect, the conceptual IARs would get "in the way" of learning instance-to-instance associations. The IARs the subjects brought to the laboratory were strong and persistent, and because of the particular arrangement of the words in the high-similarity list, the IARs inhibited specific associative learning of the words that elicited them. Of course, the subjects eventually overcame this difficulty without too much trouble; learning did proceed throughout the fifteen trials. It is interesting to note that retarded subjects are not influenced negatively by categorical similarity (Wallace & Underwood, 1964), apparently because retardates do not spontaneously produce conceptual IARs when asked to learn word lists.

Figure 7.1.
Learning of the two lists shown in Table 7.1. Data from Underwood and Schulz (1961).

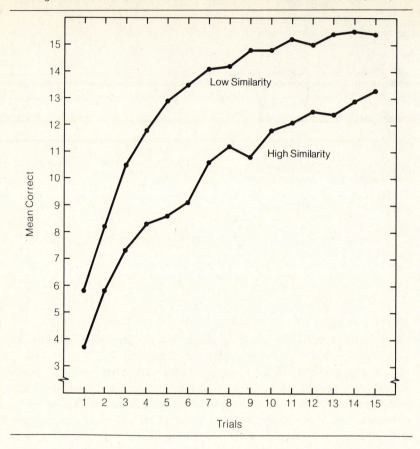

If conceptual IARs can produce interference in learning paired-associate lists, it would seem likely that by appropriate arrangement, the IARs could produce overall facilitation in learning. This expectation has been supported (Underwood, Reichardt, & Malmi, 1975). Two conditions from among the several used will be described. There were twenty-four pairs in the list. The stimulus terms were the numbers 1 through 24, and on each trial they were presented in ascending order of magnitude. Thus, unlike the usual paired-associate procedure, the order of the pairs was constant. The twenty-four response terms, listed in the order in which they were paired with the numbers were: *robin, owl, bobolink, trout, guppy, bullhead, apple, lemon, fig, rose, lilac, marigold, trumpet, tuba, bugle, guitar, banjo, fiddle, knife, bayonet, dagger, rifle, cannon, shotgun.* It can be seen that the response terms consist of three instances of each of eight concepts (birds, fish, and so on), and that the bird names are paired with the numbers 1–3, the fish names with numbers 4–6, and so on. Further study of the response terms reveal that there are higher-order concepts involved in that the first six names are animals, the next six plants, the next six musical instruments, and the last six weapons. Finally, at a still higher conceptual level, the first twelve words represent animate things, the last twelve inanimate things.

One group of thirty subjects (E Group) learned the list as described. A C Group of thirty subjects learned a list in which the numbers and words were paired randomly. Anticipation learning was used, and learning was continued until eighteen correct anticipations were given on a single trial. The mean numbers of trials required to learn the lists to the criterion were 2.50 for the E Group and 6.96 for the C Group. The question should be raised as to whether this difference occurs because the structured list facilitates learning, because the unstructured list makes learning more difficult, or some combination of both. In either case, of course, IARs will be involved.

The evidence given by the overt errors indicated that it was highly unlikely that a negative effect produced by conceptual IARs was involved in the learning by the C Group. This does not mean that the subjects were unaware that there were several instances of each of several concepts in the lists. Rather, it appears that they are able to select information from memory that is appropriate for the demands of the task. In a manner of speaking, the control subjects were able to set aside the conceptual information that was inappropriate to the task demands.

In the case of the E Group, the conceptual names facilitated learning because they restricted the number of possible stimuli to which a given word was appropriate. The subjects learned an eight-item serial list of concept names and then learned the placement of each of the instances within each concept. It should be mentioned that other conditions in the experiment made it possible to tease out the influence of the three conceptual levels on the overall learning. It was estimated that 80 percent of the facilitation was produced by the lowest conceptual level (birds, fish, fruit, and so on), with the remaining facilitation produced by the two higher levels.

A comparison of the results of the present E Group and those for the E Group of the previously described study may be necessary. In the earlier experiment, negative effects were observed for the E List, whereas in the present experiment, strong positive effects were found for the E Group. The critical difference probably lies in the position (spatial) attribute. This attribute would function in the present experiment because the pairs were always presented in the same order, and the stimulus terms (numbers) were aligned with successive positions. In the previous experiment, the pairs were presented in different orders from trial to trial; hence position was unreliable as an attribute. This difference seems to be supported in the present experiment in a condition not earlier described. In this condition the order of the pairs varied from trial to trial, although the relationship between the number stimuli and the conceptual relationships between the words and numbers remained intact. The learning of this list was much more difficult than the learning of the list in which a constant and sequential order of the numbers was maintained over trials.

These considerations underline a point relating to similarity manipulations. This point is that many manipulations of similarity will introduce both positive and negative forces in the learning. What we observe is the net effect of these forces. This point will be refined in Chapter 8 when we discuss intralist similarity manipulations.

Crossed Associates

In a cross-associate list the experimenter uses a series of pairs from word-association tables, the pairs consisting of the stimulus words used in the word-association test and a response given with high frequency to each of the stimulus words. Thus, the pairs might be *bitter-sweet, cup-saucer, table-chair, rough-smooth*, and so on. From such pairs, a crossed-associate list is produced by pairing the stimulus and response terms randomly. The pairs resulting might be the following: *bitter-chair, cup-sweet, rough-saucer, table-smooth*. In an experiment the learning of these crossed pairs would be compared with the learning of a control list (C List) that had the same stimulus terms as above (or the same response terms), but in which none of the items was associated with each other.

The results from such experiments usually show that the crossed-associate list is more difficult than the C List. For example, Spence (1963) constructed twelve-pair E and C Lists, and presented each for ten anticipation trials to two independent groups of subjects. There were 160.60 mean total correct responses for the subjects learning the C List and 138.45 mean total correct responses for the subjects who learned the E List. This difference is reliable statistically. There seems to be no reasonable explanation for such a finding other than to assume that the presence of IARs interfered with learning. These IARs are the associations between the stimulus terms and the response terms as taken from the word-association norms. Although the words were not paired in the list, the associations (IARs) must have been activated by the presence of both of the words in the list. Both of the words must be in the list in order to produce the interference. The C List, of course, consists of words which have strong associates, but the response terms of the strongly associated pairs are not in the list.

RECOGNITION

IARs and False Alarms

One source of false alarms in word-recognition studies can be identified through IAR theory. It is easy to understand the application of the theory when the technique is running recognition. In running recognition subjects are presented a series of words, and for each word the subjects must make a YES-NO decision as to whether the item had been presented earlier in the list. IAR theory assumes that the false alarms occur because the frequency of the word has a positive value as a result of having occurred earlier in the list as an IAR to a word which was in fact present in the list. For example, suppose the twentieth word in the list is *buy* and fortieth word is *sell*, this being the first occurrence of *sell*. Suppose further that a number of subjects respond YES to *sell*. The IAR theory assumes that when *buy* was presented, *sell* was elicited as an IAR. Therefore, *sell* has a situational frequency above zero for subjects who produced it as an IAR. This could lead the subject to respond YES when *sell* is presented, resulting in a false alarm.

Several matters should be mentioned about the many experiments that have been performed using running recognition to study the causes of false alarms. First, a C Word is commonly placed close to each E Word, the E Word being the assumed IAR. The C Words act as controls in the sense that they are presumed not to be elicited as an IAR by any previous word in the list. The number of false alarms on the C Words serve as a base; to demonstrate false alarms due to IARs, the frequency of false alarms must be greater for the E Words than for the C Words.

The second point to be made is that IAR theory does not pretend to account for all false alarms, but it *does* presume to account for the false alarms produced by associative relationships of the type described above. False alarms may also be produced by acoustic similarity and perhaps by other forms of similarity. The IAR theory simply does not have anything to say about false alarms produced by such factors because they do not involve the implicit occurrence of an associate and the subsequent presentation of that associate in the test list.

A third point has to do with the magnitude of the false recognition effect produced by IARs. In any absolute sense the effect is small. This appears to be, but is not necessarily, at odds with the theory. In the first place, we would use word-association norms to indicate the total number of false alarms that might be anticipated. If, in the word-association norms, the critical stimulus word produced a given response for only 40 percent of the subjects, it must necessarily follow that no more than that percentage would produce false alarms in running recognition. That is, we would not expect more subjects to produce a given IAR in running recognition than in the word-association test. So then, in the above illustration, 60 percent of the subjects cannot be expected to give "our" false alarm because they did not produce the expected IAR during the initial presentation of the critical stimulus word. But, it might be argued, why should not we observe a 40 percent occurrence of false alarms? In answering this question we must recognize that subjects must have *some* discrimination between words presented for study and words that were "thought of." If this were not the case we would undoubtedly have great difficulty in conducting our day-to-day affairs. Nevertheless, it would not be unreasonable to expect that the number of false alarms would be directly related to the number of subjects who produced a given IAR in word-association procedures. This expectation has indeed been supported (e.g., Moates & Koplin, 1967; Marshall, Rouse, & Tarpy, 1969).

As a rough measure, we could say that the error rate for E Words is usually about 10 percent higher than for C Words. A number of techniques have been used to increase this number. In a study by Vogt and Kimble (1973), in which the tests used were based on each subject's own associations, the false alarm rate ranged from 35-40 percent, depending upon whether the presentation was aural or visual, whereas the control rate was 19 percent. It has also been shown that if critical stimulus words are presented more than once before the test word is shown, the number of false alarms increases, although with very frequent presentations (e.g., seven times), there is a decrease in false alarms (Hall & Kosloff, 1970). Just what happens to the IAR with several presentations of the critical stimulus words is not clear at this time. There is some evidence that the IAR may occur only at the first presentation of the critical stimulus word and then infrequently as the critical stimulus word is given continued presentation (Vereb & Voss, 1974). However, the fact that false alarms increase with up to at least two occurrences of the critical stimulus word would not seem to support the idea that the IAR occurs primarily on the first occurrence of the critical stimulus word.

It has been shown that false recognitions can be produced by using laboratory-established associations (e.g., Saegert, 1971). The subjects first learn a list of paired associates. Then, a long list of single words that includes some of the stimulus terms from the paired-associate list is shown for study. It is assumed that when the stimulus terms are presented in the study list the subjects implicitly produce the response term they had just learned in the paired-associate list. On a recognition test, therefore, false alarms should occur to the response terms of the paired-associate list. Such false alarms have been observed. In the Saegert study these false alarms occurred only when a twenty-four-hour interval separated the learning of the paired-associate list and the presentation of the study list.

We pointed out earlier that retarded subjects are believed not to produce IARs spontaneously. If this is true, one would predict that retardates would not produce false alarms to associates in the running recognition procedure. Or, if both C and E Words are presented to both normal and retarded subjects, the two variables should produce an interaction: the normal subjects should show a difference in the number of false alarms to C and E Words; the retardates should not. Wallace (1967) used fifteen E Words and fifteen C Words (there were other filler words). For normal subjects the mean number of false alarms was 3.4 for the E Words, 1.6 for the C Words. The corresponding values for the retardates were 3.0 and 2.4. The interaction was as predicted.

Earlier we discussed briefly the proposition that we must be able to distinguish to some degree between external and internal events which become a part of a memory. The IAR is an internally generated event that the subject may actually believe was presented earlier as an external event. The prediction of false alarms by IAR theory is preceded by the assumption that subjects do no always clearly discriminate between internally generated events and external events. To repeat an earlier remark, it is fortunate that we have *some* discrimination between sources of memories (external or internal), else our mental life would most likely be positively chaotic.

Recent investigations have attempted to assess the degree to which the memories form external sources and those from internal sources do in fact get confused. (e.g., Johnson, Raye, Wang, & Taylor, 1979). For example, these investigators showed that the number of times subjects imaged an object (internal) increased to some extent the judgments of frequency with which a picture of the object had been actually displayed (external). Roughly speaking, subjects judged a picture displayed twice to have been displayed about 3.5 times if in addition the subject had imaged the object eight different times. It is too early to tell just where this imaginative research will take us, but it may eventually help us to understand just how probable it is that a given IAR will become confused with an externally presented event.

Background Frequency

In the previous chapter it was stated that high-frequency words are likely to produce more errors than low-frequency words in recognition. Later in this chapter we will deal with the fact that in free-recall learning, high-frequency words produce better recall than do low-frequency words. Thus, the effects of the background frequency of words are just the opposite for recall and recognition. (As will become clear shortly, the generalization usually made about recognition and word frequency is not quite correct). Such crossover interactions have, as might be expected, intrigued a number of investigators. Here we will center our attention on the relationship between recognition and background frequency and later consider the effect on recall. Many explanations have been proposed as to why low-frequency words yield better recognition than do high-frequency words. A book edited by Brown (1976), dealing with contrasts between recognition and recall, is probably the best single source of theories which purport to account for the effect of background frequency on recognition. We will not deal with these other conceptions; rather, we will proceed along our parochial way and give our interpretation of the word-frequency effect using IAR theory. Two studies will be described; the first will show that the usual generalization about word frequency and recognition is a simplification. The second study will show just how IARs may "act" to produce the word-frequency effect.

The Facts. Three issues regarding methods of studying the effect of word frequency must be pointed out. *First,* mixed study lists should not be used. With mixed study lists (mixed in the sense of containing both high- and low-frequency words) the subjects may not allocate their study time equally across high- and low-frequency words. *Second,* to avoid problems that may arise if beta or criterion differences occur, the forced-choice test is advised. *Third,* the characteristics of the new words in the forced-choice test are fundamental in determining the relationship between word frequency and recognition. What shall the frequency of the new words be? It would seem that in order to get the full empirical picture, the new words must be both low- and high-frequency words. Thus, a minimum of four conditions seem necessary, these conditions being H-H, H-L, L-H, and L-L, in which the first letter refers to the frequency of the words in the study list (high or low) and the second letter to the frequency of the new words in the forced-choice test list. It may be noted that a mixed test list would be a perfectly feasible instrument; in fact, it might be judged a little preferable to the unmixed test lists which were used in the experiment now to be described.

Underwood and Freund (1970b) gave their subjects fifty study words at a one-second rate. Then, a paced test was used in which the subject was allowed two seconds to choose the old word from each of the fifty test pairs. The four groups (H-H, H-L, L-H, L-L) each consisted of thirty subjects. The response measure was the percent error on the fifty tests. The results are shown in Figure 7.2.

The first fact to be noted is that high-frequency words do not always yield poor recognition performance. When high-frequency study words are paired with low-frequency new words, performance is almost perfect. Only when high-frequency study words are tested with high-frequency new words does a severe drop in performance occur. For low-frequency words, on the other hand, it is of little consequence what the frequency of the new words is. Overall, summing over type of new word, performance *is* poorer for high-frequency words than for low, but that generalization has tended to cover up some important differences.

Our interpretation of the results as seen in Figure 7-2 is based on IAR differences which occur as a function of word frequency. If a random sample of high-frequency words is examined, one finds that the number of associations among the words is far greater than for an equivalent sample of low-frequency words. A greater number of associates results in greater IAR "action." This action needs to be noted in detail:

1. IAR frequency is assumed to sum with situational frequency.

2. As a simple means of handling the arithmetic of the matter, we will assume that an IAR will add .5 frequency units to situational frequency.

3. In the H-H condition the subject studies high-frequency words and is tested with new high-frequency words. The IAR to a study word may be another word in the study list, so that the situational frequency will be 1.5. On the recognition test the discrimination is between an old item with a

Figure 7.2.
Forced-choice recognition errors as determined by the background frequency of the old and new words. Data from Underwood and Freund (1970).

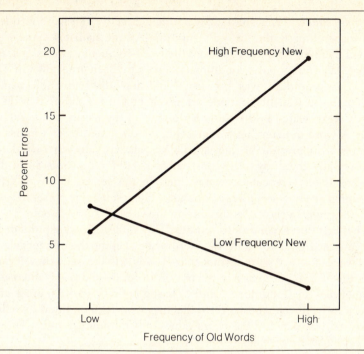

frequency of 1.5 and a new item with a frequency of zero. On the other hand, the IAR to a study word may be a new word on the test. In such a case, the discrimination is between 1.0 and .5. Thus, in the H-H condition, we have contrary factors operating. However, the positive factor will have a relatively small effect because adding .5 frequency units to a value of 1.0 doesn't make the discrimination far easier than it would have been without the IAR. The discrimination between .5 and 1.0 (when the IAR is a new word) would be a very difficult one, hence would dominate the small positive effect described. Condition H-H should produce many errors.

4. Low-frequency words may not produce IARs during the study trial. If an IAR is produced it is likely to have a higher frequency than the word producing it, but it is unlikely to be at a high level of frequency.

5. The H-L condition is easier than either L-H or L-L because the interitem associations among the H words will result in some of the H words having a frequency value of 1.5, so that the discrimination is between 1.5 and zero. This is an easier discrimination than that between 1.0 and zero, which is the situation for L-H and L-L.

Thus, IAR theory can account for the results shown in Figure 7.2. However, the theory is at a disadvantage in that the presence of IARs is entirely hypothetical. What is needed, it seems, is a study in which the words in the study list and in the test list are known to have certain associative relationships. The Bach (1974) study fitted this requirement.

The Bach Study. This study does not deal directly with word frequency and recognition. Rather, it deals with the IAR mechanisms that are presumed by theory to have produced the word-frequency effects as seen in Figure 7.2. The six basic conditions as given by Bach are shown in Table 7.2. The procedure was the usual old-new discrimination using a forced-choice test. Illustrations are given of the six different ways the words were related in the study series and of the nature of the tests for each. A word in parentheses represents the presumed IAR; X indicates a new test word presumably unrelated or associated to any other word in the list. Actually, the study series consisted of 123 different words, since all six conditions were repeated several times in the series. The words were presented at a two-second rate for study. The test list was presented at the same rate, with a choice required from the subjects for each pair.

The first three conditions outlined in Table 7.2 were intended to increase the frequency of the old word while keeping the frequency of the new word at zero. Assuming that an IAR adds .5 to the frequency, it can be seen that Condition 2 has a frequency of 1.5 for the old word, whereas the frequencies for Conditions 1 and 3, based entirely on RRs, are 1 and 2 respectively. It would be expected that the errors for Condition 2 would be about halfway between the errors values for Conditions 1 and 3. This was the case.

Conditions 3, 4, and 5 were intended to increase the frequency of the old items while holding the frequency of the new items constant at .5 fre-

Table 7.2. Conditions and Results of the Bach (1974) Study

Condition	Study Series	Test Pair	Assumed f Old	Assumed f New	Percent Error
1	Table[a] . . .	Table-X	1.0	0	20
2	Table (Chair) . . . Chair (Table)	Table-X	1.5	0	16
3	Table . . . Table	Table-X	2.0	0	11
4	Table . . . King (Queen) . . .	Table-Queen	1.0	.5	33
5	Table (Chair) . . . Chair (Table) . . . King (Queen)	Table-Queen	1.5	.5	27
6	Table . . . Table . . . King (Queen) . . .	Table-Queen	2.0	.5	21

[a]IARs are not shown when they are irrelevant.

quency units. One obvious expectation is that the performance on Conditions 1, 2, and 3 combined should be better than the overall performance on Conditions 4, 5, and 6. This is borne out. Furthermore, the error values for Conditions 4, 5, and 6 are precisely what would be expected by IAR theory. The Bach study can be used to support the IAR interpretation of the word-frequency effect on recognition as shown in Figure 7.2.

FREE-RECALL LEARNING

Interitem Associations

The issue to be discussed concerns the effect on free-recall learning of presenting lists in which words are associated because of cultural usage. As usual, such associations are inferred from word-association tests as discussed earlier. Interitem associations have been manipulated in several different ways. The common feature is to choose items that are associated, place them in a free-recall list, and see if learning differs from a control in which interitem associations are minimal in number. We sometimes speak of manipulating the "strength" of interitem associations, but this refers only to differences in the percentage of subjects producing common responses to different stimuli. For example, if to the stimulus word *gorilla*, 53 percent respond *ape* and 9 percent respond *monkey*, *gorilla-ape* are said to be associated more strongly than are *gorilla-monkey*. However, in some studies the variable is the number of different words that elicit (to some degree) a particular word. We need to examine some experiments.

Jenkins, Mink, and Russell (1958) constructed four free-recall lists, each having twenty-four words. These twenty-four words consisted of twelve pairs which, across the four lists, differed in associative strength. At one extreme the strength was very high in that on the average, 76 percent of the subjects in the word-association procedures had produced the same response. An illustration of such a strong association is *man-woman*. At the other extreme the associations were weak in that only 12 percent of the subjects on the average had given the common response. An illustration is *comfort-chair*. The four levels of strength were 76, 43, 32, and 12 percent. Within each of the four levels, the twenty-four words were randomized subject to the restriction that the words in associated pairs could not occupy adjacent positions. A single study-test cycle was given, with the rate being one second per word and in which four independent groups were used, one for each list.

The results may be seen in Figure 7.3. Little need be said about them; clearly, as the strength of interitem associations increased, the number of words recalled increased.

The second technique for manipulating interitem associations in free recall will be illustrated by a study reported by Rothkopf and Coke (1961).

Figure 7.3.

Single-trial, free-recall performance as related to associative strength of twelve pairs randomized across positions in the twenty-four-word lists. Data from Table 2 of Jenkins, Mink, and Russell (1958).

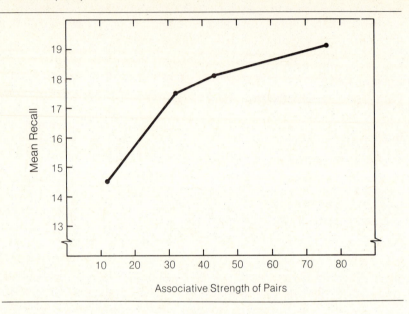

They presented their subjects ninety-nine words at a five-second rate. Word associations had been taken for all ninety-nine words so that it was possible to determine the number of different words that elicited each of the ninety-nine words in the word-association procedures. No attention was paid to the strength of the associations; if the word-association norms showed that at least 1 percent of the subjects had produced the same response, it was included as an associate. The number of different words within the list that elicited another word in the list (in word-association norms) was then viewed as an independent variable, with values ranging from zero to sixteen. The results showed that recall after the single study trial increased directly as the number of eliciting words increased. Expressed as a correlation, the relationship between number of associations impinging on a word and its recall was .62.

A third technique involves using lists in which all of the words are associates to a single word. It is to be expected that words that are associates of the same word will be associated to some extent to each other. Such lists are learned more rapidly than are control lists (e.g., Heckelman & Spear, 1967). An intermediate step between pairs of associates (as in the Jenkins et al. study) and associates to a single word would be the use of small groups of words that are interassociated, but in which the words across the small groups are not associated. Such lists also produce positive effects in learning (e.g., Matthews, 1966).

Interpretation. The interpretation of the results of such studies as reviewed above is perhaps obvious in terms of IAR theory. If an IAR is a word in the list, that word not only has a presented frequency (RR) but also an implicit frequency, and recall is a direct function of the frequency of presentation. Thus, as was given in detail in discussing the Bach study, IARs may augment direct presentation of a word.

There is probably no very critical test of IAR theory as applied to the manipulating of interitem associations. However, a most remarkable study by Deese (1959) produced results which seem to be particularly friendly toward IAR theory. Deese presented his subjects thirty-six twelve-word lists, each for a single study and test trial. Each list consisted of the twelve most frequent responses given to thirty-six words in word-association procedures. Note that the stimulus word was not in the list; only the twelve most frequently produced associates of the thirty-six stimulus words were used in the lists. Deese collected the reverse associations—he determined for each list how frequently the twelve words elicited the stimulus word which had produced them in the first place. The thirty-six lists differed, of course, in terms of the frequency with which the stimulus word was elicited. Deese calculated the correlation between the frequency with which the stimulus words appeared as *intrusions* in recall and the frequency with which the stimulus words in the list elicited these intruding stimulus words. The correlation was .87. As discussed earlier, subjects can, to some unknown extent, distinguish between IARs and words actually presented. However, it seems that in the Deese experiment the subjects completed the study trial with the belief that the critical stimulus word (which we assume occurred as an IAR at least once) was in the list. Deese's study has been replicated by Hess and Simon (1964) using children as subjects and the correlation was found to be .74.

We believe the data involving interitem associations are quite compatible with IAR theory. Earlier we reported that free recall is higher for words with high background frequency than for words with low background frequency. The difference would be expected by IAR theory because high-frequency words have a greater number of interitem associations than do low-frequency words. The argument need not be repeated.

Conceptual Relatedness

In dealing with interitem associations, we asked about the role of the association between two words on the learning of the two words. Conceptual relatedness, as an independent variable, asks about the recall of two or more words when these words belong to the same concept, or category, but are not in themselves directly associated. Thus, *apple* and *banana* are members of the same category and therefore may elicit the same category name as an IAR, but *apple* does not usually elicit *banana* in word-association tests, nor does *banana* elicit *apple*. So, then, we wish to examine the effect of conceptual relatedness of words on their free recall.

Lists could be constructed by "thinking up" words which belong to the same and different categories. However, in the long run it seems a little better to have a common source of words from which all investigators can draw and which also includes certain normative-type information. Many subjects, therefore, are asked to "think of" instances of concepts. The most frequently used category norms are those Battig and Montague (1969) derived from the responses of 442 students at the Universities of Maryland and Illinois. These students were given thirty seconds to write as many instances (exemplars) of a category as they could, with fifty-six different category names being used.

The essential results of this study are presented as tables for each of the fifty-six concepts. In each table the concept instances or members are listed in decreasing order of frequency given by the 442 subjects. *Iron, copper,* and *steel* were the three most frequently given names for the concept of metals; *dog, cat,* and *horse* were most frequent for four-footed animals; and *knife, gun,* and *rifle* were the most frequently given instances when weapons were requested.

Given that we have these tables, how do we construct lists to determine if conceptual relatedness influences free recall? It has been customary to construct an E List consisting of several different instances of several different concepts. However, it is possible to have all items in a list be instances of a single concept. The learning of such a list occcurs more rapidly than the learning of a list in which there are no conceptually related words (Ekstrand & Underwood, 1963). To repeat, it is simply more customary to use several different concepts with several different instances of each concept. For example, a twenty-four-word list might be used in which there are six instances of four different categories. How are the words arranged in the list? At the extremes there are two arrangements. First, the words may be *blocked*, by which is meant that all instances of a given concept occur in adjacent positions. Thus, in our twenty-four-item list, the first six items might be names of flowers, the second six names of metals, and so on. The other extreme arrangement is to have the items randomized in the list, subject to the restriction that no words representing the same concept can occur contiguously. There are "in-between" techniques for arranging the words, depending upon the intent of the experimenter. For example, Puff (1966) used ten items from each of three categories, and the independent variable was the number of times any word was directly followed by another word from the same category, the four levels being 0, 9, 18, and 27. The first is a random list, the last a completely blocked list.

In choosing words from the tables for constructing the E List, it seems evident that we should not choose words that are directly associated. That is, we should not choose such words if we want a "clean" determination of the effect of conceptual relatedness unconfounded by interitem associations. To use *cat* and *dog* as members of an animal category produces a confounding because *dog* and *cat* elicit each other with high frequency in word-association procedures.

Assume that we have constructed our E List. The next question concerns the words that should be chosen for the C List, a list in which conceptual relatedness should be minimized, but in which the words are to be like the E Words in every characteristic except relatedness. The most certain way to accomplish this is to use exactly the same words in both the E and C Lists. Of course, this cannot be done by using a single E List and a single C List, but it can be done by constructing many different lists and summing across them. In Chapter 8, we will show how this may be done. In actual practice, investigators have seldom gone to such extremes. That the results across a number of studies have shown consistently that the single-trial free recall is higher for the E List than for the C List makes it seem quite unlikely that the results could be attributed to some variable or variables other than conceptual relatedness. The usual outcome may be illustrated in a study done by the author (Underwood, 1964b). There were four sixteen-word lists, two E Lists and two C Lists, all learned by a single group of thirty-seven subjects.

The lists are shown in Table 7.3 in the order in which they were learned by the subjects. The two E Lists as shown in Table 7.3 have a blocked arrangement, but in fact they were presented in random order on the study trial, each word being presented for five seconds. The mean numbers of words correctly recalled are shown for each list at the bottom of the table. The superiority of the recall of the E Lists over the C Lists is evident, a

Table 7.3. Lists Used to Study the Influence of Conceptual Relatedness on Free Recall

	C List	E List	E List	C List
	apple	Bob	France	daisy
	football	Bill	England	wall
	emerald	Joe	Russia	bee
	trout	John	Germany	second
	copper	rabbi	bluejay	knife
	theft	priest	canary	bus
	hat	bishop	sparrow	geology
	table	minister	robin	maple
	cruiser	cow	measles	arm
	trumpet	horse	mumps	hammer
	doctor	dog	polio	salt
	head	cat	cancer	tent
	wine	rumba	nitrogen	cobra
	blue	foxtrot	oxygen	mountain
	gasoline	tango	hydrogen	window
	cotton	waltz	sulphur	rain
Mean Correct	11.08	14.57	14.86	11.35

superiority that is roughly 30 percent. As is usually found with E Lists, clustering in recall was almost complete.

It was mentioned earlier that blocked versus random presentation may be a relevant independent variable. The results across many experiments show that blocked presentation gives better recall than does random presentation in about half the studies (Puff, 1974). A study by Cofer, Bruce, and Reicher (1966) may be used to illustrate the positive effect. Their list consisted of forty words, with ten instances of each of four concepts. The instances were those given with high frequency in normative procedures. In one case the words were blocked, and in another the order was random. The exposure duration was also varied, being one, two, or four seconds. The results, shown in Figure 7.4, indicate a small superiority of the blocked order of the words over the random order at all three exposure levels.

Interpretation. We assume that a common IAR to the words is the category name (Wood & Underwood, 1967). To illustrate, assume that there were four names of flowers in a block:

Figure 7.4.
The influence of exposure duration and blocked versus random presentation of categorized lists on free recall. Data from Table 2 of Cofer, Bruce, and Reicher (1966).

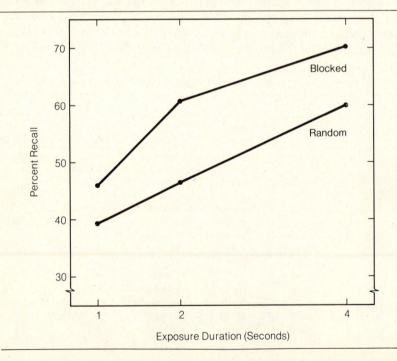

rose	←——→	flower
tulip	←——→	flower
daisy	←——→	flower
violet	←——→	flower

When the word *tulip* is shown and the IAR *flower* occurs, the subjects remember that another flower had just been presented, and by a backward association from *flower* to *rose*, the latter gets rehearsed for the second time. When the subjects make the IAR *flower* to *daisy*, they are led back to both *rose* and *tulip*. When *violet* is presented, all three previous words in the blocks may be rehearsed if the exposure duration is sufficiently long.

All of the above applies to the E List. We assume that with the C List there is some displaced rehearsal just as in the E List, but it is neither as frequent nor as systematic as it is for the E List. Furthermore, because the category names of the words in the E List occur with relatively high frequency (implicitly), the recall of the category name should be high. Once the category name is recalled, the recall of the particular instances may follow.

The interpretation of the blocked-random effect is straightforward. Given a random presentation of words for a given concept, the likelihood that the subject will be able to recover the last previous instance of a concept is reduced because of forgetting which may occur during the presentation of the list. Thus, the efficiency of the displaced rehearsal is reduced.

Tests. The IAR theory as sketched above for the influence of conceptual relatedness in free-recall learning makes one very clear prediction that appears to be unique to the theory. This prediction is that recall should be inversely related to the serial position of the concept instances for a given concept. The first instance should be better recalled than the second, the second better than the third, and so on. This follows from the fact that the number of displaced rehearsals should be greater for the first instance than for the second, more for the second than the third, and so on. Indeed, it is even likely that the latter instances of a concept may be more poorly recalled than control items holding the same positions because so much time has been "taken away" from the latter E Words to rehearse the earlier items.

The first test was made by Wood and Underwood (1967). The materials used by these investigators need to be explained. They made use of nouns and sense-impression adjectives that may be used to describe those nouns. The particular sense-impression adjectives used to describe nouns were determined by a procedure similar to the word-association test (Underwood & Richardson, 1956). The subjects were given nouns one at a time and were asked to provide the first sense-impression response that occurred to them as a description of the noun. Sense impressions refer to such characteristics as size, shape, color, height, texture, and so on. With some practice, subjects can be taught to narrow their word associations to include only sense impressions. Tables were then constructed to show the frequency with which a given object is described by each of several adjectives. For example, a baseball was most frequently described as "round," although with less frequency it was described as being "white" and "hard."

The above materials were used to choose nouns for the lists such that there were conceptually related nouns in the list. More specifically, five different colors were used, and as will be seen, these color names became the IARs. For example, the color black describes *derby, coal, asphalt, coffee,* and so on. The color red describes *bricks, lips, measles,* and *beets.*

Sense-impression responses have a particular property that makes them valuable for certain kinds of research. This property is that subjects normally do not elicit the color name as an IAR. That is, when they see *derby* in a list, they are most likely to say to themselves "hat"; when they see *measles* they are most likely to produce an IAR such as "illness" or "disease" rather than "red." This allows an investigator to use the same words in the E List and in the C List. For the E List, however, he will tell the subject about the nature of the conceptual relationships. In the present study, this was done by having a small rectangle of color occur with each

Figure 7.5.
Free recall as a function of list length and categorized (E Group) versus noncategorized (C Group) lists. Data from Table 2 of Wood and Underwood (1967).

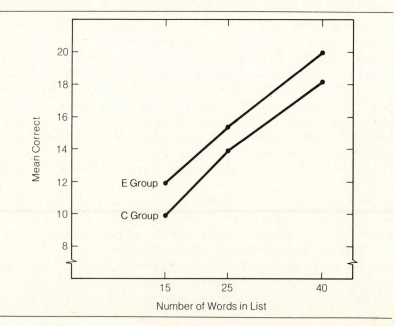

word. Thus, for *derby*, a black rectangle occurred; for *measles* a red; for *sulphur* a yellow; for *moss* a green; and for *chalk*, a white rectangle was used. The subjects were told that these colors might help them learn the lists, and it was clear from the results that the subjects immediately saw the way in which the nouns were related. The subjects given the C List, on the other hand, did not detect the relationships. To repeat: the E Lists and C Lists consisted of identical words, but the subjects given the E Lists viewed the words as having conceptual relatedness because of color commonality.

Three different list lengths were used: fifteen, twenty-five, and forty words. In all lists there were five different concepts (colors). Therefore, the number of instances under each concept varied, these being three, five, and eight for the fifteen-, twenty-five-, and forty-word lists, respectively. There were, then, three groups given the C Lists and three groups given the E Lists. The blocked-random variable was also manipulated but it had a borderline effect statistically and will not be considered here. The rate of presentation was five seconds per word.

The results are shown in Figure 7.5, in which length of list is plotted against mean correct recall after a single study trial. The fact that mean recall increased as list length increased is to be expected and is given no attention here. The difference in learning the E Lists and C Lists represents the influence of conceptual relatedness as defined for this study. The differences are not large, but they are consistent across the various list lengths.

The critical result is concerned with recall as a function of the position of the word within the series of concept instances. We will illustrate how the data were handled by looking at the fifteen-item list with blocked presentation, as shown in Table 7.4. The theory predicts that the first item

Table 7.4. One of the Lists Used on the Wood and Underwood (1967) Study

Position in List	Word
1	derby
2	coal
3	asphalt
4	bricks
5	lips
6	measles
7	forest
8	moss
9	seaweed
10	canary
11	custard
12	sulphur
13	chalk
14	sheep
15	diaper

in each block will be given correctly more times than the second, and the second will be given more frequently than the third. To make use of all of the data, items holding positions 1, 4, 7, 10, and 13 are summed to give a measure of recall for the first item in the blocked concepts. Likewise, the scores for items in positions 2, 5, 8, 11, and 14 were summed to get the recall for the item holding the second position in the series, and items 3, 6, 9, 12, and 15 provide the sum for the third position. Such summations were done separately for the E Lists and for the C Lists. Primacy and recency effects would have opposite and hence neutralizing effects on the sums, but in any event since the words are exactly the same in all positions for the E and C Lists, the prediction should use the recall by position of the C List as the base against which to assess the position effect for the E Lists.

The results are shown in Figure 7.6. Looking at the findings for the fifteen-item lists first, it is seen that recall for the E Lists decreased across the three positions as expected by the theory, whereas for the C List there was no clear trend. The results for the twenty-five-item lists give little support to the IAR interpretation, but with the forty-item list the results are quite as expected by theory, even to the point of finding poorer recall for the latter items in the sequence for the E List than for the C List.

Just why the twenty-five-item lists failed to show the expected position effects is not known. Three further studies have confirmed the findings for the forty-item lists when there were eight instances of each concept (Wood, 1968; Underwood & Freund, 1969a; Shaughessy, 1979). In addition, the later study showed that the general superiority of the first concept instances in a block cannot be accounted for as a von Restorff phenomenon. Thus, except for the findings for the twenty-five-item list, the evidence does support the IAR theory.

The sense-impression materials provide some distinct advantages for the investigator for manipulating conceptual relatedness. The question arises, however, as to whether the results of such studies can be used to generalize to the more usual conceptual manipulations in which we deal with animal names, names of vegetables, names of metals, and so on. A study by Greitzer (1976) provided an affirmative answer, and his results give strong support to the application of IAR theory. Greitzer used a list of 120 words, with twenty-four categories of five instances each. Duration of exposure was also varied, being three, five, or seven seconds. For all three durations, Greitzer found a decrease in recall across the first four instances of the concepts, with a slight inversion for two of the durations for the fifth instance. Although there was no C List, the experimenter used five buffer concepts at the beginning and end of the list, so that the position effects were based only on the fourteen concepts in the body of the list. In a second experiment, Greitzer varied the number of words within a concept (two, three, or five instances). For all three lengths, the recall showed a decrease across position without a reversal. Greitzer concludes that an intracategory rehearsal explanation can account for the data, an explana-

Figure 7.6.

Free recall of words from blocked categories as a function of the position of the words within the block and of the length of the list. The lists were categorized for the E Group but not for the C Group. Based on Wood and Underwood (1967).

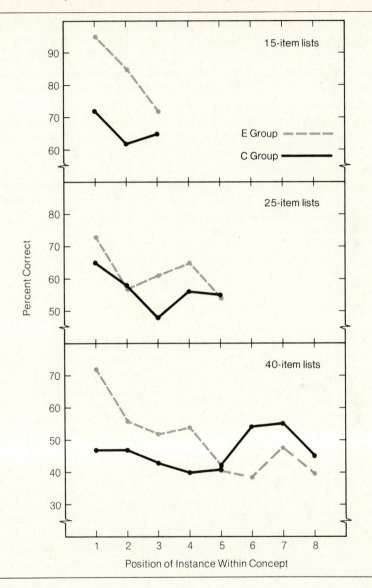

tion which coincides with IAR theory. All in all, it seems that IAR theory as applied to conceptual relatedness does a sufficiently satisfactory job of handling the data to warrant its retention and perhaps further application.

SUMMARY

Implicit-associative responses (IARs) were assumed to occur as subjects attempted to learn various types of word lists. These IARs were further assumed to become a part of memory for the word that produced them. The particular IARs that occurred were identified by using normative data from word-association procedures. Depending upon the type of lists, IAR theory would predict a positive effect on learning and in others negative effects. This was true for certain types of conceptual IARs. The inhibiting effect of crossed associates in a paired-associate list was attributed to IARs.

The IAR theory was used to account for some of the false alarms which occur in recognition tests, and for the fact that background frequency influences recognition and recall differentially. Several different types of free-recall experiments were described in which IARs could be used as the interpretative framework. These involved lists with direct associates, with words which were conceptually related, and with words which were related by sense impression commonalities.

8

Task Variables

Certain task variables exert extremely large effects on the learning of verbal materials. By task variables are meant any systematic variation in the nature of the items given to the subjects for learning. If one thinks about this for a moment, the conclusion will be reached that there could be a striking number of task variables. Let us see why this is so. Many, many characteristics of words could be quantified, crudely or precisely. These values could be used to construct lists which differ on the particular characteristic of interest. Then we could see if learning or retention differed as a function of the characteristic. Words can be reliably scaled for affectivity, intensity, vividness, power, activity, abstraction, and so on. Words differ in length, in form class, and in frequency of use. It would seem that the richness and variety of the characteristics of words would require attention of investigators for many years if the intent was to determine which characteristics did influence learning and which did not. Further, when we start dealing with pairs of words, or phrases, or sentences, the number of different potential characteristics increases at an astronomical rate.

Before examining the effect of some task variables on learning, it is necessary to consider the problem that may arise from the use of mixed lists in studying the influence of task variables. This matter has been mentioned in previous chapters but was not dealt with in a definitive manner. An effort will be made toward that end now.

MIXED VERSUS UNMIXED LISTS

Remember that a mixed list is one in which the task variable of interest is manipulated within a list. Ten concrete and ten abstract words might be randomized in a free-recall list with the intent of determining whether there are differences in the rate of learning concrete and abstract words. In an unmixed list, on the other hand, all items are homogeneous with respect to the variable of interest, so that different lists are used for the different levels of the independent variable. Thus, rather than mixing concrete and abstract words together in a single list, two lists would be used, with one consisting of all concrete words, the other consisting of all abstract words.

The potential problem with a mixed list is that subjects may detect or identify the different levels of the independent variable within the list. They may then choose to give more of their study time to one level than to the other by displacing rehearsals. The subjects may establish priorities as to which group of items (e.g., concrete or abstract) will be learned first. If this happens for an appreciable number of the subjects, and if these subjects choose to concentrate their initial efforts on the same group of items, the results would suggest that there were differences in learning as a function of the different levels of the independent variable. But, these differences could be the result of the priority-of-learning choices rather than intrinsic differences in the difficulty of the items at the different levels.

How realistic are these concerns about displaced rehearsal in mixed lists? To answer this question we will turn to three sets of data. We will look for cases in which the materials have been presented for learning by mixed lists and also by unmixed lists. The critical question is whether the two types of lists produce different estimates of the influence of the task variable in question. Subjects may, of course, displace rehearsal in learning unmixed lists, but this cannot itself lead to differential learning of the lists representing different levels of the independent variable. If, however, a mixed list shows a difference in learning for a given task variable when an unmixed list does not, the conclusion is that subjects learning the mixed lists displaced rehearsal initially so as to spend more time on the items representing one level of the independent variable than on another. Thus, the effects may be due entirely to study-time differences and not to differences in difficulty of the items representing different levels of the independent variable in the mixed list. There must obviously be some consistency among subjects who do displace rehearsal in terms of priority. That is, the subjects who do displace rehearsal must choose the items from the same level of the independent variable to rehearse if differences as a function of the differential rehearsal are to be found.

Some Studies

Paired-Associate Learning.   Postman and Riley (1957) presented their subjects with rather unusual paired-associate lists. There were three lists, all consisting of eight pairs. One of the lists consisted of what will be called "like" pairs. Four of the pairs were paired CVCs, and four were paired two-digit numbers. Thus, List L (like) had pairs in which the stimulus terms and response terms of each pair were from the same class of materials. A second list (List UL) had eight unlike pairs in which numbers and CVCs were paired, with half the items being CVC-number pairs and the other half being number-CVC pairs. The third list (List M) was a mixed list with respect to the like-unlike variable. Half of the pairs were like pairs and half were unlike pairs.

The three lists were presented to three different groups of subjects. Anticipation learning was used with the rate being 2:2 seconds, and with the learning being continued until the subjects correctly anticipated all response terms on a single trial. The mean numbers of trials to this criterion were 23.88, 23.00, and 23.81 for List L, List UL, and List M, respectively. Obviously, these three means do not differ statistically. However, when the learning of List M was examined for the like and unlike pairs separately, a large difference was found. The like pairs were all learned first on the average on trial 15.75, whereas the unlike pairs were first all correct on trial 22.81. Thus, when *all* items in a list were like items and when all items in another list were unlike items, there was no difference in learning of the two lists. But, when the list contained half like pairs and half unlike pairs, the like pairs appeared to be much easier to learn than the unlike ones. If this were true, though, why was it not observed in the comparison of the scores for the unmixed lists? The most appropriate conclusion would appear to be that in learning the items in the mixed list, the subjects (for whatever reason) tended to concentrate their time and efforts toward learning the like items before learning the unlike items. This does not mean that they completely ignored the unlike items initially, but it does mean that the time and effort were not divided equally between the two types of items. We must note that had these investigators used only List M, the conclusion would undoubtedly have been that the like items were easier to learn than were the unlike items. The results for the unmixed lists deny such a conclusion.

Free-Recall Learning. Theoretical expectations based on IAR theory would predict that words with high-background frequency would be learned more rapidly in free recall than would words with low-background frequency. As pointed out in Chapter 6, words of high frequency have many more interitem associations than do words of low frequency. These interitem associations will produce frequency inputs via IARs to augment the situational frequency, thus producing better recall for common words than for uncommon ones. It turns out that this prediction is confirmed when unmixed lists are used, but quite the opposite result may be observed when mixed lists are used. This has been reported by several investigators; Duncan's study (1974) will be reviewed here. Twenty-four high-frequency words made up the high-frequency list, with twenty-four words also making up a low-frequency list. Twelve words from each list when put together formed one mixed list, and the remaining twenty-four words formed a second mixed list. Single-trial free recall was used.

From the results for the two mixed lists, it was found that the mean recall for the high-frequency words was 9.70, and the corresponding value for the low-frequency words was 11.03. The mean recall for the unmixed list of high-frequency words was 10.90, for the low-frequency words it was 8.93. The interaction between type of list and word frequency was highly reliable statistically. Again, then, there is a choice of two quite different conclusions. With unmixed lists high-frequency words were better recalled than low, but with mixed lists the results were just the opposite.

One interpretation of these results is that in the mixed lists the subjects spend more time studying the low-frequency words than they do in studying the high-frequency words. It is as if most of the subjects quickly note the difference in the two classes of words and decide to allot more time to the most difficult words.

Verbal-Discrimination Learning.   The independent variable in two studies by Kausler (1973) was the orthographic distinctiveness of pairs of homophones. A pair such as *earn* and *urn* would be said to have high orthographic distinctiveness, while distinctiveness for *real* and *reel* would be low. Using pairs of homophones which had been rated for orthographic distinctiveness, Kausler constructed a mixed verbal-discrimination list consisting of three levels of distinctiveness. The homophones were paired, one member of each pair having been designated as the correct word, the other as the incorrect. There were four pairs for each level of distinctiveness, and following an initial guessing trial, nine anticipation trials were given. The results seemed to indicate that orthographic distinctiveness of the pairs had an influence in that the higher the distinctiveness the greater the amount of learning across the nine trials.

In a second experiment, three unmixed lists were used, each consisting of twelve pairs with the differences in the level of distinctiveness for the three lists being equivalent to the differences of the three levels in the mixed-list study. For this second experiment, the differences in the rate of learning were far from being statistically reliable, although the ordering of the means across trials was the same as for the mixed-list results. Nevertheless, the fact remains that had only the second experiment been carried out, the conclusion would have been that orthographic distinctiveness of homophone pairs was not a pertinent variable. If only the first experiment had been carried out, the conclusion would have been quite different. As it is, it seems to this observer that because the unmixed-list experiment failed to demonstrate a reliable effect of distinctiveness, it is unlikely that the variable is a relevant one.

These three studies lead to a conclusion that the manipulation of a task variable by a mixed-list design may give us a faulty reading of the influence of the variable. Differences as a function of a variable may actually represent differences in allocation of rehearsal time and not intrinsic differences in the difficulty of the items at the various levels defining the independent variable. For some task variables the same general results are found for both mixed and unmixed lists, although no one has studied carefully the quantitative aspects of differences produced in the two types of lists. To say that the same results are obtained with mixed and unmixed lists does not deny that unequal allocation of study time has occurred for the mixed list. If extra time is given to the least difficult items, the direction of the differences will be the same for both the mixed and unmixed lists. The differences produced by the different levels of the independent variable, though, should be greater for the mixed than for the unmixed lists. As noted earlier, such a careful comparison of the magnitude of differences produced by the independent variable for the two types of lists has not yet been carried out. The study of rehearsal strategies is a topic of interest in its own right and one which might well make use of mixed lists. However, if the central interest of an experiment is that of determining the influence of a task variable, there seems to be little justification for using a mixed list. The unmixed list will provide an unambiguous assessment.

MEANINGFULNESS

We already have an acquaintance with meaningfulness because we have seen how nonsense syllables (CVCs) and consonant syllables (CCCs) have been scaled. If we construct a list of CCCs of low-association value and a list of the same number of three-letter words, we can be sure that the learning rate for the two lists would differ markedly. The CCCs might be QJF, RZL, XKH, GWC, MVD, PNB, and the words might be BED, DIG, ROT, MAN, DYE, HUT. If the two lists were used as response terms in paired-associate lists, or as items in a free-recall or serial list, the differences in the number of trials required to learn them would be great. The words might require at the most a few trials; the CCCs, many trials.

Why are these two lists so different in difficulty? As a convention we say that they differ in difficulty because they differ in meaningfulness. The problem with this answer is that it has not been possible to identify a critical factor which could explain the differences in difficulty. What we find is that meaningfulness may be defined operationally in several different ways, and each can be shown to be reliable as a definition. Perhaps of greater importance is that many of these scales of meaningfulness, based upon different operational definitions, will correlate highly with each other. To illustrate, let us look at two items, QJF and MAN. How do they differ? Here are some of the ways:

1. The time taken to produce an association (word) to each.
2. The number of different associates (words) produced in a given period of time.

3. The ease with which they may be pronounced.
4. Number of meanings given in a dictionary.
5. The frequency of the letters per se.
6. The frequency with which the bigrams (QJ and JF versus MA and AN) occur in words.
7. Degree to which each suggests a concrete object.

There are others, but these are sufficient to illustrate our point. Which one of these characteristics is responsible for the differences in learning? Being good experimentalists, we say that we will find out which characteristic is critical by doing studies in which we hold all characteristics constant except for one, which we will vary. However, when we attempt to do this we run into problems because the characteristics are correlated. For example, the intercorrelations among the first three characteristics might be found to be not less than .90 when a number of items is involved. This means that we could search and search among many CCCs and among many three-letter words trying to find items on which the first two characteristics listed above are equivalent, but which differ on the third, and we would very likely be unsuccessful. Even if we found a few such words and a few such CCCs, they would probably not be representative of words and of CCCs, and they might well differ on many, many characteristics.

The above situation is quite a realistic one. The author once worked with twenty-seven three-letter units, varying from very difficult CCCs to common words (Underwood, 1966). These items were rated on the number of associates elicited, on pronounceability, and on ease of learning. A different group of subjects was given several free-recall study and test trials on the twenty-seven-item list. Among these four measures, the lowest correlation was .88. This is to say that each characteristic predicted the learning difficulty almost perfectly, and each scaled characteristic correlated with the other two almost perfectly.

Two major points evolve from this discussion. First, for a property of words such as that called meaningfulness, it is essentially impossible to find a single characteristic that is responsible for the effect on learning. Multiple, highly correlated characteristics prevent us from using the power of the experiment effectively to detect a critical characteristic (if there be one). That is why we must speak of meaningfulness as being a highly important variable for learning but one which has been very resistant to decomposition into a single fundamental or basic property. We speak of it as a general variable, meaning that many different identifiable characteristics underlie it.

The second issue incorporated in the work done on meaningfulness in an attempt to determine a single basic factor reveals a particular failing we have as experimenters and as theorists. We find a property of a verbal unit that can be reliably scaled, and we also find that it predicts learning. We then start preparing a theory about how the particular scaled characteristic produces its influence on learning. The problem with such an approach is that there are undoubtedly a number of other characteristics by which the items differ that could be scaled reliably and would predict learning well. The mistake we make in carrying forward our theorizing is to assume that the behavior of the subjects who did the scaling has some sort of direct representation in the learning behavior. It is very unlikely that this is true, particularly when words are involved. What we need to do (in the abstract) is to identify some factor that could account for the effect of meaningfulness and at the same time subsume all of the more detailed characteristics found by various scaling procedures. In the case of meaningfulness we do not have such a general factor.

It is somewhat ironic that we cannot get at the bottom of one of the most powerful variables that exists. Meaningfulness as a factor in learning cannot be ignored simply because we lack the critical skills to decompose it. It is a general task variable of which we must be continually aware because it is a potentially confounding variable when we start trying to understand other task variables.

There are occasions when the critical component of a task variable can be identified. Intralist formal similarity is one such variable and will be discussed at length later. Another is called distinctiveness of orthography. Orthographic distinctiveness was discussed briefly in the chapter on recognition when it was noted that the distinctiveness variable has a positive effect. Words such as *lymph* and *khaki* are rated as having high distinctiveness, whereas *leaky* and *kennel* are not so rated. Recall is also correlated with distinctiveness ratings. But now, we must ask if orthography is *the* critical characteristic in producing the differences in recognition and recall. The words *leaky* and *lymph* may well differ on characteristics other than orthography, and one or more of these other characteristics may be responsible for the differences in learning.

It so happens that for the orthographic characteristic, certain manipulations will produce some rather pointed decisions on this issue as to what is causing what (Hunt & Elliott, 1980). These investigators showed that when the words were printed in capital letters, distinctiveness no longer influenced learning. This strongly suggested that something about the configuration of the letters as they appear in lowercase is critically involved. Certainly, if the high- and low-distinctiveness words also differed on semantic dimensions that might produce differences in learning, changing to capital letters should not erase the difference. Further experiments demonstrated that if the words were presented aurally, the distinctiveness effect was lost, pointing again at the visual configuration of the words as being the true independent variable. Thus, it seems that with this task variable at least, it is possible to arrive at strong conclusions as to the particular characteristic that produces the phenomenon of interest.

These studies on distinctiveness also allow a more substantive conclusion, namely, that nonsemantic attributes may be importantly involved in recall and recognition. Other investigators, using quite different approaches, have arrived at the same conclusion (e.g., Slamecka & Barlow, 1979). We must consider all types of attributes as potential contributors to recall and recognition. And, even if we conclude that a given attribute was not involved in recall or recognition performance, it does not follow that the attribute was not a part of memory (Galbraith, 1975). It may simply not have been selected by the subject at the time the memory test was administered.

Effect of Meaningfulness

We asserted earlier that meaningfulness has a powerful effect. This is hardly sufficient as an empirical summary. Nevertheless, because meaningfulness is not a topic on which contemporary investigators are working, we will be very brief. In one experiment (Underwood & Schulz, 1960), the meaningfulness of the response terms in paired-associate lists was varied. There were four levels of meaningfulness, represented by low-meaningful CCCs (0–21 percent association value), moderately meaningful CCCs (67-79 percent), moderately meaningful CVCs (47-53 percent), and three-letter words. There were eight pairs in each list, and the stimulus terms were the numbers 2 through 9, assigned randomly to the response terms in each list. The amount of letter duplication was the same among the four lists, a matter of considerable importance as we will later see. The subjects were given twenty anticipation trials.

In Figure 8.1 we have plotted the results using the mean total correct responses as the response measure. The four levels of meaningfulness are equally spaced along the baseline, although we have no information regarding the psychological distance between the successive lists. However plotted, it will be apparent that meaningfulness has the powerful influence generally attributed to it. Almost three times as many correct responses were produced with the three-letter words as with the low-association CCCs.

Now, let us assume that we "turned the lists over," so that the three-letter units were stimulus terms, and the numbers were response terms. What would the results look like? From the findings of many investigators, we can predict with high confidence that there would be differences in difficulty among the four lists, but these differences would be relatively small and perhaps not statistically reliable. We would expect a positive slope of the line relating meaningfulness and learning, but the slope would be far less steep than that shown in Figure 8.1.

Why should the slopes of the two lines differ? Two matters should be discussed in trying to answer this question. The first has to do with differences in the functions of the trigrams (a general term for all three-letter units) when they are stimulus terms and when they are response terms. We briefly mentioned this in an earlier chapter. When the items are

Figure 8.1.
Paired-associate learning over twenty trials as a function of the meaningfulness of the response terms. The four successive levels of meaningfulness were 0–21 percent CCCs, 67–79 percent CCCs, 47–53 percent CVCs, and three-letter words. Data from Table 21 of Underwood and Schulz (1960).

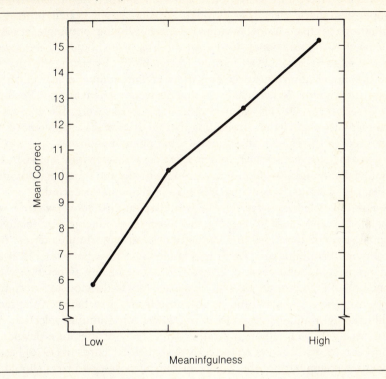

response terms the subjects have to produce them, and to produce them requires that the letters within the syllables be associated so that the three letters are integrated or unified. When the items are stimulus terms, production is not required; all the subject has to do is make a consistent recognition response to each item. In a sense, when the items are stimulus terms, many of the sources of difficulty which plague a learner when the items are response terms are simply not present.

The second matter is something of a refinement of the first. We noted that all the subjects had to do when the trigrams are stimulus terms is to establish a consistent recognition response to each. A consistent recognition response could be established by using only the first letter of the trigrams because there were no repetitions among the first letters. That was also true of the third letters. If some number of the subjects made the functional stimulus a single letter, the effects of meaningfulness could be attenuated or eliminated in that all of the stimulus terms in the four lists would become much more equivalent in difficulty.

As theorists we often attribute certain types of behavior to the subjects in order to account for our data. This is a reasonable assumption when formulating a theory, but all too frequently we forget about the possibility of testing directly the behavior in question. In the present case we are supposing the subject goes through a rather sophisticated process of blunting the effects of low meaningfulness by singling out single letters to be used as the functional stimuli for the lists. We should ask if subjects really do such things. We can quite easily find out by testing the subjects on the single letters (unexpectedly) after a certain number of learning trials with the trigrams. When such experiments were carried out (e.g., Postman & Greenbloom, 1967) it was very clear that subjects were able to respond correctly to single letters, indicating that the trigram as a whole need not be used as the functional stimulus. This phenomenon has come to be known as *stimulus selection*. When there is a discrepancy between the nominal stimulus (the stimulus as presented) and the functional stimulus (the true stimulus), we say that stimulus selection has occurred.

Stimulus selection is far more general than implied above, where it was pointed out because it may be involved in producing the relatively small effect of variations in meaningfulness among stimulus terms. Any compound stimulus may result in stimulus selection. For example, if the stimulus compound consists of two CVCs, one of low-association value and one of high, the subject will be more likely to develop an association between the easier item and its response terms than between the more difficult item and its response term. Work on stimulus selection has essentially ceased, although a rather large body of literature developed between the early sixties to the early seventies. Richardson (1976) has an admirable summary of the work. For our purposes, two facts should be remembered. First, subjects do sometimes exhibit sophisticated encoding strategies, and stimulus selection is one such strategy. Second, we must remember the existence of stimulus selection so that we will be alert to the possibilities that other phenomena may result from it.

CONCRETE WORDS VERSUS ABSTRACT WORDS

Words can be rated reliably according to their degree of concreteness or abstractness. Instructions to the subjects tell them that a word that refers to objects, materials, or persons should be given high ratings with respect to concreteness, whereas a word that refers to an abstract concept that cannot be experienced by the senses should be given a high rating on abstractness. We have already mentioned this variable when discussing recognition. For the present, we ask about the role of the concrete-abstract dimensions on associative learning, which is most clearly represented by the paired-associate task. The discussion will be introduced by the report of an experiment.

From the normative data produced by Paivio, Yuille, and Madigan (1968), two groups of sixteen words each were chosen. All words were about the same length (five, six, or seven letters), and across the two groups the words were matched on background frequency and upon meaningfulness. The words in the two groups differed markedly on the concrete-abstract variable. The abstract words were: *charm, safety, glory, quest, chaos, moral, death, spirit, chance, advice, power, belief, greed, outcome, truth,* and *vigor.* The concrete words were: *string, corner, letter, goblet, flesh, nutmeg, garret, mantle, boulder, tower, stain, doctor, circle, elbow, engine,* and *hotel.* The words in each group were paired randomly with the numbers 1 through 16 to form the pairs.

Four lists were used, and each may be designated by two words in which the first word refers to the stimulus term, the second to the response term: concrete-numbers, numbers-concrete, abstract-numbers, numbers-abstract. Four groups of twenty-three subjects each were assigned to learn the four lists. Three study-test trials were used to produce the data plotted in Figure 8.2.

The results indicate that the concrete-abstract (C-A) variable had only a small effect and that statistically, the magnitude of the difference was far from reliable. As would be expected, performance was better when the numbers were response terms than when they were stimulus terms. The C-A variable did not interact with the locus of the numbers. The effect of concreteness is in the direction usually found, but is small in magnitude. Perhaps if subjects had been instructed to form images to the concrete words the difference would have been magnified. The fact remains, however, that there is little support for the idea that the C-A variable is one of importance.

This experiment was undertaken to gather data for teaching purposes. It was expected that the experiment would produce two findings. First, learning would be more rapid with the concrete words than with the abstract words. Second, the effect of the C-A variable would be greater when the words were stimulus terms than when they were response terms. These expectations were based on the findings of others, particularly the extensive work of Paivio (1971).

It would be an egocentric position associated with a single set of data to suggest that investigators who have found differences in associative learning between abstract and concrete words have failed to reflect the true status of the effect of the variable in question. Yet, the fact remains that our results indicate that the C-A variable is not one of great consequence. Perhaps the lesson to be learned is the one we have been emphasizing: it is extremely difficult to identify the critical characteristic underlying most task variables. As Paivio has discussed at length, the concrete-abstract dimension is correlated with a number of other operationally distinct dimensions, and (in spite of Paivio's prodigious amount of work) it is possible that one of the correlated dimensions is "really" the

Figure 8.2.
The learning of concrete versus abstract words in paired-associate lists.

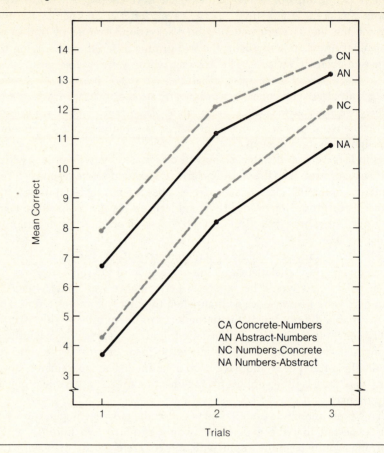

causal factor in the concrete-abstract effect when it occurs. Following the above argument, when it does not occur, the critical variable must not differ for the two groups of words formed for the experiment such as the one reported here. But let it be said that we have no understanding as to why our experiment failed to show the influence of a variable that others have reported to produce very large effects. Of course, it is possible that some investigators have found the C-A variable to be irrelevant, but the results of their experiments have not been reported. So, the whole matter becomes a bit complicated, a suitable state of affairs because drawing cause-effect conclusions when manipulating a task variable is a complicated process.

Related to the issue of the C-A variable is another variable that has been related to learning differences. Reference is made to learning when pictures, as opposed to words naming these pictures, are used as stimulus terms. The interpretation of learning with concrete words has been that an image may be formed which facilitates the learning. In the same sense, then, the picture substitutes for the image. Numerous studies have shown that picture stimuli lead to more rapid paired-associate learning than do the words naming the pictures. The situation is as difficult to handle as is the concrete-abstract difference because the differences between pictures and words are so great that those who have studied the problem intensively despair of being able to identify the critical difference(s) between pictures and words. Goggin (1982) has made a careful analysis of the problem, and her work should be consulted for a listing of the differences between words and pictures.

WITHIN-LIST SIMILARITY

We have already developed some familiarity with the variable known as intralist or within-list similarity. The IAR theory is essentially a theory about within-list similarity. Within this context we have seen that relatedness among words will usually facilitate free recall, but when specific associations are required by a task (as in paired-associate learning), semantic relatedness among items may produce negative influences in learning. For the time being, however, we are going to deal with formal similarity among verbal units. Most commonly, reference to formal similarity means the degree to which letters are repeated among the items in a list; the greater the number of repeated letters the higher the formal similarity. Perhaps a better way to say this is that as the number of different letters used to construct a list of a given length decreases, formal similarity increases. Let us look at some findings that reflect the influence of formal intralist similarity.

Sample Findings Using Formal Similarity

We carried out a study (Underwood & Ekstrand, 1967) in which subjects were asked to learn by free recall a list of only four trigrams. Actually there were two lists with essentially the same structure, used merely to be sure that some generality would attend the findings. The two lists were: KXF, XKV, FVK, VFX, and HQJ, JZH, ZJQ, QHZ. In both cases only four different letters were used to construct the four items. The subjects were given forty study-test trials on the four-item lists. At the end of the forty trials the mean number of responses correctly given was 2.2. The lists were so difficult that it seemed probable that some of the college students would never be able to learn the lists perfectly in a single sitting. It might be noted that we did not use a four-item list for low similarity (no repetition of letters) because it would be too easy to learn.

As a further illustration of the effect of intralist similarity, we will examine a study by Nelson, Wheeler, and Bircov (1970). These investigators used lists of both low and high meaningfulness. The list of low meaningfulness consisted of nonsense syllables, and the list of high meaningfulness consisted of three-letter words. For each level of meaningfulness there was a low- and a high-similarity list. The four lists are shown in Table 8.1. For the two high-similarity lists each of six letters was used four times. For the two low-similarity lists there were seventeen and nineteen different letters used. In the former case ten letters were used once and seven twice, whereas in the latter, fourteen letters were used once, five were used twice.

Serial anticipation learning was used with a two-second rate. Learning trials continued until the subject had anticipated five of the eight responses correctly on a single trial. The mean numbers of trials required to reach this criterion are plotted in Figure 8.3. Note that with low meaningfulness and high similarity, the average number of trials required to reach five correct responses was thirty-seven trials. Ignoring meaningfulness, the average number of trials required to learn the low-similarity lists was eleven whereas thirty trials were required on the average to learn the high-similarity lists. Clearly, intralist formal similarity is a powerful variable.

As a third study we will look at a further experiment conducted at Northwestern University (Schwenn & Underwood, 1968). In this experiment formal similarity was varied across seven levels. At the two extremes the difference in formal similarity was not as great as seen in the previous two studies, but we were more interested in exploring the effects of relatively small steps of letter repetition rather than extreme differences. There were seven CCCs in each list, and the levels of similarity may be identified in terms of the number of different letters used: 21, 19, 17, 15, 13, 11, and 9. A list at the one extreme was JVY, LRK, NZC, WDM, XBF, SQH, and GPT. At the other extreme one of the lists was NBM, KHM, LGK,

Table 8.1. Serial Lists Used by Nelson, Wheeler, and Bircov (1970) in Their Study on the Influence of Meaningfulness and Intralist Similarity on Learning

High Meaning High Similarity	High Meaning Low Similarity	Low Meaning High Similarity	Low Meaning Low Similarity
HAM	PAY	FAQ	QAZ
RAT	SKI	ZAJ	ZOF
RUM	URN	ZIQ	VUB
HAT	GEM	FAJ	DEJ
RUT	OWL	ZIJ	KYV
HUM	LIT	FIQ	BIW
RAM	TUB	ZAQ	CUQ
HUT	FOX	FIJ	GOX

Figure 8.3.
Mean trials to criterion of five correct responses on a single trial for eight-item serial lists as related to meaningfulness and intralist similarity. Data from Table 1 of Nelson, Wheeler, and Bircov (1970).

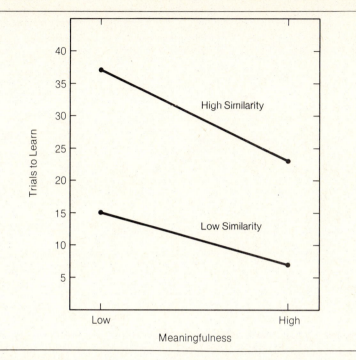

JMG, WGB, JWH, and LJN. Actually we used three different lists at each level of similarity to avoid the results being tied to the peculiarities of any one list.

There were twenty-one groups of thirty subjects each. Seven groups were given thirty free-recall trials, each group having a different level of similarity. Seven groups were given thirty trials on a paired-associate list in which the trigrams were stimulus terms and the numbers 1 through 7 were response terms. The remaining seven groups learned paired-associate lists in which the numbers were stimulus terms, the trigrams the response terms.

The mean number correct per trial across the trials for each group is shown in Figure 8.4. The left panel shows the learning scores for the seven levels of similarity when the trigrams were the stimulus terms and the response terms were the numbers 2 through 7. We can see that as intralist similarity increases among the stimulus terms, performance increases only a little at the middle level of similarity, after which it falls sharply with further increases in intralist similarity. For the results shown in the other two panels, we see that performance falls directly as intralist similarity increases. Both functions are linear, and the changes with intralist simi-

Figure 8.4.
The role of intralist similarity among CCCs in learning various types of lists. There were seven different levels of intralist similarity. Data from Schwenn and Underwood (1968). These data were not included in the original article.

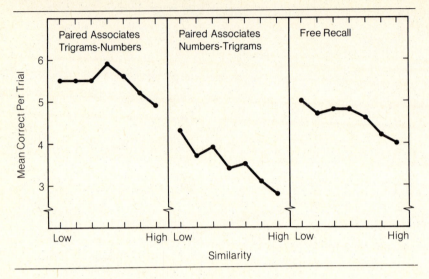

larity are highly reliable statistically. We do not understand why performance when the trigram–numbers are learned does not fall linearly with increases in intralist similarity. However, we have subsequently found the same complex relationship in quite a different case of intralist similarity (Underwood & Lund, 1980b), so we have good reason to conclude that the finding is a reliable one.

Encoding Theory and Intralist Similarity

Repeated letters among stimulus *words* may produce difficulties in learning a paired-associate list. As seen earlier, repeated letters among three-letter words may make serial learning very difficult. It is doubtful that such findings would be expected by the usual observer. One thing we like to believe is that meaning has a very powerful, positive effect in learning, and if we use meaningfulness as a representative of the dimension in question, we know that it does indeed produce marked differences in the rate of learning. Too frequently, however, the belief in the importance of meaning in learning carries with it a corollary which states that attributes of a nonmeaning nature are relatively unimportant for the young adult learner. It is this corollary which must be questioned. As discussed in Chapter 4, encoding attributes can be divided into two general classes. One is called sensory, and for words this includes the phonemic or acoustic attribute and the orthographic or structural attributes. The other class may be spoken of as semantic, and this includes associative and conceptual relationships among words or among larger idea units.

The data on intralist formal similarity when common words are involved seem to be shouting an important generalization, namely, that it is very difficult if not impossible for learners to avoid the interference resulting from sensory similarity. The sensory attributes may appear to be more primitive than do the meaning attributes. If one views the order of events that occur when we look at and comprehend a word, it becomes evident why the sensory attributes might be thought of as basic. To comprehend the meaning of the word, the acoustic or orthographic attributes must first be responded to (the representational response). The representational response may in turn be followed by meaning responses, including imaginal responses.

As was pointed out in Chapter 4, when high formal similarity occurs among words it appears that sensory encoding dominates the memory. This does not mean that the memory does not carry semantic codes, for it most assuredly does. But it does mean that particular sensory codes are apparently difficult to ignore or "keep down" when they occur in a list having many repeated letters. As a consequence, the subjects appear to have trouble in using the semantic attributes to differentiate among the words.

The presence of sensory codes in memory may be inferred from other lines of research. An example may be given from a study by Nelson and Davis (1972). Their subjects first learned a serial list until they could repeat it correctly on two successive trials. They then learned a second list made up of homophones of the words in the first list. For one group these homophones occupied coordinate positions in the two lists, i.e., if *weight* occupied the third position in the first list, *wait* occupied the third position in the second list. For a second group the homophones were randomized in positions in the second list. The coordinate group's performance was far superior to the other in learning the second list, indicating that the acoustic attribute was a part of the memory for the words in the first list.

One further illustration will be given. One might suspect that instructing subjects to use particular types of encoding (sensory or semantic) would drastically change the composition of the memory for the task. However, the results of Nelson, Reed, and McEvoy (1977) rather strongly deny this hypothesis. They conclude that, "Both sensory and semantic codes appear to be activated under each kind of encoding strategy (p.462)."

The above illustrations suggest that we must accept sensory attributes as a fundamental part of the memory. The representational response is not produced merely as a means of getting to the semantic codes; sensory attributes may lead to the semantic codes, but they have a strong life of their own. When formal intralist similarity is manipulated, the sensory codes, which overlap for the various items, prevent these items from being easily discriminated from each other. If these sensory codes cause the intralist interference, perhaps the semantic attributes cause the ultimate reduction of the interference, a reduction which seems to be necessary if the list is to be learned. The evidence currently available gives very little support to this conjecture. In one of our studies (Underwood & Lund, 1980b), we varied similarity by varying the number of words repeated among eight word triads. This manipulation clearly resulted in differential interference. At the same time we carried out another study in which, rather than repeating words, we inserted homophones in the positions that corresponded exactly to the positions held by the repeated words in the other study. Because homophones have quite different meanings, it is possible in theory for the subjects to eliminate the interference produced by the acoustic identity of the homophones. This did not happen; the interference produced by the homophones was as great as that produced by the repeated words. Further, there was no evidence that semantic encoding of the homophones became more and more dominant over trials. This conclusion is similar to that reached by Runquist and Runquist (1978). These investigators studied the role of semantic attributes in reducing interference produced by other semantic attributes: "It was concluded that learners are not able to use discriminative semantic attributes to reduce interference (p. 370)."

One of the less palatable conclusions from these and many other studies is that we seem to have a colossal ignorance as to how within-list interference, produced either by semantic or sensory attributes, is reduced so that our subjects do learn the lists we give them.

Meaningful Similarity

By meaningful similarity we refer to words that are synonymous, that are directly related associatively (e.g., *cup-saucer*), or that are members of the same category. Some negative effects on learning can be produced by manipulating meaningful similarity, but the size of the negative effects is relatively small when compared with the effects of formal similarity as discussed earlier. For example, in one study serial lists of fourteen adjectives were used (Underwood & Goad, 1951). For one list each word had the same core of meaning (e.g., *elated, gleeful, carefree, jolly, laughing, happy, pleasant, festive, sunny, blissful, genial, smiling, cheerful, hearty*) while the words in another list had minimum similarity. The mean number of trials to learn the high-similarity lists to a criterion of one perfect trial was 18.7; for the low-similarity lists the corresponding value was 13.8 trials. Although the difference is reliable statistically, it is certainly not of the size that we have come to expect when manipulating formal similarity.

As we learned in Chapter 7, meaningful similarity among words will facilitate free-recall learning. If, however, the meaningful similarity is manipulated among stimulus terms in a paired-associate list, negative effects can be observed. (Underwood, Ekstrand, & Keppel, 1965). These effects result from the need of the subjects to establish encoding differences among the similar stimulus terms, a requirement that is not necessarily present in free-recall learning. If similarity is varied among the response terms of a paired-associate list, contrary factors will be present. As in free-recall learning, similarity among the response terms will facilitate the learning of the response terms per se. At the same time, though, discriminative encoding must be established for the similar response terms, just as is true when the words are stimulus terms. It is quite possible that these contrary factors may produce results in which the measured influence of the similarity among the response terms is near zero. The general conclusion is that variation in meaningful similarity in paired-associate learning and in serial learning may not always produce a clear influence. Even if an influence is produced, it is likely to be small in an absolute sense.

Methods

Earlier we wrote at length about the problems of drawing specific cause-effect conclusions when manipulating a task variable. In the case of intralist similarity, the problems of method are somewhat diminished. Consider a case in which intralist similarity is increased by decreasing the number of different letters used among CCCs. There is no reason to believe that the items making up a high-similarity list are any more difficult than are those making up a low-similarity list. The differences in difficulty of the two lists result from differences in the levels of repeated letters across items and not to differences in difficulty of the items per se. Nevertheless, investigators frequently use more than one list to represent a given level of formal similarity among CCCs. The idea is that if for unknown reasons there is a difference in item difficulty for the two lists (over and above that due to intralist similarity), having several lists at each level will diminish the chance of the results being biased. Generally speaking, we can feel fairly certain that when we manipulate formal similarity, it is unlikely that any other task variable will be correlated with formal similarity. Hence, any differences we obtain are unambiguously attributed to intralist similarity.

When we manipulate semantic similarity, we have a more serious problem. For example, suppose we want to test the effects of meaningful similarity on serial learning using a ten-word list. For high similarity we choose five pairs of synonyms and randomize them in the ten positions in the list. For the control or low-similarity list we choose ten words that are as unrelated as we can make them according to our judgment. But, what ten unrelated words do we choose? How can we choose ten words that are intrinsically equivalent in difficulty with the words in the high-similarity list? Equating the ten words in each list according to frequency, number of letters, number of associates, concreteness, and so on, is a task whose results can never satisfy most experimentalists for reasons cited earlier when we discussed meaningfulness.

This design problem can be solved fairly easily. What we must do is use five of the words from the high-similarity list in the C List. We would choose one word from each of the five pairs of synonyms. To these five we would add five additional words of the same general characteristics (such as frequency, length, etc.) as the synonyms. Obviously, we would use a random group design, one group for each list. In the analysis of the results for the two groups, we would use only the scores from the five items which occur in both lists. Since we are comparing the scores for exactly the same items, any differences would be attributed to the semantic similarity associated with the five pairs of synonyms in the E List.

The basic idea encompassed in the above procedure could be expanded by using two sets of five pairs of synonyms. There would then be two different E Lists and two different C Lists, and across two subgroups of subjects, each of the twenty words would be used equally often in the C Lists and in the E Lists. The scores on all ten items for each subject would be used in calculating the results.

We will consider another case. Suppose our interest is in determining the effect of conceptual similarity among stimulus terms in a paired-associate list. For the E List we decide to use the names of ten animals as the stimulus terms, and for the C List we will use ten unrelated words of the same general characteristics as the animal names. We must ask whether the words in the E List, taken individually, are equivalent in difficulty to the ten items in the C List. There is no basis for giving a "yes" answer to this question; therefore, we must accept the possibility that the two lists differ in difficulty for reasons other than the intralist similarity of the words in the E List. It would be unwise to proceed with the experiment.

We can solve this design problem in essentially the same way we solved the problem for manipulating synonymity in serial lists. We would make up ten E Lists, each consisting of ten members of the same category, i.e., ten animals, ten vegetables, ten flowers, and so on. We would also make up ten C Lists, each list containing one item from each of the ten E Lists with no word used more than once. Summed across subjects, therefore, each E Word will also have served as a C Word, and differences in learning the E and C Lists must be attributed to the intralist conceptual similarity. In all of these cases, each item used in the final analysis must occur in both the E and C Lists; given this, we have an airtight test of the role of intralist similarity. In this sense, intralist similarity differs from most other task variables in that these other variables are all determined by intrinsic characteristics of the words, whereas in intralist similarity the items taken singly do not differ on intrinsic characteristics. Intralist similarity is a context-dependent variable.

OTHER TASK VARIABLES

Having been warned about the interpretative problems which seem inherent in most task variables, we will examine some further characteristics of verbal materials to see what effects they produce. This will be done without extensive comment on the issue of interpretation.

Form Class

It would seem reasonable to ask if words differing in form class (adjectives, nouns, verbs, and so on) differ in the rate at which they are learned. The evidence is that differences in learning for nouns, adjectives, verbs, and adverbs are relatively small (e.g., Cofer, 1967). On the other hand, when prepositions, articles, and conjunctions are used in paired-associate lists, learning is much slower than for the learning of noun pairs, although more rapid than the learning of CVC pairs (Epstein, Rock, & Zuckerman, 1960). In one experiment, ten-pair lists were used (Underwood & Ekstrand, 1968b). The E List was as follows: *at-day, the-job, of-war, to-hat, by-tax, on-sky, in-wit, or-sea, for-box,* and *but-car.* A C List had exactly the same response terms, but the stimulus terms were as follows: *attempt, theory, office, today, bygone, onward, instant, orange, forest,* and *butter.* A comparison of these words with the stimulus terms for the first list will show that they have identical first and second letters, e.g., *at* and *attempt, the* and *theory, of* and *office.* The subjects were given six anticipation trials, and the mean numbers of correct anticipations were 24.92 for the E List, 40.88 for the C List. For some unknown reason the conjunctions and articles and prepositions do not "stick" well, nor do other words stick well to them.

Noun-Adjective Versus Adjective-Noun

Suppose a paired-associate list consisted of such pairs as the following: *red-barn, misty-day, old-man.* In each case an adjective is the stimulus term, and a noun is the response word. The learning of a list with such pairs would be compared with the "turned over" pairs (i.e., *barn-red, day-misty, man-old*). The adjective-noun order is the one commonly used in English sentences. It might be expected, therefore, that learning of the adjective-noun list would occur more rapidly than the learning of the noun-adjective list. The opposite was found to be true. (Paivio, 1963). It was this finding that apparently led Paivio to undertake his extensive work on the effect of the concrete-abstract dimension on learning.

Vividness

Words can be rated reliably as to their vividness, and vividness is not highly correlated with meaningfulness. Is there something about vividness which would influence the rate of learning? Tulving, McNulty, and Ozier (1965) had subjects rate words on both vividness and meaningfulness, and then constructed lists which were equated on meaningfulness but differed on vividness. The list of words having high vividness was: *apron, balloon, bunny, butter, cabbage, camel, chorus, cigar, circus, comet, granny, jungle, lantern, rainbow, runner,* and *satin*. The list having low vividness was: *buyer, crisis, entry, founder, output, patron, renown, routine, rover, rumour, session, surplus, tariff, topic, treason,* and *vigour*.

The lists were presented for eight free-recall study-test trials. The results showed that the list with the words of high vividness was learned more rapidly than the list with words of low vividness, although the difference could not be described as large. It is a worthwhile exercise to examine the words in the two lists carefully to see if other word characteristics might differ for the two lists and thus account for some of the differences in learning. The three investigators who conducted the experiment were able to suggest several possible characteristics that might have been involved in addition to vividness.

A REMINDER

Task variables may produce very large effects on learning, but the basic underlying factor or factors that are responsible cannot usually be determined. The number of letters in a word (word length) is clearly a task variable. The author once asked his class to design an experiment that would be definitive with regard to word length and rate of learning, in the sense that no other variable was confounded. No student was able to present a design that passed the scrutiny of the other students. So much for task variables.

SUMMARY

Task variables refer to characteristics of the verbal units used to construct lists. Meaningfulness is one such characteristic that has been shown to have a profound effect on learning. A number of different procedures have been used to define meaningfulness, each operationally distinct from the others. The indices of meaningfulness derived from these different procedures are highly correlated; consequently, it is not possible to determine the fundamental factor(s) underlying the positive effect of meaningfulness on learning. This problem holds for certain other task variables, including the concrete-abstract variable.

Intratask similarity avoids the problem of method noted above. Formal intralist similarity among a group of verbal units is said to increase as the number of different letters used in the units decreases. Although there are some minor exceptions, learning rate decreases directly as formal intralist similarity increases. When words are used in the lists in which formal similarity is manipulated, very large effects have been found. This must mean that nonsemantic attributes dominate the semantic attributes. Meaningful similarity, varied by using synonyms or conceptually related words, influences rate of learning and is not subject to the confounding that is found with meaningfulness.

The influences of other task variables were noted briefly. These included form class, adjective-noun versus noun-adjective pairings, and vividness.

9

Transfer and Interference

In the study of learning, transfer refers to the carry-over of associations, skills, concepts, or strategies from one task to another. Each of these various factors may produce either positive or negative effects, or no effects at all in the performance on the second task. Whether overall performance on the second task is facilitated (positive transfer) or inhibited (negative transfer) will probably be determined by the summation of the positive and negative effects. All of this may sound as if matters were pat and sure when in fact, as we will see, they are not.

If we put the definition of transfer into operational form we have the following:

	Task X	Task Y
E Group	YES	YES
C Group	–	YES

If the performance of the E Group on Task Y is better than the performance of the C Group, we say that positive transfer has occurred. If the reverse is found, we speak of negative transfer.

It is a convention to divide transfer phenomena in verbal learning into two classes, nonspecific transfer and specific transfer. We will first discuss some of the findings about nonspecific transfer. With respect to specific transfer we will spend a considerable amount of time on what will be called identity paradigms, all of which may produce interference. In the process we will emphasize the role of competition as an explanatory concept, but other explanatory approaches will also be described. We will then turn to what may be called similarity paradigms because they deal with the effects of systematic differences in the similarity of the first- and second-list items.

As a next step, certain experiments in which expected positive transfer failed to occur will be examined. Finally, a rather wide variety of inter-ference phenomena will be described.

NONSPECIFIC TRANSFER

Learning-To-Learn

Suppose we have a pool of unrelated words from which we draw randomly to form two lists of the same length. The kind of list is not of importance for the moment. We then proceed to follow the operational definition given above in that the E Group learns two lists in succession, whereas the C Group learns only the second list. If the performance on the common list is better for Group E than Group C we have demonstrated learning-to-learn. And because the words used in the lists were unrelated (insofar as presumably unrelated words can be unrelated), the transfer is said to be nonspecific because it cannot be immediately attributed to particular similarity relationships between the items in the two lists. (Note that if one assumes the two lists were equal in difficulty, the C Group is not needed to reach the conclusion about transfer; the same conclusions can be reached by comparing performance on the two lists for the E Group.)

Changes in performance with practice are sometimes found to be of great magnitude. For example, Keppel, Postman, and Zavortnik (1968) had their subjects learn thirty-six lists of paired associates made up of common words. A list was learned every two days, and the learning criterion was one perfect trial. The mean number of trials to learn the initial lists was approximately eleven, whereas on the last few lists the mean was approximately four. However, it did not appear that a plateau had been reached even after thirty-six lists. Those who have studied learning-to-learn most extensively speak of it as resulting from the acquisition of instrumental skills that, while being partially specific to a given task and materials, will also generalize appreciably (Postman, 1969).

We should not anticipate that changes called learning-to-learn will always be as large as observed in the above study. Sometimes the changes are small, particularly with free-recall lists of unrelated words. In fact, if we use lists made up of words from a single category, there will be negative transfer across lists (Brown & Atkinson, 1974). It is like the PI buildup seen in the Brown-Peterson procedure (see Chapter 3) when successive triads of words are members of the same category. On the other hand, if the free-recall lists are made up of CVCs, the improvement in performance with each successive list continues for many lists (Meyer & Miles, 1953). Serial learning of CVCs has been shown to produce very large learning-to-learn effects (e.g., Ward, 1937). Verbal-discrimination learning also shows learning-to-learn for twenty-four-pair lists made up of common words (Underwood, Shaughnessy, & Zimmerman, 1972a). This is all to say that improvement across lists is a fairly general feature of human learning.

In the above experiments each list was learned to a given criterion, and clearly there is a positive correlation between the number of previous lists and the rate of learning the current list. Such data do not tell us, though, how important the level of learning on a list is in determining the magnitude of learning-to-learn. All we know is that some learning produces learning-to-learn, whereas obviously no learning will not. With respect to this matter, LaPorte and Voss (1974) carried out the critical study. Eight pairs of CVCs were used in the paired-associate lists. The number of lists was varied (one, two, or four) prior to all subjects being given the same test list to learn. In addition to the number of lists, the level of learning of the lists was manipulated, being four out of eight correct, eight out of eight, or two successive perfect trials.

In terms of the mean number of trials required to learn the test list, LaPorte and Voss discovered that the degree of learning of each list was a far more important variable than the number of lists. Number of lists produced a significant effect only on the initial trial of the test list. For example, when the subjects learned each training list to two successive perfect trials, the mean trials to learn the test list to the criterion was 7.7 trials when only one training list was used, and the corresponding value was 6.9 trials when four training lists were learned, a very small difference. These investigators conclude that their results suggest the "importance of list mastery as a factor in nonspecific transfer rather than to the number of associations acquired per se" (p. 473).

In a further study, LaPorte, Voss, and Bisanz (1974) set about to see if the nonspecific positive transfer was due to storage processes or to retrieval processes. To determine this they had one treatment in which the subjects were not tested on the training list. Rather, in a study-test procedure, the test trials were omitted and the subject did simple arithmetic problems during the times when test trials would normally be given. They found that the amount of transfer to the test list was just as great as was the transfer for the standard treatment in which test trials were given on the training list. Their conclusion emphasized the role of storage skills in producing the learning-to-learn and minimized the role of retrieval skills.

It is apparent that for some tasks, learning-to-learn is a very important variable as gauged by the differences in performance at various stages. If one thinks of the empirical work that needs to be done, the projected work becomes enormous in amount. Into the experimental matrices we must at least put the type of task, the number of training tasks, the level of learning on the tasks, the various types of paradigms (yet to be discussed), and certainly the type of material. In addition we should have separate measurements for various types of skills which have been identified as being involved in learning-to-learn and which will be expanded in number for future studies. We may hope that someone will develop an articulate theory that will cut across all of these variables; perhaps in that way the empirical stage can be reduced in amount.

Warmup

Another phenomenon of nonspecific transfer is known as warmup. It is called this because it has sometimes been viewed as analogous to warmup that seems to be an inevitable preliminary to athletic performance. The definition of learning-to-learn given above actually includes the effects of warmup, and hence is not a "pure" definition. The notion is that warmup results from the development of postural sets or adjustments. The act of learning one list may develop the appropriate postural set so that a second list would be learned faster than the first. To repeat, so-called learning-to-learn is in part due to warmup from the first list to the second. However, it is generally assumed that warmup would be complete after learning one list so that increases in performance on successive lists given immediately would be attributed only to learning-to-learn.

It is possible to separate the two sources of nonspecific transfer by using a warmup task which does not require learning. For example, in simulating paired-associate learning by the anticipation method, the subjects might be shown a neutral item every two seconds, and each time it appears the subject is asked to "anticipate" which number between one and nine will appear. However, because the numbers which appear are randomly determined there is no way for the subjects to learn; they knew it was a guessing game from the beginning. As a consequence of these activities the development of an appropriate postural set is presumed to occur, and the learning task will be facilitated if given immediately.

There is another way to distinguish between warmup and learning-to-learn provided certain assumptions are accepted. These assumptions are first that warmup is lost very rapidly with rest. Second, learning-to-learn skills are forgotten very slowly if at all. We may see how this works out by looking at a study by Mayhew (1967). Subjects were given ten study-test trials of free-recall learning on lists made up of thirty nouns. Two lists were given each day in immediate succession for three different days.

The mean numbers of correct responses per trial are shown in Figure 9.1. The saw-toothed nature of the "curve" is probably due to warmup differences. On the first list on each day there is a lack of warmup, but as the first list is learned, warmup occurs so that the full positive effects of warmup appear on the second list within each day. Between days the warmup produced by learning is lost so that the first list on a day serves to warm up the subjects resulting in an improvement on the second list each day. This effect seems quite clear for the first two days, but decreases noticeably on the third day. Learning-to-learn would be in-

Figure 9.1.
Changes in performance within and between days due to nonspecific transfer. The changes between days are identified as learning-to-learn, those within days as warmup. Data from Table 1 of Mayhew (1967).

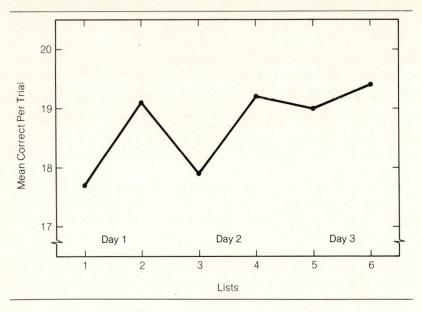

dexed by the performance on the first list on each day (without warmup), and the difference between the first and second list within each day indicates the magnitude of the warmup effect. In this experiment it is obvious that learning-to-learn was very small in amount.

IDENTITY PARADIGMS

Over the years, specific transfer as related to interlist similarity has come to be associated with paired-associate tasks and with four key identity paradigms, in three of which an item in the second list is identical to one in the first list. With the first list symbolized as A-B, the four paradigms as indicated by the second list are C-D, A-D, C-B, and A-Br. In discussing these paradigms we will frequently omit the first-list symbol (A-B) and refer only to the second-list symbol. The C-D paradigm is a control or reference paradigm having zero similarity in that no words are repeated in the two lists. It is a control in the sense that nonspecific transfer effects will be absorbed by the second list so that when performance on C-D is compared with the performance on the second list of any of the other paradigms, the differences will be attributed to specific identity relationships. Generally speaking, and using C-D as a base, it is found that transfer for all three identity paradigms is negative, with the amount increasing from C-B to A-D to A-Br (Twedt & Underwood, 1959). Some modifying factors to this statement will be mentioned later.

A-B, A-D

If an investigator wants to study negative transfer, this paradigm is likely to be used. The negative effects presumably result from the fact that having just learned A-B and undertaken the learning of A-D, the subject continues to give the B response as an implicit associative response (IAR) produced in the laboratory. Competition is said to occur. To try to learn to respond with D to A after having learned B to A sets up incompatible response tendencies with the consequent competition and negative transfer.

Variations can be made on the A-D paradigm, and still the transfer will be negative. We may consider an illustrative study done by Anderson (1981) which shows that a secondary measure may be used to detect the competition. In this paired-associate study there were twenty pairs, with the stimuli being concrete words and the response terms being the numbers 0 through 9. Anderson varied the usual A-D paradigm by assigning each of the response terms—the ten digits—to two stimulus terms, the assignment being random for each subject. The rate for the anticipation learning was five seconds for the time to try to anticipate the correct response followed by five seconds for the study of the pair. After the initial study trial, seven anticipation trials followed. The control paradigm was the usual one, A-B, C-D.

In addition to noting the correct responses, Anderson measured the latency of responding, this being the time between the presentation of the stimulus term on the anticipation trials and the response to the stimulus term. The subjects were instructed to respond as quickly as possible but, of course, to also try to produce the correct response. The latency measures were analyzed only for the correct responses.

The percentage of correct responses on each trial and the latencies for these responses for both paradigms are shown in Figure 9.2. The negative transfer in terms of correct responses is apparent in the left panel. The right panel shows that across trials the latencies to the correct responses decrease in a regular manner. One can almost "see" the subjects learning to produce the correct response more quickly as learning proceeds, and it would seem reasonable to presume that in the A-D paradigm this involves learning to reject more and more quickly the B terms from the first list.

The question arises as to whether correct responses and latency measures reflect a single underlying mechanism. Anderson's evaluation of his data led him to conclude that there was not complete overlap. One technique he used to reach this conclusion was to look at the latencies for the two paradigms when the correct performance was equivalent. For

Figure 9.2.

Negative transfer in A-B, A-D paired-associate learning as represented by the number of correct responses (left panel) and in terms of latency of responding to the stimulus terms (right panel). Data from Table 1 of Anderson (1981).

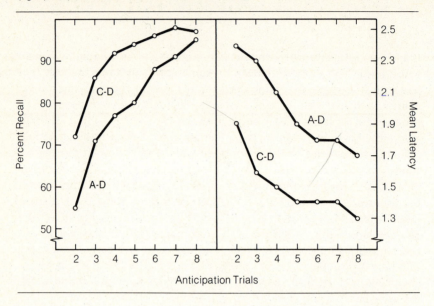

example, it can be seen from Figure 9.2 that the number of correct responses is about equivalent for Trial 2 of C-D and Trial 3 of A-D, for Trial 3 of C-D and Trial 6 of A-C, and so on. Given that the number of correct responses was equated for the two conditions by this procedure, it was found that the latencies were still longer for the A-D learning than for the C-D learning. Because of such data, Anderson concluded that the two measures do not reflect the same properties of the memory for the pairs.

We might well anticipate that the magnitude of negative transfer would be directly related to the level of learning of A-B beyond some minimum level. Thus, it might be expected that the greater the probability that the B term will occur as an implicit response in the learning of A-D, the greater the interference. This is not the case; the level of A-B learning does not influence the amount of negative transfer to a significant degree (Postman, 1962). The reason for this may lie in contradictory effects which occur as the degree of A-B learning increases. On the one hand, the increase in the degree of A-B learning will increase the likelihood that the B response will occur implicitly. On the other hand, the stronger the A-B associations, the easier it is for the subject to discriminate or differentiate between the two sets of competing responses. In this same study, Postman showed that the C-B paradigm also showed no influence of the degree of A-B learning, although there was an effect for the A-Br paradigm in that the amount of negative transfer increased a small amount as degree of A-B learning increased.

Within-List Competition. We might insert the A-B, A-D paradigm within a long list of paired associates. When this is done there is no suggestion of interference (e.g., Bruce & Weaver, 1973). This might be expected on the grounds that discrimination between the response terms is not required. Rather, the subject simply acquires two response terms for the same stimulus term. The data suggest that when A-D is presented for study, the subject may rehearse the previously studied A-B pair. Nevertheless, a slight change in the procedure will result in rather heavy negative transfer. The change is to make the A terms slightly different. In one study the stimulus terms were identical except that one was printed in lowercase letters and the other in capital letters, with the subject being required to produce each response term to its appropriate stimulus term (Underwood & Lund, 1981). The number of times each pair was presented was also varied. After studying this long paired-associate list, in which many different pairs fitted the above paradigm and in which control items (no interfering item) were present, the subject recalled as many of the pairs as possible. The results showed negative transfer for all levels of learning of the pairs, but there was no systematic relationship between the level of learning of one pair and the amount of competition on its interfering pair. It was as if the interference was generalized. It is not clear why this should be.

A-B, C-B

In this paradigm the stimulus terms in the two lists differ, with the response terms being identical. It was earlier noted that this paradigm may produce negative transfer. However, one may vary the direction and amount of transfer by varying the ease of learning the response terms. When the subjects learn A-B and then are given C-B, so-called response learning (the acquisition of the response terms per se) has taken place during A-B learning, and this would tend to produce a positive factor in learning C-B. To assess the amount of positive transfer the C-D paradigm provides the control data. In this paradigm the D items must be learned from "scratch," and if they are difficult items to learn, many trials will be required. But, as noted earlier, the B terms in the C-B paradigm will have been mastered in learning the A-B list so that in learning C-B this acts as the source of positive transfer. What this means, therefore, is that the more difficult the response terms are to learn the greater the positive transfer (Jung, 1963). So, then, there is a clear positive factor in this paradigm which, under certain circumstances, will make the overall transfer positive. With response terms that are relatively easy to learn, the overall transfer is likely to be negative.

An unanswered question concerns the mechanisms by which negative factors occur with this paradigm. One may speculate that it results from the backward association between B and A interfering with the corresponding backward association in the second list (B-C). Viewed in this fashion, the two backward associations constitute an A-B, A-D paradigm, and in some fashion it could be that interference is produced. However, there is no convincing evidence on this and there is some evidence that the backward associations are not responsible (Schwartz, 1968). This matter represents unfinished business.

A-B, A-Br

This paradigm is constituted by maintaining the A and B terms in the second list but re-pairing them. It can be seen that A-Br combines both the A-D and C-B paradigms and thus may be the sum of the negative effects for each of the two. Again, of course, because the response terms are the same in both lists, a distinct positive factor is present (transfer of response learning).

Other Identity Paradigms

Although the above four paradigms have been most frequently studied, the effects of other identity paradigms have been investigated occasionally. For example, the two paradigms symbolized as A-B, C-A and A-B, B-C have been shown to produce negative transfer when assessed against the C-D base (e.g., Goulet & Barclay, 1965). In the A-B, C-A paradigm the stimulus term in the first list becomes the response term in the second list, whereas with the A-B, B-C paradigm the response term in the first list becomes the stimulus term in the second. Again, explanations of the negative effects have tended toward the use of interference among backward associations. These paradigms are quite complicated. One would need to assess further whether in the A-B, C-A paradigm there is a positive factor (response learning, perhaps, or item differentiation) as a consequence of the stimulus term becoming a response term. The same questions would be asked about the B term in the A-B, B-C paradigm.

There is only one further identity paradigm possible, namely, A-B, B-A, and it can be seen that this paradigm would be asking about the transfer due to the backward association (B to A) acquired in learning the first list.

A Point of Method

When we conduct an experiment using more than one of the key paradigms, we do not give the lists in the order indicated by the symbols, e.g., A-B, A-D. Rather, A-B is always the second list so that under all paradigms the same list is learned, eliminating the possibility that the differences observed in transfer are due to intrinsic differences in list difficulty. So, to mimic the experimental procedure as it would be carried out, the paradigms should read C-D, A-B; A-D, A-B; C-B, A-B; and A-Br, A-B.

SIMILARITY PARADIGMS

The similarity paradigms fill in the "space" between the terms of the identity paradigms. Because of the continuity in transfer as similarity varies, we will see that in a general way we can make predictions of transfer changes as similarity changes because we know about the transfer effects for the two basic identity paradigms (A-B, A-D; A-B, C-B). We will follow these changes in similarity and transfer.

Assume that we start with the A-B, A-D paradigm and that our first step is to increase the similarity between B and D. We know that we get negative transfer with A-B, A-D. But, as the similarity between B and D increases, we would expect less and less negative transfer (or more and more positive), and when the two terms become identical, positive transfer would be at a maximum because the paradigm becomes A-B, A-B. In a similar fashion we see what would happen if we gradually decrease the similarity between the A terms in the A-B, A-D paradigm. As we move from A to A' to A" (decreasing similarity) we will reach A-B, C-D, which is the reference paradigm in which no positive transfer is expected of a specific nature.

As a further step we may use the A-B, C-B paradigm as a starting point and carry out the similarity manipulations just as was done above. If the stimulus similarity is increased between A and C, we arrive at the A-B, A-B paradigm, and if the response terms are made more and more dissimilar, we reach the A-B, C-D paradigm.

For the above manipulations of similarity, we can predict in a general way what *must* happen to transfer in the sense that we can say that transfer must move from negative to positive. The missing part of our knowledge concerns the mechanisms which change the negative transfer into positive. Suppose we have A-B, A-B' and another paradigm A-B, A'-B, in which the prime symbol indicates very high similarity. Positive transfer occurs with these two paradigms. What is producing this positive transfer? We will briefly examine two theories that attempt to answer this question after we have presented some of the basic facts for which the theories must account.

1. What is the nature of the similarity that is required in these similarity paradigms? Using unmixed lists, positive transfer may be expected with synonyms, with direct associates, and with antonyms. A common property of these three types of relationships is an associative one in that antonym responses are frequently given in word-association procedures (e.g., *low* is frequently given to *high*) and synonyms are frequently associatively related (*wind* may be a response to *breeze*). The fact that pairs of

synonyms are frequently related associatively does not necessarily eliminate the possibility that similarity of meaning per se may be responsible for some transfer effects. Yet the fact remains that the higher the degree of rated meaningful similarity between pairs, the greater the likelihood that the two words will be associatively related when tested by word-association procedures.

2. Most of the research has made use of the A-B, A-B′ paradigm, although it has been shown that positive transfer will occur with the A-B, A′-B paradigm (e.g., Kasschau & Pollio, 1967). Smith (1974) compared the two directly using synonyms. Sample pairs from both lists for both paradigms are:

A-B, A-B′:   *dirty-quiet, dirty-tranquil*

A-B, A′-B: *filthy-tranquil, dirty-tranquil*

Although Smith found positive transfer for both procedures, the amount was considerably larger for A-B, A′-B than for A-B, A-B′. Smith attributes this difference to the fact that when response terms are identical, there will be a transfer of response learning, a factor that constitutes a positive one over and beyond that which may be attributed to the similarity of the stimulus terms in the A-B, A′-B paradigm.

3. It will be remembered that for the identity paradigms, the degree of A-B learning had no appreciable influence on the magnitude of negative transfer. For the two similarity paradigms under consideration, it has been found that the amount of positive transfer is directly related to the number of A-B trials (e.g., Smith, 1974; Underwood, 1951).

4. Smith (1974) also showed that the greater the number of lists learned, the greater the amount of transfer on the final list. Thus, the learning of three lists (*dirty-quiet, dirty-peaceful, dirty-serene*) produced greater positive transfer in learning *dirty-tranquil* than did *dirty-quiet* alone.

A favorite explanation for the positive transfer observed with these paradigms is mediation between the related words. We will speak temporarily only of the A-B, A-B′ paradigm because it is not complicated by the transfer of response learning. The notion of mediation is very simple when applied to A-B, A-B′. The subject, having learned A-B, acquires A-B′ by using B as a mediator so that two associations are involved, A to B and B to B′. This can take place because of the already existing association between B and B′.

There is some auxiliary evidence to support the mediator idea. First, many subjects report that they mediated in learning the A-B′ list. Second, if mediation occurs it should take longer to produce the response term B′ than would be true if a direct association between A and B′ were involved. Thus, if the anticipation interval is very short, such as one second, performance might be retarded as compared with performance on the A-B, C-D paradigm, in which it is presumed that mediation is much less likely to occur. Some evidence supports this expectation (e.g., Richardson, 1968). Third, it might be anticipated that subjects could become skilled at using mediators. If this is true, amount of specific transfer across successive sets of A-B, A-B' lists should be greater than for the reference paradigm. Evidence is in line with this expectation (Postman, 1964b).

Evidence against the mediation hypothesis comes primarily from Smith's (1974) work. It would seem reasonable to expect that the A-B associations would grow stronger during A-B' learning if mediation occurs because A-B continues to be practiced during A-B' learning. After Smith had completed the transfer phase of his experiment, he asked the subjects to recall all of the response terms they could from the lists. They were given the stimulus terms to aid recall. Smith found that the recall of the B terms was no better for the A-B, A-B' paradigm than for the reference paradigm (C-D). It will be remembered that Smith also had conditions in which four lists were learned rather than the customary two. Smith raises the question as to what the mediator could be when the subjects reach the third and fourth lists. The several possibilities that Smith suggested were all denied by the data on response recall.

It is possible to account for the positive transfer in the similarity paradigms by using a classical generalization theory (Underwood, 1951). This theory states that whenever an A-B association is learned, stimuli similar to A also show an increase in the probability of eliciting B, the increase being directly related to the degree of similarity. Further, as A-B is learned, response terms similar to B have an increase in the probability of being elicited by A. In effect, what this theory assumes is that during A-B learning, A'-B is also learned to some extent by this parasitic-like generalization process; this is also true for A-B'. Such a theory will account for the basic data. Nevertheless, the data Smith has presented on response recall do not support the generalization theory because A-B should be strengthened during A-B' learning for either paradigm. Therefore, A-B should be well recalled following the learning of the transfer list, but Smith's data did not produce this result.

There is a further problem with the generalization theory. It is stated to reflect manipulations of synonymity. There is no easy way to include associated pairs which are not synonyms. That is, there is no way to "get" the generalization gradients in operation except by using synonymity as the similarity manipulation. It does not seem possible that direct associates (e.g., *lock-key*) which are not synonyms can be fitted in the theory based on generalization gradients in which meaningful similarity underlies the gradients.

It must be concluded that no satisfactory account of the positive transfer found with the similarity paradigms is available. It is difficult to support a conclusion that would deny any role for mediation, and it is probably true that most investigators who have studied the issues lean toward a theory that allows mediation to play some role at least. It seems that we need more analytical studies such as the one carried out by Smith (1974), a study which has figured prominently in the above discussion.

SOME FAILURES TO FIND POSITIVE TRANSFER

Three different experiments will be described in which the outcomes were unexpected. They were unexpected because positive transfer did not occur, and this failure had rather profound theoretical implications.

Stimulus Discrimination

It will be remembered that when we were discussing formal intralist similarity it was necessary to conclude that just how subjects overcome the interference so as to learn the list given them was unknown. In some way it appeared that the subjects found new attributes that allowed the needed discrimination to be made. The problem we will develop now, a problem dealing with interlist similarity, is related to the issue of the acquisition of discriminating attributes.

In the discussion of the various paradigms, we gave an account of certain transfer phenomena by using a logical analysis of the situation. It seems beyond doubt that response learning is a part of the overall learning for paired associates. Thus, in the C-B paradigm, if the response terms are difficult to learn (e.g., CCCs), the learning of the second list should be facilitated because the subject would already have learned the response terms. This is what we mean by a logical analysis, and the data have indeed shown that the positive transfer may occur with the C-B paradigm when the response terms are difficult to learn.

Now we will examine the A-B, A-D paradigm to see if there is some source of positive transfer, always using the C-D paradigm as a control. We noted that in the A-B, A-D paradigm the stimulus terms are identical in both lists. Therefore, the stimulus terms might provide a positive factor. A logical analysis might suggest that some form of stimulus learning could transfer from the first to the second list in the same sense that response learning is said to transfer. We would accept the notion that the subjects must learn to make a stable implicit response to each stimulus term before the response term could be associated with it. This learning may transfer to the second list and produce positive effects. Furthermore, from what we know about the influence of intralist similarity, it would seem that the higher the similarity, the more difficult it would be to learn a stable and discriminating code for each stimulus term in the list. Therefore, the positive effect resulting from the A-B, A-D paradigm having identical stimuli in the two lists should be directly related to intralist similarity among the A terms. The logical analysis leads to an experimental test which we will now describe.

We will need two paradigms, A-D and C-D, and two levels of interstimulus similarity, which we will speak of as low and high similarity. When the similarity is low, the positive effect in going from A-B to A-D should be relatively small, so that the overall negative effects of the paradigm should be observed. But, when similarity is high, the performance on C-D of the A-B, C-D paradigm should be severely retarded. That is, we must have high similarity among the stimulus terms in the first list (A-B) and also high similarity among the stimulus terms of the second list (C-D). Remember, we are going to compare the learning of A-D and C-D. When the subjects have learned the first list in the A-D paradigm, the negative effects of the high similarity must have in some way been overcome. Given that these are overcome, when the subject is given the second list (A-D), the stimuli are the same and the positive transfer should be very high. Subjects given C-D will have to establish a new set of discriminations among the stimulus terms, but this should not be necessary for the subjects who have the same stimulus terms in both lists. In fact, the learning of the A-D list should take place at about the same rate as that observed when the similarity among the stimuli is very low.

The expectations from the experiment are shown in Figure 9.3. Let us review. With low similarity among the stimulus terms within a list, per-

Figure 9.3.
Expected transfer effects for stimulus discrimination of the A-B, A-D and A-B, C-D paradigms when stimulus similarity is low and high.

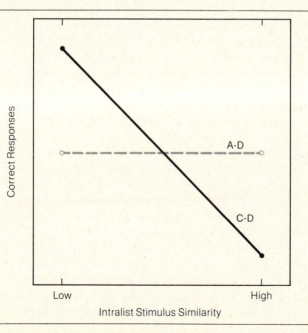

formance will be better for C-D than for A-D. This merely reflects the negative transfer usually produced by the A-D paradigm when the C-D paradigm is a control. However, the picture reverses itself when high stimulus similarity is involved. C-D learning is severely retarded, but A-D is uninfluenced by the similarity among the A terms because they have already been discriminated in learning A-B. The critical outcome of the experiment is a very sharp interaction of the kind depicted in Figure 9.3 between similarity and paradigm.

We carried out studies as indicated by the above thinking (Underwood & Ekstrand, 1968a). It is probably quite apparent what the outcome of these experiments was. We did not find the expected interaction. In fact, the slope of the two lines was essentially equivalent, there being only a hint of the interaction. The logical analysis indicated that positive transfer in the A-D paradigm "had" to be high when similarity among the stimulus terms was high. Something was wrong. The data indicated that the discriminations among stimuli which necessarily had to be developed in learning the list were completely lost when a new set of response terms was paired with the old stimulus terms in the second list. We do not have a solution to this problem.

Our findings have been confirmed by Ellis and Shaffer (1974). When, however, these investigators used complex forms as stimuli and when they used nine letters in a 3 × 3 matrix (essentially a nine-letter nonsense unit), the expected interaction appeared.

From Serial to Paired-Associate Learning

Ebbinghaus used serial learning almost exclusively in his work. He established a practice that had great endurance. For many years it was common to use serial learning when one was doing an experiment in which the type of task was of no importance. These habits persisted until about 1960 when it became fairly apparent that for analytical purposes the paired-associate task was superior to the serial task. At about this same time an experiment was reported which had a stunning effect on the thinking of many investigators.

The experiment in question was carried out by Young (1959). Young had his subjects learn a serial list to one perfect trial, and then transferred them to a paired-associate list. The pairs in this paired-associate list were made up of items which held adjacent positions in the serial list. Let the serial list be symbolized as A, B, C, D, and so on. The pairs in the paired-associate list constructed from the serial list may be identified as A-B, B-C, C-D, D-E, and so on. However, as usual, the order of the pairs was randomized from trial to trial in paired-associate learning.

From the time of Ebbinghaus, most investigators had presumed that in learning a serial list, the subjects acquired a series of associations between adjacent items, A to B, B to C, C to D, and on down through the list. Given this belief, it would appear that the positive transfer from serial learning to the paired-associate learning in Young's experiment would be heavy. In effect, the subject merely had to use the associations learned in mastering the serial list, and the learning of the paired-associate list could take place quickly—perhaps even in one trial.

The results showed very little positive transfer. In terms of the number of trials required to reach the criterion of one perfect recitation of the paired-associate list, there was no statistical difference between the E Group and a C Group that had not learned the serial list initially. How could this be? If associations existed between adjacent items in serial learning, positive transfer should have been high. The fact that it was not obviously pierced the idea that associations are developed between adjacent items in serial learning. Those of us who might be called associationists found it difficult to assimilate Young's results.

Needless to say, very critical appraisals were made of Young's methods, and many new experiments were undertaken. We may examine two of the issues. In current terminology, it might be said that the subjects actually developed associations between adjacent items in learning the serial list, but because of the change of context in moving from the serial list to the paired-associate list, the subjects (for whatever reason) did not utilize the serial associations in acquiring the paired-associate task. One possible argument against this idea was the fact that in Young's first experiment he had some of his subjects learn the paired-associate list first before moving to the serial list. The positive transfer in this case was very large, indicating that the subjects were utilizing the associations developed in paired-associate learning to perform the serial task. It would seem that if a context change was responsible for the earlier finding, there should not have been such heavy positive transfer when moving from the paired-associate list to the serial list because such a move is also a change in context.

Another way to get at this matter was to instruct subjects carefully concerning the relationships between the serial list and the paired-associate list, the idea being that such instructions would remove negative performance factors which might be expected without such instructions. Such instructions did increase the positive transfer (Postman & Stark, 1967), but the transfer was far less than might be expected if the learning was based on associations between adjacent items. There was also the possibility that subjects might respond in learning the paired-associate list by reviewing the serial list. In any event, it does not seem that change of context was a critical factor.

In having subjects move from a serial list to a paired-associate list (as Young did), the latter list becomes a double-function list. Each item from the serial list serves both as a response term and as a stimulus term in the paired-associate list. Such lists were known to be difficult to learn. Perhaps (it might be argued) the failure to find positive transfer was due to the fact that the positive effects were counteracted by the negative effects in learning a double-function list. However, an experiment in which the paired-associate list was a single-function list led to the same conclusion (Young, 1962).

How does a subject learn a serial list if not by forming associations from item to item? This question remains open. The position an item holds in the list may be involved in the learning in some way. One could view a serial list as a constant order paired-associate list in which positions are the stimulus terms, the words or syllables the response terms. Tests of such notions have not been encouraging; for example, adding the position number to each word has very little effect on the learning. The mechanisms underlying serial learning remain one of the enigmas waiting around for a fresh approach.

Perception and Learning

Tulving (1966) presented his subjects with a list of twenty-two nouns, one at a time, at a one-second rate. The subjects were instructed merely to pronounce each word as it occurred. Six such trials were given. At this point the subjects were informed that they were to learn the words, and twelve study-test trials followed. A C Group was also given twelve learning trials on the list after having had a prior list of different items which they pronounced in the same manner as had the E Group. So, the two groups learned the critical list following the pronunciation of each item six times by the E Group and zero times by the C Group.

The results showed that on the first test trial following the first intentional learning trial, the E Group obtained a mean of 10.42 correct responses, the C Group a mean of 9.25 correct responses. The difference between the two means was unreliable statistically, and the acquisition curves over the twelve trials were essentially indistinguishable for the two groups.

The Tulving experiment suggests the rather remarkable conclusion that after processing the word six times there was no "residue" that had any influence on the number of items recalled. The results indicate further that it is not appropriate to equate perception and learning. The subjects in the E Group perceived (responded to) each word six times, and still there was no influence on subsequent free recall. The Tulving result has been confirmed by Hicks and Young (1972), but only when nouns were used as the learning material. When adjectives made up the lists the performance of the E Group was clearly ahead of the C Group. Just why nouns and adjectives should "behave" differently in this situation has not been explained as yet.

These three studies illustrate how transfer techniques have been used to try to answer fundamental questions about the nature of the learning of various tasks. Some have suggested that transfer techniques may not be sensitive enough to allow us to base fundamental decisions about learning upon them. The fact remains that there are many questions about fundamental properties of learning which can be answered only by using transfer techniques. It seems likely that they will always be used because in many cases there are no other ways to answer the questions being asked.

A VARIETY OF INTERFERENCE PHENOMENA

We will now examine a variety of interference phenomena. In some cases the interference appears to be produced by established habits which are not under experimenter control. In other cases we may be able to see that the interference results from a special case of the basic paradigms. In still others, the source of the interference is obscure.

Stroop Effect

Competition may be demonstrated in several ways by using our strong predilection to make representational responses to words. The young adult, upon seeing a word, has a very difficult time not responding to it because that is what one does to words. Now, if we arrange a situation in which the subject is asked to do something else to words, interference may be observed. The classical interference task of this kind produces what is known as the Stroop effect (1935). Subjects are shown a long list of names of colors. Each word is printed in an ink color that is inappropriate for the color name. Thus, the word *red* is printed in blue ink, the word *blue* is printed in green ink, the word *green* in red ink, and so on. The subjects' task is to name the color of the ink for each successive word and to do this as rapidly as possible.

A person who attempts the above task for the first time can literally feel the interference; the naming of the ink color is in competition with a long-standing habit of reading words. The long-standing habit is A-B, the naming of the ink colors A-D. The amount by which the color naming is retarded can be assessed by comparing the results with those of a control group in which the subject names a list of color patches as rapidly as possible. In producing a Stroop effect it is not at all necessary that the words be names of colors. One could have names of animals written in different colors of ink and the interference would be almost as great as if the words were names of colors.

The persistence of an interference effect may be rather brief or, under certain circumstances, prolonged. The Stroop situation produces prolonged interference. Doten (1955) had the subjects name the ink color of 144 color words. The response measure was the time required to name the ink color of the 144 color names. There were only five different color names, hence only five different ink colors. The subjects received fifteen

Figure 9.4.
The effect of extended practice on the reduction in the magnitude of the Stroop interference phenomenon. Estimated from Doten (1955).

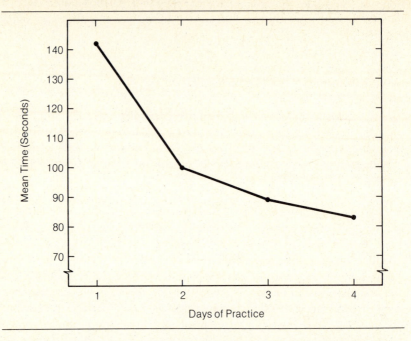

trials (a trial being the naming of the 144 ink colors) a day for four successive days. The mean times to name the 144 ink colors on the first trial of each day are given in Figure 9.4. The figure indicates that the subjects were getting better and better but after the first day the increase in naming speed was relatively small. It would have taken perhaps two or three more days for the performance to reach a point beyond which no further changes would occur. Clearly, the Stroop effect is a powerful one. Doten also noticed that having practiced naming the ink colors, the reading habit was temporarily interfered with.

Our strong propensity to read words can be shown to produce interference in situations other than that devised by Stroop. We may present the subject a series of pictures of common objects and superimpose on each object the name of a different object. The subjects' task is to name the object pictured. Thus, we might have a picture of an automobile with word *tree* printed in large letters over the car. The subjects' task is to name the object pictured as quickly as possible. It is commonly found (Lupker, 1979) that naming time is longer with the word present than without it present. Again, it appears that we have difficulty "setting aside" the word and attending only to the picture.

Another way of inducing this competition resulting from our tendency to respond to words has been worked out in the author's laboratory. One group of subjects is given a list of the letters of the alphabet in random order. The task is to code these letters as rapidly as possible. The code is the simple one of aligning the number system with the letters in order. The subject first finds the letter *a* and assigns it a value of 1, then the letter *b* is assigned 2, and so on. The total time to encode all of the letters may be used as the response measure. A second group is given a list of words, each starting with different letters, and the words are ordered in a list in accordance to first letters in exactly the same order as the list of single letters. The task of this second group is the same as that of the first; they are to find the word beginning with *a* and assign it 1, then find the word beginning with *b*, assign it 2, and so on as rapidly as possible. It is found that it takes longer to code the first letters for the list of words than to code the list of letters. It is presumed that the subjects read the words and that this consumed time that would not be consumed for the list of letters. Again it appears that we respond to words in the way we are accustomed to responding to them: we read them.

Output Interference

A number of loosely related procedures are all said to produce output interference. As a general statement, output interference is interference that results from the act of recalling. Or, to say this another way, recalling produces forgetting. A great variety of procedures have been used (see Roediger, 1974, for a description of the various procedures); two will be reviewed here.

A common procedure is to construct a rather long free-recall list in which there are blocked categories of items. For example, Smith (1971) used a list of seven categories with seven instances in each category. The subject saw the list once and then recall was requested. On recall, the subject was given a predetermined order of the category names and was required to recall in that order. A period of thirty seconds was allowed to recall as many items from each category as possible. Across subjects, both the order of the categories as presented for study and the order for recall were systematically varied. The results may be seen in Figure 9.5, where the mean number of words recalled in each successive category is given. There is some loss across the successive categories.

The second illustration comes from Roediger and Schmidt (1980). They presented their subjects with a twenty-pair list. One member of each pair was printed in capital letters, and these twenty words were the target words. The other members of each pair were printed in lowercase and were related in some way (usually by being synonyms) to the target words. The subjects were told that they would have to recall the target words when the lowercase words were used as cues. The lowercase word was always presented above the target word. The pairs were presented at a three-second rate, and following the one study trial, cued recall took place, with

Figure 9.5.
Output interference in the recall of a list of seven categories of seven instances each (blocked). The experimenter specified the order in which the categories were to be recalled. Data from Table 2 of Smith (1971).

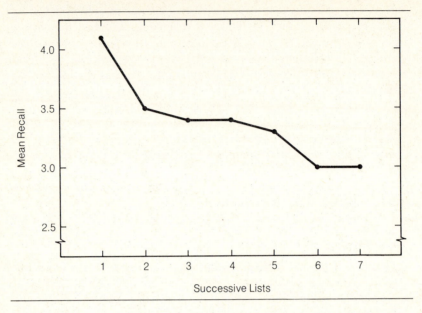

ten seconds allowed to recall each target word when the cue word (lower-case) was shown. Across subjects the order of presenting the cue words was systematically varied. After completing the learning and recall of one such list, a second list was given under exactly the same conditions, although, of course, the words used were different from those making up the first list.

The results may be seen in Figure 9.6, where the percent recall for five successive blocks of four items each is plotted. There is no doubt that performance generally decreases with each successive recall attempt.

Both of the experiments reported here may suffer from a problem of method. Obviously, the amount of output interference (as inferred from gradually lower recall) is perfectly correlated with an increase in the length of the retention interval. Could it be that the so-called interference really represents merely a retention curve? Probably not, but certainly it needs to be evaluated experimentally. Furthermore, even if all of the loss attributed to output interference cannot be accounted for by "normal" forgetting, it would seem that all studies of output interference should use a forgetting control to assess adequately just how much of the loss should be attributed to interference.

Assuming that there is a reliable phenomenon called output interference, to what is it to be attributed? There is no obvious way by which the classical paradigms (e.g., A-B, A-D) can be identified with this situation.

Figure 9.6.

Output interference in the cued recall of twenty items. Each of the five output positions consisted of four items. The two unrelated lists were learned in immediate succession. Data from Table 2 of Roediger and Schmidt (1980).

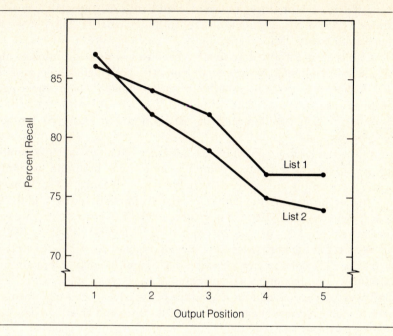

That is, what is A in the various recall attempts? If anything, it appears that both of the experiments described here fit the noninterfering paradigm, A-B, C-D.

The Ranschburg Effect

It will be remembered that in the memory-span technique, the subjects are presented a string of digits or letters for a single presentation under instructions to recall the items in the order presented. Suppose there were two strings as follows:

String 1:   7 2 5 1 9 6 8
String 2:   7 2 5 1 2 6 8

These two strings are identical except that the digit 2 occurs twice in the second string whereas no digit is repeated in the first string. Which of these two strings is more likely to be recalled perfectly? Experiments indicate that performance on the string with the repeated digit will be inferior to that on the string without repetition. This inferiority will be primarily caused by the subject's omitting at recall either the first or the second occurrence of the repeated digit, although most frequently there is a failure to produce the digit the second time. This phenomenon is called the Ranschburg Effect (after its discoverer), and in keeping with previous practice it will be identified here as RE. It appears that in some way the repeated number produces a form of interference. Of particular interest is the fact that we usually think that repetition enhances recall, but the RE appears to be one clear exception.

A little more information about procedures is needed. Subjects may recall orally or they may write their responses; both methods produce the RE. Although subjects are asked to recall the items in their proper positions, investigators may score the protocols by a free-recall criterion or by a serial-position criterion, and the RE is normally observed for both scoring methods.

As one thinks about possible relevant independent variables, a number of possibilities arise (a more complete review may be found in Jahnke, 1969). Perhaps the most obvious variable is the "distance" or lag between the two occurrences of the item. The relationship between lag and the RE is a rather complicated matter (e.g., Lee, 1976). If the two occurrences are in adjacent positions (e.g., 7225168) there is a "reverse" effect in that the subjects recall the item twice for almost all strings. As lag increases from zero, the RE begins to emerge with a lag of approximately three to four producing the maximum RE. Increases in lag beyond this optimal level will lead to a reduction in the magnitude of the effect because problems of primacy and recency begin to confound the situation when the length of the spans are seven to eight digits, the lengths commonly used.

It should not be supposed that the RE is found only with letters and numbers (the traditional memory-span materials). It may also be found with common words under certain conditions. If numbers are used for the spans, the pool is limited to ten, and across many trials each number is used many times. If this same requirement is imposed on words—if a pool of only ten words is used—the RE will be found. If different words are used for each string, there will be no RE (Jahnke, 1972).

Theory. What could produce the RE? Some form of interference is one possibility. However, one of the more clever explanations suggests that the effect is due to a guessing bias and has nothing to do with interference (Mewaldt & Hinrichs, 1977). These investigators assume first that the subject recognizes a failure to recall a given item in a given position. Frequently in the recall of the string, the subject is given a recall sheet on which there are seven boxes (one for each digit), and each box is to be filled in from left to right. If the subject cannot fill in a given box, guessing may occur for that position in the series. Such a guess is likely to be a number that has not already been given. It can be seen that a guess of this nature would *not* help the score for the E strings (strings with repeated numbers) if the guess occurred in one of the positions held by the repeated item. On the other hand, a guess for a C string (no repeated items) could be correct, hence could improve the score for the C strings. In short, the guessing hypothesis indicates that the RE is due to an elevated score for the C strings resulting from guessing, not because of a reduced score for the E strings. If this theory is correct there is no need to talk about interference or even refer to the RE as a learning or retention phenomenon.

The question, then, is how this theory squares with the facts. The answer is that the evidence is mixed. Some subjects guess (make more overt errors) more than others, but those who guess a lot do not show a larger RE than do those who guess infrequently (Jahnke, 1974). It would seem that the guessing hypothesis would have to predict that the greater the number of guesses, the bigger the RE. Along a similar line, Walsh and Schwartz (1977) instructed subjects in one case to guess freely if they did not know an item for a particular position, and in the other case another group was asked not to guess but to leave the space blank if they did not know the correct response. These different instructions had their intended effect in that the number of overt errors made differed. The magnitude of the RE, however, did not differ statistically as a function of the instructions, although the differences were in the direction expected by the guessing hypothesis.

On the other hand, some data has been found to support the guessing hypothesis. The failure to find the RE with an unlimited pool of words (as noted earlier) could be used as indirect support of the guessing theory. With an unlimited pool of items the likelihood of guessing correctly is extremely low. Investigators have attempted to manipulate guessing habits by varying the number of strings in which repetition does occur. (Hinrichs & Mewaldt, 1977). The idea is that the greater the amount of repetition, the greater the likelihood that a subject, in guessing, will include repeated items in the guesses and therefore reduce the magnitude of the RE. Some positive evidence has been found, but it is not sufficiently strong to conclude that the entire RE is due to guessing, although a part might be so attributed.

A number of investigators have suggested the possibility that RE results from interference. If this is true, it should be noted that interference would have to occur between strings because the RE does not occur when different items are used for each successive string. Such between-list interference could be mediated by any one of the three identity interference paradigms discussed earlier, provided that the position of the item is a fundamental part of span learning.

Prefix and Suffix Effects

Like the RE, prefix and suffix effects occur in conjunction with memory-span procedures. We will look first at the prefix effect, and an early study by Conrad (1960) will introduce us to this curious phenomenon. The subjects were given strings of eight digits. In a C Condition the usual memory-span technique was followed in which serial recall was attempted immediately after the last digit was read. In the E Condition the subjects did exactly the same except that just before recalling the string they had to speak the digit "zero" (prefix). They did this for all strings given in the E Condition. For the C Condition 72.5 percent of the strings were reported correctly, whereas for the E Condition the corresponding value was 37.5 percent. In short, a fraction of a second delay before recalling, a delay filled by the saying of "zero," reduced recall almost in half. Actually, it is usually found that the recall of seven-digit strings with a prefix is correct with about the same frequency as the recall of eight-digit strings without the prefix. The loss produced by the prefix is general in the sense that a small loss is observed at all serial positions.

It might be suggested that the prefix effect occurs simply because of the delay involved in recalling the digits as a consequence of having to say the prefix and that normal forgetting of the digits is to be expected. The evidence is not entirely conclusive on this issue (Baddeley & Hull, 1979), but the weight of the evidence is against the forgetting interpretation, at least as a sole cause of the effect.

A second set of operations also produces a prefix effect. In this procedure, the redundant prefix (e.g., the zero) is placed first in the string as it is read, but the subjects do not have to reproduce it at recall. It appears that the magnitude of the negative effect is much the same for the two methods (Jahnke, 1975).

The suffix effect is produced by having the zero at the end of the string, but it is not recalled. A comparison is made with the recall of the string in which the zero (the suffix) was not present. In contrast to the prefix effect, the loss produced by the suffix is usually limited to the last two or three digits in the series, and sometimes only to the last one. The suffix effect has also been shown with lists of common words (Harris, Gausepohl, Lewis, & Spoehr, 1979). The subjects in the E Condition in the experiment knew that they did not have to recall the last word in the series. They were given a string of eight words followed by a suffix word. Subjects in the C Condition received only the eight words. For the last three positions in the list, recall was much higher under the C Condition than under the E Condition.

It will be remembered that we are in the process of looking at a variety of phenomena which might be considered to be due to interference. For the prefix and suffix effects, a number of writers have referred in general terms to these effects being a product of interference. As yet, however, there has been no clear statement of what is interfering with what, and that interference is actually present is not obvious to this author. Some have talked about the redundant item interfering with the organization of recall, but again the mechanisms are not evident. It does not appear that any of the classical interference paradigms can be applied. The fact that the prefix and suffix effects cannot be readily analyzed in terms of interference should not be taken to mean that the memory span is not subject to interference, because it clearly is. It has long been known, for example, that memory span performance is poorer if the strings are made up of highly similar letters (acoustically) than if made up of dissimilar letters. Thus, these findings are quite in line with the role of formal similarity in list learning as discussed in the previous chapter.

Single Task to Simultaneous Learning

In an earlier chapter we discussed a procedure wherein two or more lists are learned simultaneously. For reasons which are of no relevance here, we studied simultaneous learning following the learning of each list in isolation (Underwood & Lund, 1980c). And again, while the procedures and materials do not easily translate into interference paradigms, the magnitude of the effects which will be called interference effects are exceedingly large and compelling. The experiment will be described, starting first with the lists used.

Figure 9.7.
Free recall of a list of twenty pairs. The E Group was first given a study-test trial in isolation (alone) and then two study-test trials in which three lists were learned simultaneously. The C Group was given only the two simultaneous learning trials. Data from Underwood and Lund (1980).

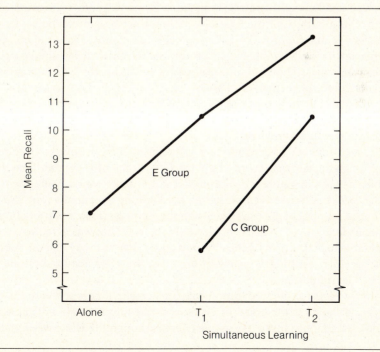

One list consisted of twenty-one pairs of male and female first names, e.g., *Harold-Elizabeth*. On any given study trial each pair was presented twice, and at recall the subjects were required to recall the pairs. Another list consisted of forty-two two-word phrases, e.g., *printed-page*. This list was tested by a YES-NO recognition test in which twenty-four new phrases were mixed with the forty-two old phrases. The third list was made up of animal names. Seven of the animal names were presented once, seven twice, and seven three times. On the tests the subjects made absolute frequency judgments, and for this seven new animal names were mixed with the twenty-one old ones.

There were forty-two presentations on the study trial, and during simultaneous learning one item from each of the lists occurred as a presentation. The rate was twelve seconds per presentation. When the lists were learned alone, the rate was four seconds. Two groups of subjects were used. The E Group was given one study-test trial on each of the three lists in isolation (alone). Then, two trials were given by simultaneous learning (T1 and T2). For both isolated and simultaneous learning, the order of testing was recall of the name pairs first, then the frequency judgments, and finally the recognition test. The same order occurred when the three lists were learned alone. The C Group merely had two study-test trials under simultaneous learning. The subjects knew from the beginning of the experiment the steps that would be taken, the nature of the lists, and how each list would be tested.

We will look at the recall results first. Figure 9.7 shows the mean recall on all three trials for the E Group, and on the two simultaneous-learning trials (T1 and T2) for the C Group. The critical finding is the complete transfer of the learning shown on the isolated trial to the simultaneous-learning trials. The level of performance on T1 for the E Group is essentially identical to that on T2 for the C Group. In both cases one trial preceded, but it was an isolated trial for the E Group and a simultaneous-learning trial for the C Group. The subject moved from one type of learning to another without loss.

The frequency judgments were scored as hits; this is simply the number of times the subject recorded the true frequency of the items. The mean hits, as seen in Figure 9.8, are plotted in the same way as were the recall data. On the isolated learning trial, the E Group averaged about 20.5 hits (out of 28 possible). However, when the items became a part of simultaneous learning (T1), performance fell to a level that was essentially comparable to that shown by the C Group on T1. This is to say that the subjects apparently lost the frequency information they had acquired on the isolated learning trial.

Two plots for the recognition data are given in Figure 9.9, with the false alarms shown in the upper box, misses in the lower box. In both cases the isolated trial produced a negative effect, although the effect was not com-

Figure 9.8.
Mean hits in frequency judgments with (E Group) and without (C Group) an initial trial alone prior to simultaneous learning. Data from Underwood and Lund (1980).

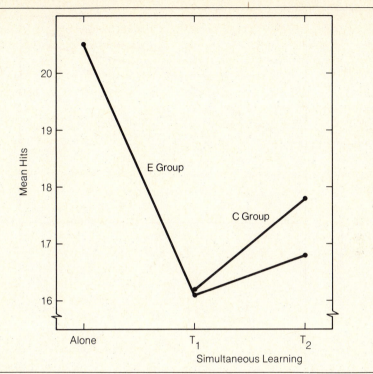

plete (as was true for the frequency judgments). Still, statistically speaking, the two groups did not differ on T1 and T2 for the false alarms, although they did for the misses.

It should be pointed out that the heavy positive transfer in recall, as compared with the heavy negative transfer for the frequency judgments and for recognition, once again indicates that the attributes of memory utilized in recall and recognition must have very little overlap. Why should the subjects' performance on T1 for frequency judgments and recognition indicate that what was learned on the isolated-learning trial did not transfer? We have not as yet found a reasonable answer to this question. It could be speculated that the attributes determining performance on the isolated trial were quite different from those determining performance on T1 and T2. But, why should they change? Again, while we might speak of interference in a general way, it has not been possible to apply the paradigms of negative transfer to this situation.

Figure 9.9.
Misses and false alarms in recognition memory with (E Group) and without (C Group) an initial trial alone prior to simultaneous learning. Data from Underwood and Lund (1980).

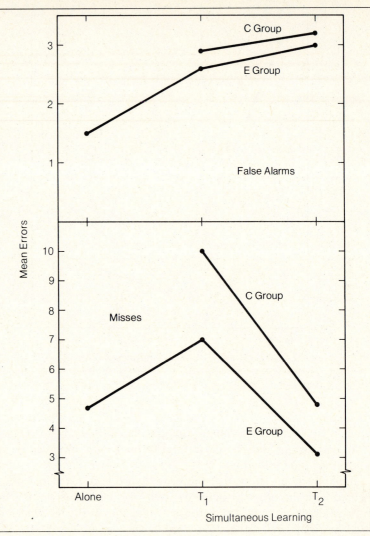

SUMMARY

Transfer refers to the carryover of learning from one task to another. This carryover will sometimes produce positive effects, sometimes negative effects. Transfer may be divided into two classes. Nonspecific transfer refers to positive transfer that may be attributed to warmup or to learning-to-learn. Specific transfer refers to either positive or negative transfer that is attributed to specific similarity relationships between the two tasks. The bulk of the data on specific transfer has resulted from four paired-associate paradigms identifying the similarity relationships between the two lists. If A-B identifies the first list, the four paradigms may be identified as C-D (control or reference paradigm); A-D, in which the stimulus terms in the two lists are identical, the response terms different; C-B, having different stimulus terms but the same response terms, and A-Br, in which the stimulus and response terms are the same in both lists but the pairings differ. These paradigms may also be used to identify various transfer situations in which paired-associate lists are not used.

We presented three illustrations of cases in which positive transfer was expected but did not occur. One case indicated a failure of transfer of stimulus discrimination, another a failure of transfer from serial learning to paired-associate learning, and a third in which no positive effect was found in free-recall learning as a consequence of having pronounced all words in the lists six times each prior to free-recall.

A variety of presumed interference phenomena were described. These included the Stroop effect and variants, output interference, the Ranschburg effect, prefix and suffix effects, and interference in moving from single-task learning to simultaneous learning.

10

Forgetting

This chapter will center on the empirical and theoretical matters dealing with forgetting. There are a number of preliminary points to be made primarily as a means of establishing the orientation and delimiting the scope of the presentation.

1. As many others have pointed out, when we study learning across trials we are really studying the interplay between learning and forgetting, with the performance score on any trial being the net effect. That is to say that as we study learning in the laboratory we are dealing with a microinteraction between learning and forgetting comparable to the macrointeraction summed across the life of the organism. While it is a good idea to remember that such interactions exist, they need not frighten us. When we observe learning we observe a case in which the anabolic or positive component is more powerful than the catabolic or negative component, but this does not give us insight into either learning or forgetting. These insights, if they are to arise, must arise from other sources.

2. It is common, in studying forgetting, to give one or more learning trials and then at some later point in time administer a memory test and say that we are studying forgetting. How long must this interval be? This is an arbitrary matter, of course. If the learning is carried out in discrete trials, we might say that if we use a retention interval that is longer than the interval between trials, we will speak of studying forgetting. These are not really serious matters, although there are some terminology usages that may lead to confusion. Some investigators use the terms short-term memory and long-term memory in very specific ways. Short-term memory may mean a retention interval of perhaps thirty seconds or less, and any interval longer than thirty seconds is said to be dealing with long-term memory. This could mean that if the subjects were given a single study trial on a relatively long free-recall task, the items at the beginning of the list would be said to involve long-term recall; those at the end, short-term recall. Other investigators might think of long-term recall as dealing with intervals of hours or days or weeks. There is no sure antidote for such

sources of confusion. We simply have to be careful in our reading that we get in touch with the terminological biases of each author.

3. The minimum operations for demonstrating forgetting require two conditions. Under both conditions equivalent learning is given, but they differ in the length of the interval between the end of learning and the memory test. If on the memory test performance is poorer after the longer retention interval than after the shorter, forgetting is said to have occurred. In the usual experiment the shorter retention interval may be at most a few seconds in length.

4. We are already aware that interference may occur in various ways during learning. We must recognize that interference may also be inferred in various studies in which forgetting is the phenomenon of interest. However, the strongest case for interference as a factor in forgetting is made by studying forgetting as a function of interference which is inserted into the situation. As we will see, the transfer paradigms examined in the previous chapter also serve as paradigms for introducing interference into the study of forgetting. Two forgetting phenomena result from the use of interference as an independent variable and we will later spend a considerable amount of time on these two phenomena.

5. It will be remembered that certain general memory models assume that there is no forgetting. The fact is, however, that functional forgetting does occur and to try to describe it is the enterprise of the moment.

FORGETTING CURVES

Ebbinghaus used relearning as a measure of retention, so we may look at a study that used this measure. Finkenbinder (1913) used twelve-item serial lists made up of difficult nonsense syllables. Learning was carried until the subjects anticipated all items correctly on a single trial. The retention intervals varied from one hour to three days, with ten different intervals being used. The measure of retention—or of forgetting—was the number of trials to relearn to one perfect trial divided by the number of trials required to learn to one perfect trial in the first place. If all intervals showed forgetting (as they did), all of the ratios would be less than one.

It has been common practice to use a number of short retention intervals and fewer of the longer intervals. In plotting results from such experiments, using an arithmetic baseline for the values of the independent variable (length of retention interval) will result in a severe "squeeze" for the short intervals. One may avoid this by expressing the intervals as logarithms. This has been done in Figure 10.1, resulting in a near linear relationship between the relearning measure (RL/L) and the log baseline. Note that at the longest interval (seventy-two hours) the subjects required half the number of trials to relearn as was required for original learning.

As a second study we may examine the retention of a free-recall task

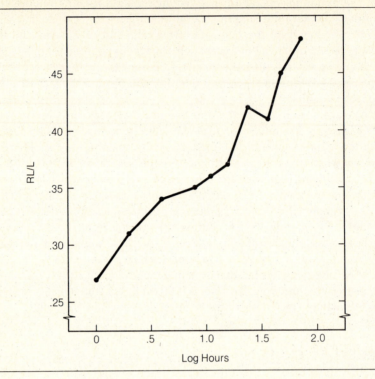

(Williams, 1926). The subjects were given a fifty-word list by the method of complete presentation, with five minutes allowed to study the list. All subjects were given an immediate recall test (at which an average of twenty-five words was recalled), and then different groups recalled again after one, two, three, five, or seven days. The immediate recall was used as a base to determine the percentage recall for the different groups (see Figure 10.2). For these data an arithmetic plot of the retention intervals serves quite well, and the plot shows a gradual loss over the seven days.

In another free recall study (Underwood, Zimmerman, & Freund, 1971), subjects were shown common words at a three-second rate. In a long study list, items were presented 1, 2, 3, 4, 5, or 6 times, there being twelve words at each frequency. One group of subjects was given an immediate test, another after twenty-four hours, and a third after seven days. The percent recall for each interval is shown in Figure 10.3, in which study frequency is used as the baseline. As might be expected, recall increased directly as the number of study occurrences increased, although after seven days the amount recalled was very small and the relationship between study fre-

Figure 10.2.
Forgetting of fifty-word, free-recall lists over seven days as measured by recall. Data from Table II of Williams (1926).

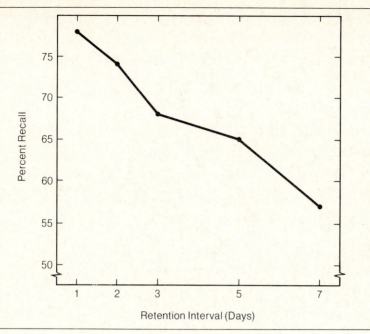

quency and recall very weak. In fact, after seven days the average subject recalled only 6.83 items out of the possible seventy-two. The subjects also produced a mean of 7.08 intrusions after seven days.

Whitely and McGeoch (1928) asked about the long-term retention of six stanzas of poetry, each stanza consisting of four lines. The subjects studied the poem for fifteen minutes by the method of complete presentation, after which an immediate test was given. Then different groups were tested 15, 30, 60, 90, or 120 days later. The measure was the number of lines correct. The retention scores were calculated as the percent delayed recall of immediate recall. As may be seen in Figure 10.4, somewhat over 35 percent of the forgetting occurred during the first fifteen days, but even after 120 days 28 percent of the lines were correctly reproduced.

One more study will be examined, a study which goes out of the laboratory for the learning (Bahrick, Bahrick, & Wittlinger, 1975). These investigators used 392 subjects, varying in age between seventeen and seventy-four years. A requirement was that each subject had to have been a member of a high school graduating class in which there were at least ninety students. The 392 subjects were divided into nine groups which differed in terms of amount of time since high school graduation, these intervals ranging from three months to about forty-eight years. In a

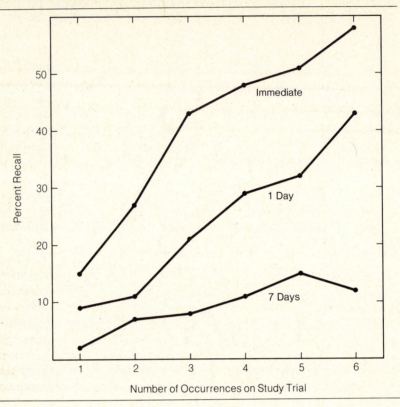

Figure 10.3.
Recall of free-recall lists after zero, one, and seven days as a function of frequency of study of the words. Data from Underwood, Zimmerman, and Freund (1971).

free-recall test the subjects had eight minutes to write the first and last names of all members of their graduating class. To be counted correct, both names had to be given. We have plotted the mean number of names recalled, using a log baseline (see Figure 10.5). It should be repeated that the length of the retention interval was determined by the age of the subgroups; the older the subjects the longer the retention interval. One could object that these groups may differ on factors in addition to age, e.g., the number of people (over ninety) in the graduating class. The investigators were quite aware of such problems, but the adjustments that were made did not appreciably change the nature of the forgetting curve.

Further illustrations need not be given. It is quite obvious that there is a phenomenon called forgetting, and perhaps the illustrations are completely redundant. Whether or not we "really" forget is not a matter of discussion here. The evidence indicates that with the passage of time, without practice, there is usually a decrement in performance in verbal

Figure 10.4.
Forgetting of lines of poetry over 120 days. Data from Table 1 of Whitely and McGeoch (1928).

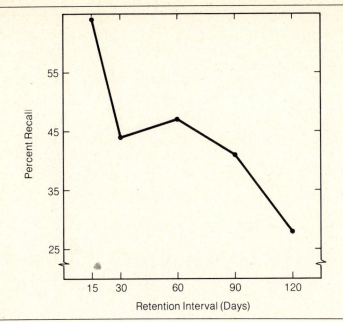

tasks (although there are some exceptions to which we will turn at a later point). Many investigators have shown that giving successive recall tests without feedback will almost always show that some items not recalled earlier will be subsequently recalled, but it would be a very rare event to show that all items could be recovered.

SINGLE-LIST SITUATION

Consider the case in which subjects are given a single list of paired associates to learn, and memory for the list is measured after one day or one week. Ideally, our subjects should be naive to the laboratory (for reasons that will emerge later). If the list is learned to the point that the subject can give all items correctly on a trial, we may expect roughly 20 percent forgetting after one day and 50 percent forgetting after a week. This is not to imply that these values will be inevitably found, although as will be seen, there is considerable constancy in the loss with time and not many variables will change it. To look at variables that might change it is our first step. Obviously, by definition, the length of the retention interval is a major variable. What other variables influence forgetting?

Figure 10.5.

Forgetting of names of high-school classmates over forty-eight years as measured by recall. Data from Table 4 of Bahrick, Bahrick, and Wittlinger (1975).

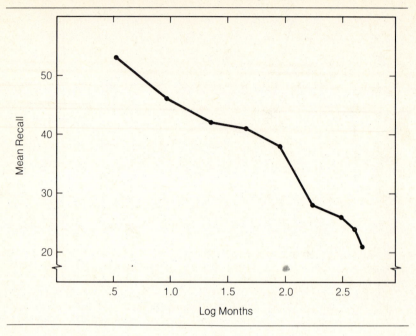

Relevant Variables

Level or Degree of Learning.   Generally speaking the greater the number of acquisition trials, the less the rate of forgetting. This statement seems straightforward enough, but it really doesn't tell us much; indeed, it might be somewhat deceiving. If we have a twenty-pair list and one group is given two acquisition trials, another ten, the latter would have higher recall than the former. However, such a comparison is "unfair" because more items would have been learned in ten trials than in two trials, so recall should be higher for the ten-trial group. How, then, do we determine if level of learning is a relevant variable?

In the above illustration we could use two control groups which are given immediate retention tests. We then can calculate a percent recall score by dividing the twenty-four-hour recall by the immediate recall and multiplying by one hundred. These two percentage scores would indicate the amount of forgetting after two and after ten acquisition trials. However, it could be argued that such comparisons are not very meaningful. The argument would run about as follows. The items that are correct after two learning trials are, as a group, easier to learn than those that were correct as a group after ten trials. Perhaps this difference in ease

Figure 10.6.
Schematic picture of the learning of paired-associate lists when trials are massed and when twenty-four hours fall between the learning of each block of two trials (spaced). Suggested by Keppel's (1967) findings.

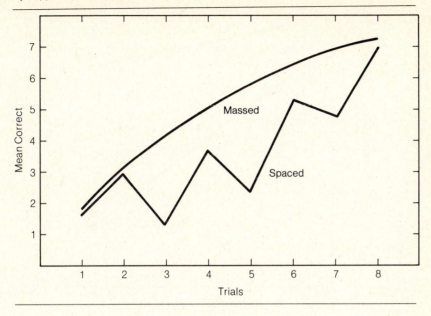

of learning is correlated (either positively or negatively) with rate of forgetting. This argument tells us that it is unclear as to whether we have a fair test of the influence of the level or degree of learning.

The only unambiguous way to study forgetting as a function of the degree of learning is to use overlearning procedures. In overlearning, all groups are given learning trials until all items are correct at least once. Then, for different groups, varying numbers of additional learning trials are given and recall is requested after twenty-four hours. Recall is expected to be a direct function of the number of overlearning trials.

The fact that degree of learning may produce an affect on forgetting advises us to keep this variable constant when we are studying the influence of other variables on forgetting. If, for example, we inquire about the influence of meaningfulness on rate of forgetting, we must be sure that the level of learning is equivalent for the two or more lists (representing different levels of meaningfulness) before the retention interval is introduced. This is not always easily accomplished because the rates of learning may differ sharply for lists with different levels of meaningfulness. In a sense, it is difficult to stop the learning on the different lists so that the degree of learning is equivalent. Various techniques have been devised for handling such problems (Underwood, 1964a), but the detail involved does not recommend a review of these techniques here. The important fact to

Figure 10.7.

Forgetting of paired associates as a function of massed and spaced learning and length of the retention interval. Data from Keppel (1967).

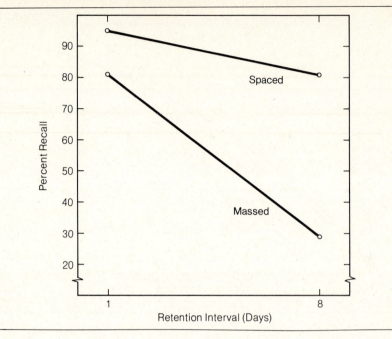

remember is that to assess forgetting as a function of some independent variable requires that the degree of learning be neutralized for the various conditions.

Spaced Learning. One of the most potent variables influencing forgetting is spaced practice. Earlier it was noted that a form of spacing that had received considerable attention was the effect of time between successive trials on learning. Thus, we might have zero, one, five, or ten minutes between successive learning trials and ask about the influence of this variable on both learning and retention. A number of experiments have shown that in paired-associate tasks such intervals have very small effects on learning and on forgetting. However, if we increase the length of these intervals to hours or days, the outcome is, by any gauge, startling. We will examine a study by Keppel (1967).

The list used by Keppel was made up of eight CVC-adjective pairs. All groups were given eight anticipation trials on the list. Two of the groups had all eight trials at a single sitting. One of these groups recalled the list after one day, the other after eight days. The other two groups had two learning trials per day for four days, following which one group recalled after one day, the other after eight days. Thus, for these two groups the

Figure 10.8.

Successive recall performance during the acquisition of a fifty-pair list for six sessions when zero, one, or thirty days separated the sessions. Recall thirty days following the sixth session is also shown. Data from Table 2 of Bahrick (1979).

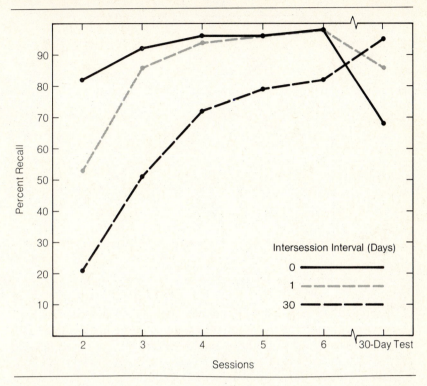

spacing during learning was twenty-four hours between each two anticipation trials.

Figure 10.6 is a stylized picture of the acquisition trials under massing and spacing. Note that the spaced condition produced a saw-toothed "curve" as a consequence of the microinteraction between learning and forgetting. Forgetting occurs over the twenty-four hours inserted after trials 2, 4, and 6, but the forgetting appears to become less and less as learning proceeds. We have just warned about the problem of testing forgetting for different conditions if the level of learning differs. It can be seen that if performance on the last trial is used as an index, the learning under the two conditions was roughly equivalent.

Percentage of recall is shown in Figure 10.7, where it is clear that the rate of forgetting of the spaced list is far less than the rate for the list learned by massing. The differences are so great that it seems beyond doubt that if one wants to minimize forgetting, learning should take place by widely spaced practice.

Keppel's results suggest that there may be an optimum set of conditions

Figure 10.9.

Paired-associate recall after two and forty-five minutes for subjects that were closely observed during learning and for subjects that were not closely observed. Data from Deffenbacher, Platt, and Williams (1974).

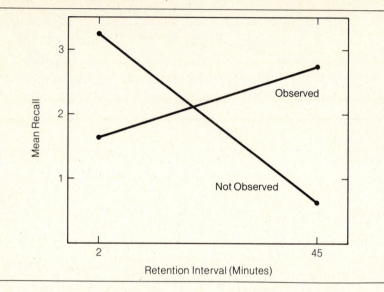

of distributed learning that will minimize the rate of forgetting. Perhaps two days is too short for maximum retardation of forgetting. Perhaps with other materials two days might be too long. Very little has been done to answer such questions, although the recent work of Bahrick (1979) is an exception. One of his studies will be described.

The paired-associate list contained fifty pairs. These lists were learned by what is known as the dropout method. Alternate study and test trials are used. Items correct on the first trial are omitted on all subsequent study and test trials, so that the list gets shorter and shorter as learning proceeds. Bahrick terminated learning when all stimulus terms had been responded to correctly once. There were three conditions. In one (a massed condition), the subjects learned the list six times in immediate succession. These are spoken of as six sessions. Thus, after the trial in which all items had been given correctly once, the list was given again in its entirety, and the dropout procedure continued until all items had been given correctly in that session. This continued for six sessions; that is, all subjects learned the list six times by the dropout procedure. For a second group, one day intervened between each of the six sessions, and for a third group, the interval was thirty days. We may think of these last two groups as having distributed practice, the distribution interval being one day in one case, thirty days in the other. On all sessions after the first, the subject was asked to recall as many items as possible before relearning began. Retention was tested thirty days after the sixth session for all three groups.

Figure 10.10.

Recall as related to concrete and abstract stimulus terms in paired-associate lists. Data from Table 1 of Butter (1970).

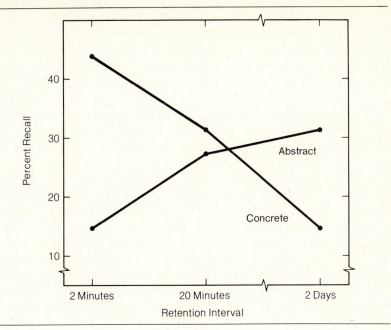

The measure used was the recall, starting with the second session. These recall measures are plotted in Figure 10.8. The one critical fact is that recall after thirty days increased directly as the intersession intervals increased. Thus, the massed group recalled only 68 percent after thirty days, while the distributed group, having thirty days between sessions, recalled 95 percent. Again, these data tell us that long-term distributed practice is a key to long-term maintenance of memories.

Simultaneous Learning.   A relatively recent discovery is that if two or more lists are learned simultaneously, forgetting rate is less than if the lists were learned singly (Underwood & Lund, 1979). In the experiments it was found that if three lists were learned simultaneously, recall after twenty-four hours was 38 percent better than for the same list learned alone.

Arousal.   Arousal refers to a heightened state of tension or attention, nervousness, or apprehension. The empirical question is how arousal affects forgetting. A number of studies have produced essentially the same findings; we will first illustrate these by examining an experiment by Deffenbacher, Platt, and Williams (1974). The subjects were given six pairs to study for one trial. The stimulus terms were the following CVCs of zero association value: TOV, CEF, QAP, JEX, LAJ, and DAX. The response terms were the numbers two through seven. Four groups of subjects participated. For two of the groups the experimenter stood just behind the subject's right shoulder to observe the subject trying to learn the pairs on the single learning trial. For the other two groups the experimenter sat at a nearby desk with his back to the subjects as they were given the study trial. One group receiving each treatment was tested two minutes after the study trial, and one was tested forty-five minutes after the study trial.

The results, as seen in Figure 10.9, show an unusual crossover interaction. The subjects who were observed closely during the learning trial (and presumably whose arousal was thereby increased) had poor recall after two minutes, but high recall after forty-five minutes. The group that was not observed showed just the opposite effect.

The CVCs used in the experiment above had been used by several other investigators. Furthermore, some of the syllables are associated with high arousal and some with low arousal, when the psychogalvanic response is used as an index of arousal, and results similar to those in Figure 10.9 have been found when the low- and high-arousal syllables are plotted separately. Just why nonsense syllables should produce differences in arousal is not evident. As a further fact in the evaluation of the effect of arousal, Butter (1970) discovered that concrete and abstract words produce different levels of arousal, with the abstract words generally producing more arousal than the concrete words. Correspondingly, the abstract words showed an increase in recall across a two-day period, and the retention of the concrete words fell across the same period. These results may be seen in Figure 10.10.

Similar results have been observed by Schnorr and Atkinson (1970) with quite a different method. The subjects were shown ninety-six concrete noun pairs at an eight-second study rate. Only a single study trial was given. A recall test followed, also paced at an eight-second rate, and a second recall test followed one week later. The variables of interest were the position of the items in the study list and length of the retention interval. The study list was divided into four segments of twenty-four pairs each to implement the position variable.

The results are shown in Figure 10.11, where immediate and one-week recall is related to position of the pairs. Although not as dramatic an interaction as seen in the just preceding figures, its presence is reliable. The authors related their finding to differences in arousal that occur as a function of study position.

Taken as a whole, the results relating arousal to retention are quite remarkable in the sense that they completely reverse forgetting. Especially surprising is the fact that with abstract words recall is greater after two days than after two minutes. There have been reports of failure to observe the arousal-retention phenomenon (Saufley & LaCava, 1977). But, as pointed out earlier, the crossover interaction has been found by several different investigators working in different laboratories, and there is no

Figure 10.11.
Recall of paired nouns on an immediate and a one-week test as related to position of the pair in the study list. Data from Table 1 of Schnorr and Atkinson (1970).

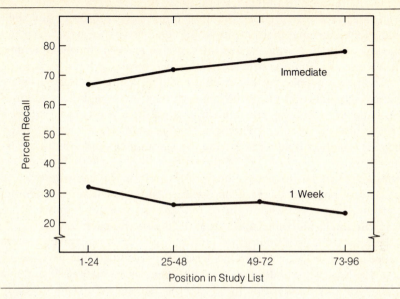

way to ignore the data. Technically, to observe better recall following a retention interval than that shown on immediate recall defines *reminiscence*. Evidence of small amounts of reminiscence over very short retention intervals (e.g., two minutes) have sometimes been reported, but the magnitude of the reminiscence effect does not approximate that shown by the studies in which arousal is manipulated.

Interfering Tasks. Forgetting is heavily influenced by the learning of interfering tasks. Because the variable is of particular importance for theory, it will be given extended treatment later.

Irrelevant Variables

The list of relevant variables—variables that influence the rate of forgetting—is a short one. Some investigators may believe that more variables should be added to the list. However, if the variables are limited to those that produce a substantial effect, or that have consistently shown to have an effect of any magnitude, the list is probably fairly complete. For example, one might add concrete-abstract to the list, for a few studies have shown an effect; on the other hand, other studies have not shown effects.

No attempt will be made here to give an exhaustive list of variables that have been found not to influence rate of forgetting. Many of these variables have a striking effect on learning (e.g., meaningfulness, intralist similarity) but have no influence on forgetting. And, of course, there probably have been many unpublished experiments that showed no difference. Nevertheless, it is perhaps worthwhile to present briefly a sampling of studies that show that even though a variable may produce wide differences in learning, retention may be equivalent.

In Chapter 5 we described depth-of-processing procedures and their influence on learning. Nelson and Vining (1978) have shown that deep and shallow processing, while having the expected marked effect on learning, do not result in differences in recall after one week.

It will be remembered that double-function, paired-associate lists are exceedingly difficult to learn. When each item serves as both a stimulus term and as a response term, similarity is maximal and internal interference is heavy. Young and Thomson (1967) carried out a study to determine if retention differed following the learning of single- and double-function lists. There were eight paired adjectives. A single function list required 13.6 trials to achieve one perfect trial on the list, whereas 35.8 trials were required to reach one perfect performance on the double-function lists. There were eight paired adjectives. A single-function list from the single-function list; 5.3 from the double-function list.

Epstein (1972) used three-word units as response terms in an eight-item paired-associate list. The stimulus terms were two-digit numbers. In one case the three-word units made sentences (e.g., *wild horses gallop*), and in a second condition all words in all eight sentences were randomized to produce relatively meaningless three-word units (e.g., *stars hard gallop*). Learning was carried to six correct responses on a single trial. Different groups had retention tests after five hours, one day, or one week. The mean number of trials to learn to the criterion with sentences as response terms was 7.00; for the random triads the corresponding value was 14.69 trials. Despite this large difference in learning, there was no reliable evidence that retention differed for the two types of lists.

A mnemonic found effective for children's learning of paired associates is to put the two words in a sentence frame. If the pair was *horse-dog* the sentence might be "The horse chased the dog." The sentence frame is given to the subjects before the learning trials are initiated, with the subjects strongly urged to try to think of the two words in the sentences. Olton (1969) showed that recall one week after learning did not differ for two groups of subjects (one given the mnemonic, the other not) despite the fact that the learning rate differed.

For reasons that are irrelevant here, we (Underwood & Erlebacher, 1965) once carried out a study in which the stimulus terms in a paired-associate list consisted of five letters, but the order of these letters varied from trial to trial. On one trial the stimulus term might be SBCAN, on the next trial, CBNSA, then BNASC, and so on. The variable stimuli made the learning far more difficult than that observed when the letters remained constant from trial to trial, but the twenty-four-hour recall did not differ.

We all know that in studying learning we may anticipate large individual differences in the rate at which learning occurs. Yet, individual differences appear to have little effect on the rate of forgetting. If, for example, a group of subjects is given a list to learn to a criterion of one perfect trial, there will be wide individual differences in the number of trials taken to reach the criterion. However, the correlation between the number of trials to learn and the number of items correctly recalled after twenty-four hours will probably not differ significantly from zero. This would indicate only that individual differences in learning and individual differences in forgetting are not correlated. Such data do not tell that there are no reliable individual differences in forgetting. But, this can be inferred from other data (Underwood, 1964a). A group of subjects is given a constant number of learning trials on a given list, and recall is taken twenty-four hours later. The correlation between the number of correct responses in learning and the number correct at recall will be quite high. What this indicates, it seems, is that the level or degree of learning so dominates recall that other variables, including individual differences in forgetting, simply have very little influence.

RETROACTIVE INHIBITION

It was noted earlier that a major variable in producing forgetting is the presence of an interfering task (or tasks). If that interfering task is acquired before the target task is learned, the interference is spoken of as proactive interference or inhibition. If the interfering task comes after the target task, the interference is spoken of as retroactive interference or inhibition. For each of these two phenomena, the interference paradigms (e.g., A-B, A-D) discussed in the previous chapter are frequently used. Because retroactive and proactive interference have quite different histories, we will first discuss them separately.

Retroactive inhibition (RI) is most readily defined by the use of E and C Groups as follows:

E Group: Learn Task A   Learn Task B   Recall Task A
C Group: Learn Task A   - - - - - - - - -   Recall Task A

If the recall of List A is poorer for the E Group than for the C Group, RI has been demonstrated.

The discovery of RI took place at about the turn of the century, and hundreds of studies have aimed at determining the effect of variables on RI or making particular theoretical tests. If one studies the RI paradigm it will become obvious that the number of potential variables is very large. For example, the amount of RI would surely be related to the level of the similarity between the two tasks. In thinking about similarity as a variable we would include the various transfer paradigms discussed in an earlier chapter as well as the various kinds of similarity that we have identified as formal, meaningful, and conceptual. The first learned task in the RI paradigm is frequently called the original learning (OL), and the second task the interpolated learning (IL). We could vary the number of trials on OL

Figure 10.12.

Retroactive inhibition of paired-associate lists having the A-B, A-D relationship as a function of the number of interpolated lists. Data from Underwood (1945).

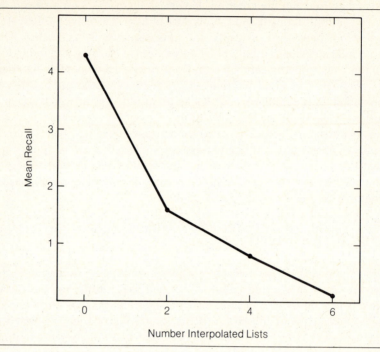

or on IL, and we could vary the number of lists making up IL. Temporal variables abound; the time between OL and IL, the time between OL and recall, and the time between IL and recall each might be manipulated. Then, of course, the nature of the tasks can be varied, from words to paragraphs. Retroactive inhibition has been shown to occur with a great variety of tasks. In fact, the failure to find RI would be a distinct event.

Needless to say, we are not going to attempt to summarize the literature on the effects of all of these independent variables on RI. Rather, we will get some "feel" for the phenomenon by looking at several rather diverse studies.

Some Studies

We must first recognize that an enormous amount of forgetting may be produced in a very short period of time by interfering tasks. This may be illustrated by a study in which the independent variable was the number of interpolated lists (Underwood, 1945). The lists were made up of ten pairs of adjectives, these lists being learned by the anticipation procedure. The original list (OL) was presented until the subject produced six correct

Figure 10.13.

Retroactive inhibition in serial lists as a function of the similarity of nouns occupying identical positions in the original and interpolated lists. Data from Table 1 of Johnson (1933).

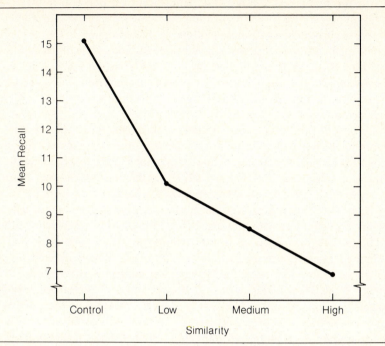

anticipations on a single trial. For a C Condition, twenty-five minutes passed between the end of OL and its recall. The experimental conditions involved the learning of two, four, or six interpolated lists, each presented for four anticipation trials. Subjects in these conditions also recalled OL after twenty-five minutes. The relationship between OL and the IL lists was A-B, A-D, but with two IL lists the symbols would be A-D, A-E, with four, A-D, A-E, A-F, A-G, and with six IL lists, A-D, A-E, A-F, A-G, A-H, A-I. Thus, with six interpolated lists, the subjects studied seven different response terms to each stimulus term.

The results of this study in terms of recall are shown in Figure 10.12. All three interpolated conditions produced RI, with the magnitude increasing directly as the number of IL lists increased. With six lists in IL, forgetting as measured by recall was almost complete. Out of twenty-four subjects in this condition, only three recalled one or more items from OL.

Johnson (1933) studied the relationship between RI and the similarity of meaning of words in OL and IL. The words were abstract nouns, twenty-one in each of the lists. Synonyms had been scaled for similarity so that the similarity between the items in OL and those in IL was identified as high, medium, or low for three different conditions. The synonymous pairs of words occupied identical positions in the two serial lists. That is, if in the high-synonymity condition the two words were *laughter* and *mirth*, if *laughter* occupied position 8 in OL, *mirth* occupied position 8 in IL. The criterion of learning for both OL and IL was one perfect trial. Recall of OL always occurred twenty minutes following its learning.

The mean number of items recalled as a function of similarity is shown in Figure 10.13. With the highest level of similarity, only 6.9 words were recalled on the average, whereas the average for the control was 15.1, well over twice as many as the number recalled when the words were highly synonymous.

Retroactive inhibition is not limited to word lists. A number of investigators have shown that RI will occur if two prose passages are learned, providing there are some conflicting associations in the two passages (e.g., Anderson & Myrow, 1971; Crouse, 1971). Conflicting associations in prose passages would be carried by sentences in the passages, of course. It could be anticipated, therefore, that RI could be produced by using lists of conflicting sentences without these being embedded in a passage. A study by Bower (1978), who used lists of twenty unrelated sentences, will be examined for evidence on RI between sentences. Bower likened simple sentences to an A-B association in which the subject of the sentence is A, and B is the verb phrase. Thus, in the sentence "The teacher sold his house," *teacher* is A, and *sold his house* is B. Given this unique perspective, it can be seen that a list of interpolated sentences each could form an A-B, A-D paradigm with sentences in the first (OL) list. Thus, if the sentence in OL was "The teacher sold his house," the IL sentence could be "The teacher shot a deer." Or, an A-Br paradigm could be formed in another condition, such as: "The teacher sold his house," and in IL, "The lawyer sold his house," where in the OL the sentence having the lawyer as subject might have been "The lawyer paced the race." As a third condition, no sentence subject occurred more than once in IL and OL, and no verb phrase occurred more than once; hence the two lists formed an A-B, C-D paradigm. Finally as a fourth condition, the IL list was omitted to provide a control. All A terms in all sentences were names of professions. To increase the magnitude of the interference, Bower used two successive interpolated lists for each of the three paradigms.

Learning was by the anticipation method in which the subject learned to give B (verb phrase) when A (profession name) was shown. A dropout procedure was used in which a sentence was omitted from further study once the verb phrase had been correctly anticipated. Learning of the IL was for three anticipation trials for all items following an initial study trial. Of course, since there were two lists for IL, each list was given for a study trial followed by three anticipation trials.

The first measure of RI used (the only one to be considered here) consisted of asking the subjects to give the B terms from the first-learned

Figure 10.14.
Retroactive inhibition using simple sentences under various paradigms. Data from Table 1 of Bower (1978).

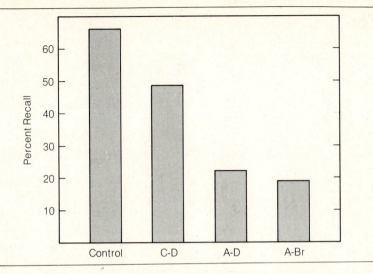

list when A was shown. This test was paced at a two-second rate. Bower's findings are summarized in Figure 10.14. It is obvious that RI was very severe for the A-D and A-Br paradigms, although even the difference between the control and C-D was reliable statistically.

Why should an A-B, C-D paradigm produce RI as it did in Bower's study and as has also been observed with the usual paired-associate lists? A comparable situation in free-recall learning would be the case where the items in the two lists had no apparent similarities. Such a study has been done by Postman and Keppel (1967) using two lists of twenty nouns each in which "meaningful similarity was minimized both within and between lists" (p. 204). The original list was presented for four study-test trials and the independent variable was the number of study-test trials for IL, these being zero, two, four, and six trials, with the first obviously being the usual control for RI. There was a thirteen-minute period between the end of OL and the test of RI.

At recall the three groups having IL were asked to recall as many items as possible from both lists. The central interest here is in the recall of the first list; the mean number recalled for each condition is shown in Figure 10.15. The recall of OL decreased as the number of IL trials increased, although it would appear that further trials on IL would not have increased RI appreciably. The same relationship has been shown many times with paired-associate lists. At the moment it is important to recognize that RI does occur in free recall of unrelated words, much as is true for the case of paired-associate lists of unrelated words. The magnitude of RI in free

Figure 10.15.
Retroactive inhibition in the free recall of unrelated lists of twenty nouns as related to degree of interpolated learning. Estimated from Postman and Keppel (1967).

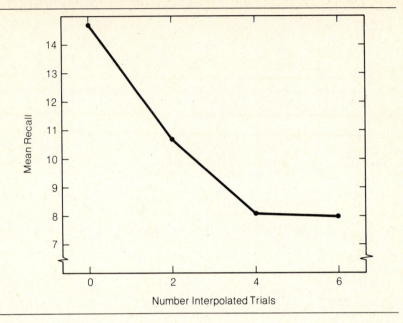

recall can be increased, of course, by manipulating certain similarity relationships (e.g., conceptual relationships) between the two lists (Shuell, 1968).

The studies we have examined attest to the generality of RI. Still another broad area of investigation, that of short-term memory, also produces evidence of RI. One study demonstrated the influence of acoustic similarity on short-term recall (Wickelgren, 1965). The subject was given a serial list of four letters, at the rate of .5 seconds per letter. This can be considered OL. As IL the subjects were presented a series of letters at the same rapid rate and asked to write them. The subjects were not asked to learn these letters in IL. Wickelgren showed that if the IL letters were acoustically similar to the letters in OL, recall of OL was less than if the IL letters were acoustically dissimilar.

In a second procedure, two-item paired-associate lists consisting of nouns as stimulus terms and CCCs as response terms and forming an A-B, A-D paradigm produced greater RI (greater forgetting of A-B) than did a control group (Forrester, 1969). The work of Levy and Jowaisas (1971) illustrates a third procedure. They presented their subjects a single CCC for one second, with its recall being requested after varying intervals. These interpolated intervals were filled by having the subjects shadow (say aloud) interpolated items as they were presented. These interpolated items were either other consonants (high similarity) or numbers (low similarity). Recall of the CCC decreased as the number of shadowed items increased, but the decrease was greater for the interpolated consonants than for the interpolated numbers.

PROACTIVE INHIBITION

Compared to RI, study of PI (proactive inhibition or proactive interference) has had a relatively short history, and empirical knowledge about PI lags far behind that for RI. Whitely (1927) discovered PI but it was not until 1936 that it was named (Whitely & Blankenship, 1936). We have some knowledge of PI as a result of work with the Brown-Peterson procedure as described in Chapter 3. The definition of PI, using E and C Groups, is as follows:

E Group: Learn Task A   Learn Task B   Recall Task B
C Group: - - - - - - - - - -   Learn Task B   Recall Task B

If the recall of the C Group is greater than the recall of the E Group, PI is demonstrated.

We must at first observe one critical variable, namely, that PI in retention requires that an interval of no learning occurs between the learning of Task B and its recall. Recall of Task B might be viewed as simply another learning trial on the task. However, once the interval between the end of the learning of Task B and its recall is greater than the intertrial interval used in learning, PI may occur. This means that PI is a direct function of the length of the interval between the learning of Task B and its recall.

A question may be raised as to how long the retention interval must be before PI may be detected in significant amounts. It has been measured after twenty minutes using an A-B, A-D paradigm (Morgan & Underwood, 1950) and after fifteen minutes in free recall of lists of unrelated words (Shuell & Koehler, 1970). Thus, PI "sets in" rather rapidly once the learning of the target task is terminated. Furthermore, in some studies the magnitude of PI reaches its maximum rather quickly. For example, Postman and Hasher (1972), using free recall, found significant PI after fifteen minutes with no further increase between fifteen minutes and forty-eight hours. Slamecka (1961) measured PI following the serial learning of abstract sentences. The PI was as great at fifteen minutes as it was at twenty-four hours. Thus, while PI must increase with time following learning, the increase may level off after a short period of time.

Some Studies

In the case of RI, as the degree of learning or number of trials on the interpolated list increases, RI increases rather sharply to a high level and

Figure 10.16.

Proactive inhibition of paired-associate lists of adjectives as related to number of successive lists and to the length of the retention interval. Data from Greenberg and Underwood (1950).

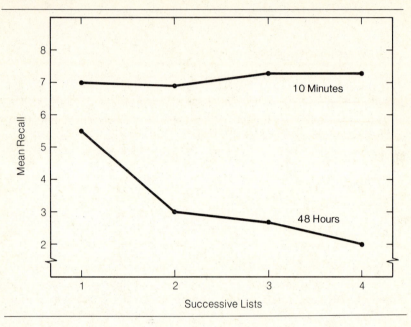

then reaches a plateau. We might suspect that the same relationship would be present for PI if the degree of learning of the interfering list (the prior list) is increased from a low to a high level. This expectation is not supported. Clearly, the level of learning of the interfering list will have some influence on PI. With zero level of learning of the interfering list there is no PI; with "some" learning there is. Here again, however, it appears that PI "sets in" very quickly and reaches its maximum at a relatively low level of learning on the interfering list. Studies dealing with serial learning (Postman & Riley, 1959) and with paired-associate learning (Underwood & Ekstrand, 1966) have found very minor effects of the degree of learning of the interfering tasks. Just why this insensitivity prevails is not known.

On the other hand, PI is very sensitive to the number of interfering lists. Three studies will be briefly reported. Subjects in an experiment by Greenberg and Underwood (1950) learned lists of paired associates, each list consisting of ten pairs of two-syllable adjectives. The criterion of learning was eight correct responses on a single trial. After forty-eight hours the first list learned was recalled. The subject then learned a second list of words unrelated to those in the first list, and this second list was also recalled after forty-eight hours. This continued for four lists. Another

Figure 10.17.
Proactive inhibition after five hours as a function of the number of successive free-recall lists of adjectives learned. Data from Table 1 of Wipf and Webb (1962).

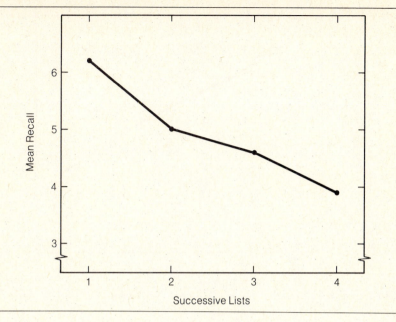

group of subjects learned and recalled the same four lists, but the retention interval for each list was ten minutes rather than forty-eight hours. One list was learned and recalled each day for four successive days. The recall results for the two groups are shown in Figure 10.16. Recall of the subjects having the ten-minute intervals remained essentially constant for the four lists, i.e., PI did not "set in" within ten minutes for these lists. With the forty-eight-hour retention interval, recall decreased directly as the number of lists learned and recalled increased. The first list serves as a control (no prior lists). It should be emphasized that the words were unrelated and did not form any one of the negative transfer paradigms discussed in the previous chapter.

Wipf and Webb (1962) used the response terms from the Greenberg-Underwood lists to form four free-recall lists. Learning was carried to eight correct responses and the retention interval was five hours. As may be seen in Figure 10.17, recall declined with each successive list. Again it should be noted that these words were two-syllable adjectives and were unrelated to each other.

In a study by von Wright and Salminen (1964), the subjects learned either zero, two, five, or eight lists prior to learning the target list—the list to be recalled. The materials were pairs of CVCs. The target list was always recalled after twenty-four hours. Figure 10.18 shows again that

Figure 10.18.

Recall of paired CVCs after twenty-four hours as a function of the number of prior lists learned. Data from Table 1 of von Wright and Salminen (1964).

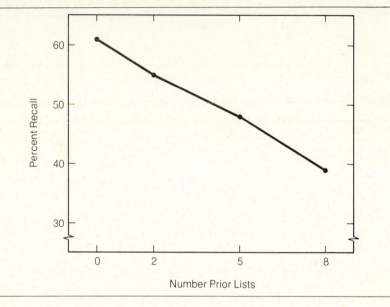

recall decreases steadily as the number of prior lists learned increases.

One further fact about these studies of cumulative PI should be noted. If the subjects at the time of recall are provided with the response terms for the target list, no evidence of cumulative PI is obtained (Underwood, Broder, & Zimmerman, 1973). It is the inability to recall the response terms that produces the cumulative PI.

Beginning in the 1960s, the evidence such as described above on PI in long-term memory was complemented by the work using the Brown-Peterson paradigm. It will be remembered that the buildup of PI can be produced in just a few minutes using the Brown-Peterson procedure. However, we may examine some data by way of a reminder of the nature of PI in the task. Blumenthal and Robbins (1977) used short prose passages as their material. On any one trial, the steps were as follows: First, the passage (a page in length) was presented for study for two minutes. Then the subject worked on a crossword puzzle for two minutes following which three minutes were allowed for a test over the passage. A minute later another passage was given, and so on. The two minutes used for working on the crossword puzzle was obviously the retention interval with the work on the puzzle used to prevent rehearsal.

One group of subjects had four successive passages from the same subject area, e.g., music or sports; we may speak of these passages as having high similarity. Another group had four passages from different or

Figure 10.19.
Proactive-inhibition buildup in the Brown-Peterson paradigm as related to the similarity of four successive prose passages. Data from Table 1 of Blumenthal and Robbins (1977).

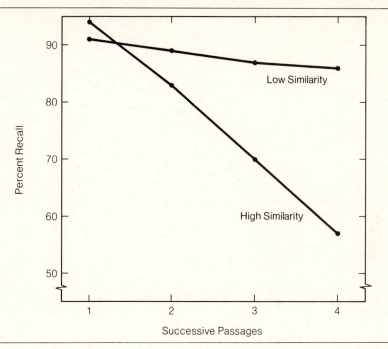

low-similarity subject areas, e.g., history, physics, music, and sports. It would be expected that PI would be much greater for the high-similarity group than for the low-similarity group, and as Figure 10.19 shows, this was the case. In the same sense that PI in long-term memory may produce heavy forgetting, there is also a startling decrement using the Brown-Peterson procedure when there is similarity between the successive stimuli. However, there are differences that should not be overlooked. The results for low similarity seen in Figure 10.19 show at best only a slight decline across lists. For the list studies with retention intervals of twenty-four or forty-eight hours there is a heavy loss across lists even when the items are unrelated. The results for the low-similarity list as seen in Figure 10.19 are not a consequence of the use of prose passages because the results are essentially the same as if unrelated word triads are used (e.g., Russ-Eft, 1979). Nevertheless, there are cases where a sharp loss is seen across successive word triads in the Brown-Peterson procedure, even when the words in successive triads appear unrelated. We saw such a case (Lachar & Goggin, 1969) in Figure 4.1 when word length was varied. The semantic and acoustic similarity among the words in the successive triads was described as low. It may be that some sources of similarity (or sources of interference) among words are difficult to detect. Disregarding these apparent contradictions, further comments about the short-term and long-term procedures are in order.

In the long-term studies the learning of each successive list is carried to the same criterion. On the other hand, in the Brown-Peterson procedure there is no control over the amount learned. Rather, all items are presented for the same period of time for study and the level of learning is unknown. Suppose, for example, that the falling curve (for high similarity) seen in Figure 10.19 is due to negative transfer. That is, suppose that the level of learning is lower for each successive passage. If this is true, then we are not dealing with differences in forgetting, but rather with differences in level of learning attained. It could be, of course, that both level of learning and forgetting due to competition at recall are occurring—we simply do not know. Thus, we return to the problem discussed earlier when we concluded that unless degree or level of learning was equated before the retention interval, we may have a confounding.

The above is just a part of a more general issue that has engaged a number of investigators working with the Brown-Peterson paradigm. Basically the issue is whether the buildup of PI across similar tasks is due to a learning deficit or a retrieval deficit. We just noted above that it could be a learning deficit. Others have concluded that it may be a retrieval problem which, if so, makes it a matter of forgetting only, unconfounded by differences in learning. Nevertheless, it does not seem possible to arrange procedures that will allow a clear decision concerning learning and storage differences versus retrieval differences. An inquiry by Radtke and Grove (1977) may be consulted for more discussion of this difficult problem.

GENERAL INTERFERENCE THEORY

Some History

In days rather far past, forgetting theory made use of such terms as trace decay, fading trace, loss of strength by disuse, the wasting effects of time, and so on. Such statements might be viewed as other ways of noting that forgetting occurs, but more importantly these statements may implicate time as a causal factor in forgetting. These ways of viewing forgetting were challenged in 1932 by McGeoch who pointed out:

> In scientific descriptions of nature time itself is not employed as a causative factor nor is passive decay with time ever found. In time iron, when unused, may rust, but oxidation, not time, is responsible. In time organisms grow old, but time enters only as a logical framework in which complex biochemical processes go their ways (p. 359).

As a substitute approach for theorizing about forgetting, McGeoch offered retroactive inhibition as a model, a model which makes interference produced by competition the major cause of forgetting. McGeoch's article had a profound influence; very quickly the notion that interference was heavily involved in forgetting was widely accepted. It should be noted that McGeoch did not include PI as a second model; it was not until about 1960 that PI became coordinate with RI as a model of forgetting.

Interference as produced by competition can perhaps be most clearly conceptualized by using the A-B, A-D paradigm. If after having learned two lists with identical stimulus terms the subject is asked to give the first-list response associated with A, the association A-D may prevent the recovery of the A-B association. In an extreme case the two conflicting response tendencies may both be blocked. Although the A-B, A-D paradigm may be considered the prototypical case of competition, competition must be considered in a broad context so that interference may be produced by competition of response tendencies from apparently unrelated stimuli. Von Wright (1959) more thoroughly discusses the ways in which competition may occur, although we do not have much data on the variables influencing the magnitude of competition.

In 1940 Melton and Irwin proposed a two-factor theory of retroactive inhibition. They first accepted competition at recall as one source of the RI loss. Beyond this, they proposed that during interpolated learning the associations in the first task become weakened or extinguished or unlearned. Eventually, techniques were worked out which were presumed to measure unlearning without contamination from competition (Barnes & Underwood, 1959). Subjects learned A-B and A-D. Then on the memory test they were given the A terms and were asked to produce *both* response terms (B and D). There was no pacing; essentially unlimited time was given the subjects to produce the response terms, the idea being that with these procedures there would be no competition. The results showed that when A-D was learned to a high level the subjects could recover only about 50 percent of the B response terms.

The above technique for measuring unlearning was used in many studies designed to produce an understanding of the variables that affect the magnitude of unlearning. Unfortunately, investigators began to report that competition may occur in the testing phase. One can infer that competition may have occurred if PI is measured in the unlearning test. Because the second list (A-D) could not have been unlearned, any observed decrement (beyond that observed for the control condition in which only A-D was learned) had to be attributed to some factor other than unlearning, presumably, therefore, to competition. Now, if competition is occurring on the unpaced test, the so-called unlearning of the first list may be due to competition, at least in part. The analysis of forgetting in the RI paradigm was thrown into disarray by the possibility that competition may occur on the unpaced test.

On logical grounds, unlearning and competition need not be considered independent factors. Given that there is unlearning (the amount of which we now seem unable to estimate), representing a weakening of the first-list associations, its consequence could be that of changing the amount of competition. More particularly, because the second-list associations have not been unlearned, if both lists have been carried to the same criterion of learning, the second-list associations should be stronger than those in the first list, hence could dominate (interfere with) the first-list associations. This logic presumes that competition is some function of the relative response strengths of the conflicting response tendencies, and this (as seen in the previous chapter) has not always been found to be true (e.g., Runquist, 1957; Underwood & Lund, 1981).

All of the above is to say that at the present time the underlying mechanisms involved in the interference observed in RI and PI are simply not known. That is why it seems necessary to speak of a general interference theory.

The General Theoretical Problem

We need to review some of the facts presented earlier. First, we identified several variables that have been found to produce differences in the rate of forgetting of a list learned alone (singly-learned list) in the laboratory. Second, we saw how RI and PI represent cases of severe forgetting which may be attributed to interference between the two or more lists used. Given these two sets of observations, it can be seen that to use PI and RI as general models for all forgetting, we must show that the forgetting of the singly-learned list is due to RI and PI. But, we must be more specific than that. We must say that the forgetting is produced either by interference from an interpolated task learned outside the laboratory or from a prior task learned outside the laboratory, or from both.

At the present time the theorizing is "stuck" at this point. We have not been able to identify the interfering associations acquired outside of the laboratory which produce the loss in the singly-learned list. It is an act of faith in nature's consistency that we generalize the facts of interference as observed in RI and PI and say that all forgetting must be due to interference.

An interference model of forgetting could be said to be one in which there is no forgetting in the sense that traces become weaker. Performance on a given task may suffer a decrement (interference), but that need not imply that there was any change in the strength of the trace interfered with. On the other hand, several possibilities could be included in the model to make it more flexible with respect to this matter. For example, unlearning may produce a permanent weakening of the trace. Or, one could assume that once a task is interfered with, the probabilities of subsequent interference are increased, thereby producing a weakening of the trace from a different source. Furthermore, because the passage of time reduces the validity of the cues for discriminating between memories in a psychophysical sense, there could be an increase in interference without a corresponding decrease in the strength of the memory traces.

One further matter. We saw how arousal influenced recall in unexpected ways; in particular we say that recall performance actually increases over time if arousal was high when learning occurred. At the present time it is not evident how an interference approach could handle this finding. Poor immediate recall under high arousal must reflect a performance decrement (as opposed to a learning decrement). It is quite possible that this could result from interference effects, but the details of how this could happen are obscure.

SUMMARY

Forgetting occurs during a period of no practice following the learning of the task tested for retention. The effects of several variables that influence the rate of forgetting were reviewed: (1) generally speaking, the higher the level or degree of learning, the slower the forgetting; (2) spacing the learning over days decreases forgetting; (3) forgetting is less rapid if two or more tasks are learned simultaneously than if the tasks are learned in isolation; (4) arousal decreases immediate retention but facilitates long-term retention; (5) forgetting is profoundly accelerated by the learning of other lists that interfere with the target list, the paradigms for introducing the interference being called retroactive interference and proactive interference. Several studies were reviewed to illustrate that there are a number of variables that do not influence forgetting despite the fact that these variables influence learning.

Studies were examined to show how the magnitude of retroactive and proactive interference is influenced by a number of different factors, and included in these studies were experiments in which sentences had been used as the learning material. Both proactive and retroactive interference were shown to occur in various short-term memory procedures. It would seem possible to use proactive and retroactive models to account for all forgetting, but no satisfactory theory along this line has been offered.

11

Basic Processes

In the past chapters we have seen how a number of independent variables influence the rate of learning of the various types of lists of words or other verbal units, but at no point did we face the question of how it is that our subjects are able to recall even one word from a free-recall list, or how it is that they can produce a response term to the appropriate stimulus term in a paired-associate list. In Chapter 4 we discussed various transformational attributes (mnemonics) and how they are undoubtedly involved in some of the learning carried on by the young adult. However, transformational attributes do not eliminate new learning, although they may minimize its amount. Even with heavy use of transformational attributes there is always some new encoding or decoding that must take place.

The above should not be taken to imply that most of the learning we observe in college students is through the use of transformational attributes. For example, when subjects are interrogated about the manner in which they learned each paired associate in a list, for many of the pairs the subjects cannot report mediated associations (or other mnemonics), thus indicating that many of the pairs were probably learned by rote. For example, in a study by Adams, Marshall, and Bray (1971), a list of twelve CVC-adjective pairs was learned, with the subjects requested to report any mediators used to relate the stimulus and response terms in each pair. Roughly speaking, the subjects reported mediators for about half the pairs; for the other half of the pairs the subjects apparently did not use any mnemonics.

There is a further point to be made about the use of transformational attributes. As has been said before, transformational attributes make use of already learned associations to acquire new ones. Our interest in this chapter is how these old associations were learned. And no matter how far we might regress (the old ones were acquired through the use of still older ones), there would seem to come a point where associations were established without the help of transformational attributes. It will be remembered that with college students, semantic processing (produced by "depth" procedures) of low-meaningful units did not facilitate their learning, nor did procedures that facilitated the incidental learning of words facilitate the learning of low-meaningful units. One might view the college student faced with the task of learning CCCs in much the same way that we might view children as they first try to learn three-letter words.

How, then, are associations formed when transformational attributes play at best a minor role? The attempt to answer this question leads us directly into an examination of the role of temporal contiguity in associative learning.

CONTIGUITY

Discussion of the role of temporal contiguity (or proximity) in mental life has a long history, from the ancient Greeks to contemporary writings. Bringing experimental data to bear on the issue is decidedly recent. Even as late as 1932, Robinson, in examining principles involved in learning, gave contiguity a role but cited no evidence other than some conditioning experiments with rats:

> The fact that two psychological processes occur together in time or in immediate succession increases the probability that an associative connection between them will develop—that one process will become the associative instigator of the other (p. 72).

Robinson took the edge off of his law of contiguity by saying that contiguity did not insure that associations would develop, indicating that frequency (number of contiguous occurrences) may be an important modifier of the law. This seems to mean that some minimal number of trials of contiguous occurrences is necessary for learning to be demonstrated. Contiguity, in Robinson's thinking, became a necessary condition for establishing associations, but insufficient alone. Frequency is a very weak modifier; obviously there must be at least one trial for contiguity to have an opportunity to operate. Furthermore, if we think in terms of the contiguity of verbal units we can see that the amount or strength of the association would not only depend upon the number of trials but also on other factors, such as meaningfulness. If we think of the possibility of two items becoming associated when they had *not* occurred contiguously, we might well become convinced that contiguity is fundamental for learning, regardless of how the rate of development of the association may be determined by other variables.

We will look at data which presume to help us reach a decision on the way we should view temporal contiguity and association formation. We will examine some negative cases first, and then some positive ones.

Negative Cases

Thorndike (1932) reached the following conclusion:

> . . . mere sequence does little or nothing in and of itself. Ten or twenty or a hundred such repetitions of B after A will not appreciably increase the probability that A will evoke B (p. 65).

Two of Thorndike's many experiments will be described to indicate how he reached the above conclusion. In one experiment the subjects were read a series of short declarative sentences, sentences that were quite unrelated. Each sentence had the name of a person and a related person, carrying out some act. For example: "Francis Bragg and his cousin played hard." This sentence might have been followed by "Norman Foster and his mother bought much."

There were ten such sentences and they were read ten times to the subjects under the following instructions: "Listen to what I read with moderate attention, as you would listen to a lecture (p. 66)." After the tenth reading, the subjects were asked to answer some questions. Among the questions were those which asked for the first word in a sentence when given the last word of the just preceding sentence. To illustrate, using the two sentences above, the subjects would have been asked what word followed "hard." The correct answer is "Norman." Thorndike found that only 3 percent of the subjects were able to give the correct responses to such questions, a number that he indicates was at a chance level. He reasoned that if contiguity alone was critical, "hard" and "Norman" would have become associated.

In another experiment, a long list of word-number pairs was read to the subjects. Four of the pairs occurred twenty-four times, and on each occurrence the *number* in the preceding pair was always the same; a given number was paired with more than one word. In effect, then, the number of the preceding pair and the word of the following pair occurred in close temporal contiguity twenty-four times. Again, Thorndike reasoned that if contiguity was important, the two units should have become associated, but the data indicate that they did not.

Undoubtedly the subjects in Thorndike's experiments expected a memory test, but it would be quite unlikely that they expected to be quizzed on the items which Thorndike viewed as being crucial to contiguity testing. But contiguity per se should not be judged by such matters; if contiguity is critical for learning, and if two units are presented contiguously, associative formation should occur regardless of what the subjects expected. Thorndike's data clearly suggested to him that contiguity was not an important principle of learning.

As a second negative case we will examine a study by Glenberg and Bradley (1979). The Brown-Peterson short-term technique was used. The subjects were led to believe that the critical task was to remember four-digit numbers over short retention intervals. On a trial the sequence of events was as follows: A warning signal was followed by a four-digit number which was followed immediately by two words shown for two seconds. The subjects were required to rehearse aloud these two words during the retention interval. The rehearsal was paced by a "beep" and the retention intervals were 1.33, 6.67, and 13.33 seconds, which allowed one, five, and ten rehearsals of the pairs, respectively. This type of rehearsal, in which the subjects are required to keep certain units in mind by rehearsing them, is called maintenance rehearsal. At the end of the retention interval the subjects were asked to recall the four-digit number.

After being given twenty-one trials, the subjects were tested (unexpectedly) on the words they had rehearsed. The pairs of words were all different. On the test one member of each of the twenty-one pairs was given as a cue with the subjects requested to provide the other member of the pair. The mean number of words correctly recalled was essentially zero, the percentages being .01, .04, and .01 for the three rehearsal intervals in order. On a second test the subjects were given all of the forty-two words and were asked to pair them appropriately. These pairings were correct above a chance level, but there was no clear relationship between the number of rehearsals and the number of correct pairings. In another experiment in this same report, Glenberg and Bradley showed that recognition of the individual words was at a level beyond chance, so it was not as if the rehearsal had no effects on memory. The final conclusion of the authors was that ". . . contiguity alone is not sufficient for association formation (p. 97)." It should be noted that the study reviewed here was not the only one that led up to this conclusion; in earlier studies (e.g., Glenberg & Adams, 1978) much the same findings were reported.

Positive Cases

Murray (1970) reported results that led to the conclusion that pairs of CVCs may become associated as a result of contiguous occurrence. The guise for presenting the syllables was a probability-learning task. On a given trial a CVC was projected to the left side of a screen and the subjects were required to spell it aloud. A second syllable was then shown on the right side of the screen, and it too was spelled. Then the subjects were to guess whether a red light would or would not be lit. They had earlier been informed that the presence of the syllables was to distract them from learning the "rules" that determined whether the light would or would not come on.

The independent variable was the length of the interval between the appearances of the two CVCs, these intervals being one, two, four, or seven seconds. This was a between-groups manipulation. There were ten CVC pairs and each was presented ten times. The question, of course, is whether the two syllables became associated and, if so, whether there was a relationship between the level of association and the interval between the two CVCs. To test for this, following the probability-learning trials, the subjects were given four study-test trials on the ten pairs under intentional-learning instructions. The tests used an associative matching procedure in which the CVCs that had occurred on the left side of the screen were shown in one column, those that had occurred on the right side, in another column. The test was to match the CVCs to form ten pairs. Control groups had the CVCs mispaired during the paired-associate learning trials.

For the experimental groups, the mean number of correct matches decreased as the time between the spelling of the two CVCs increased. Roughly, the mean numbers correct on the four trials were 14.6, 13.0, 11.3, and 10.8 for the four intervals in order of magnitude. No gradient was apparent for the control group, and the average number of matches across the four trials was a little less than eight correct. The data for the control groups may have involved interference from the incidentally established associations in probability learning, but this fact would not, of course, deny the conclusions that associations were established.

It will be remembered that in verbal-discrimination learning the two words constituting a pair occur simultaneously. We may ask if these two words become associated. Because the subjects do not have to learn these pairings in order to master the verbal-discrimination task, it would seem that any associations established between the two words would represent incidental learning, hence, a case of learning by contiguity.

In a study by Zechmeister and Underwood (1969), the twelve-pair lists of low-frequency words were given either five, ten, twenty, or thirty-five acquisition trials. To reach one perfect recitation on this list required about seven trials; thus, it is apparent that except for the five-trial condition, much overlearning was involved. After verbal-discrimination learning, tests of associative learning were made. One test involved intentional paired-associate learning of the pairs. These results showed that paired-associate performance was much better with ten verbal-discrimination trials than with five, but that performance improved very little beyond ten trials. Other groups were given associative matching, and the number of correct pairings increased directly as the number of training trials increased, with the group having had thirty-five training trials giving a mean of eleven correct pairings (out of twelve possible). Thus, it would appear that a considerable amount of associative learning occurred in verbal-discrimination learning. We presume that this learning was incidental, although we have no direct evidence on this matter.

In another study (Underwood & Lund, 1980a), the initial task was the simultaneous learning of two free-recall lists. In such a task, it will be remembered, one item from each of two easily discriminable lists of words are presented together for study; then another pair is presented, and so on down through the lists. After such a study trial, recall is taken for each list separately. Because the subject studies two words simultaneously, the two words might become associated as a result of the contiguous occurrence.

In this particular study, one free-recall list consisted of sixteen four-letter nouns typed in capital letters. The other list was made up of sixteen nouns of at least two syllables, typed in lowercase on the memory-drum tape. The procedure called for five simultaneous learning trials followed by a test for associative learning for the pairs of words occurring together on the study trials. This was done by having a paired-associate list of sixteen pairs in which half the stimulus words were the short nouns, and half the long nouns. There were four conditions. In all four the paired-associate lists (the tests for associative learning) were identical; differences among the conditions were determined by the pairings in simultaneous learning, as follows:

Condition A. The items paired on the paired-associate list were the items studied together in simultaneous learning. If associative learning occurred, the paired-associate list should be acquired rapidly.

Condition I. The two words occurring together on the five simultaneous learning trials were *not* paired on the paired-associate list. If associative learning occurs in simultaneous learning, negative transfer should be expected on the paired-associate list.

Condition V. On each trial of simultaneous learning, a different pairing of the long and short words occurred, and these pairings were all different from the pairings on the paired-associate list. Again, negative transfer was expected if associative learning occurs in simultaneous learning.

Condition C. In this control condition, the words in simultaneous learning were completely different from those in the paired-associate list. This condition served as a control only for nonspecific transfer.

The paired-associate list was presented for eight anticipation trials following one study trial. The mean numbers of correct responses on each trial are shown in Figure 11.1. Using Condition C as a reference, it can be seen that Condition A produced heavy positive transfer, with about 14.5 correct responses being given on the first anticipation trial. Conditions V and I both produced negative transfer. The results for all three of these conditions would be expected if associative learning occurred during simultaneous learning. We were also able to provide evidence that most of the subjects did not intentionally set about to associate the two items in the pairs in simultaneous learning. Such could have been expected if the subjects employed a strategy of using each item in a pair in simultaneous learning to cue the other when recalling the lists separately. Our conclusion was that associative learning occurred during simultaneous learning as a consequence of the contiguous pairings.

An Assessment

It must appear that strictly on the basis of available data we cannot reach a crisp decision on the role of contiguity in association formation. Probably very few investigators would argue against the proposition that close

Figure 11.1.
Learning of a paired-associate list as a function of various conditions of contiguity occurring earlier during simultaneous learning. Data from Underwood and Lund (1980).

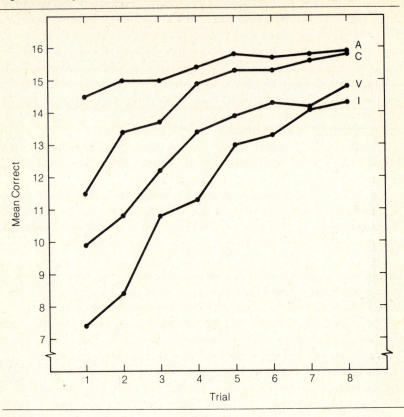

temporal contiguity is a necessary condition for the formation of associations. The critical issue is whether or not it is a sufficient condition, or whether some other factor must attend the contiguity. With respect to verbal learning no reasonable attending factor has yet been suggested. Thorndike (1932), it will be remembered, rejected contiguity as a sufficient condition, and suggested that the attending factor is *belonging*. The idea, somewhat vague, was that "this goes with that." In some sense this idea suggests that associative learning has already occurred. Robinson (1932) suggested that a factor such as frequency had to be present before contiguity would produce associative learning. As mentioned earlier, it is difficult to understand his reasoning because a contiguous occurrence of two events *is* a frequency and there is no way to avoid it. Furthermore, if one takes the position that associative learning is not an all or none process, then it must be the case that more than one contiguous occurrence of two events will result in a stronger (or more probable) association than would one contiguous occurrence.

The attribute approach assumes that contiguity is a sufficient condition for learning. Many of the attributes are a result of associative learning, and a raw (nonmediated) association is the beginning by which a given word may develop a number of different types of information or attributes which may enter into subsequent memories. To take this position in the face of some negative evidence (as reviewed earlier) rests on several considerations which will now be noted. Some restatements of previous points will be included.

1. That contiguity is a necessary condition for associative learning seems to be generally accepted. This implies a further acceptance of highly selective mechanisms in behavior. It is difficult to imagine what we would be like if the acquisition of associations was not sharply limited by the imposition of contiguity as a necessary condition for learning.

2. If there is a critical condition that must attend temporal contiguity before association formation occurs, why is this critical condition so difficult to identify? Perhaps some might suggest reinforcement of some kind as being the critical attending factor, but even in the animal learning literature a number of studies make the presence of this attending factor unlikely as a requirement for learning.

3. It may be that conditions can be arranged in which temporal contiguity alone will not produce learning. The maintenance-rehearsal technique as used by Glenberg and his associates may be one such condition. Still, one might argue that more trials would have produced some associative learning; item learning did occur because recognition was influenced, and there was some evidence of associative learning in the associative-matching data. Nevertheless, the matter is not handled satisfactorily by this route because we would necessarily be saying that the amount of learning that occurs by temporal contiguity differs for different situations. This automatically implies a modifying (attendant) factor, which has not been identified. We cannot easily dismiss the lack of association formation observed in these maintenance-rehearsal experiments.

4. What *can* be concluded is that contiguity must be a sole determinant of associative learning in most situations. It is the primary factor underlying the acquisition of associations in the paired-associate task. As noted earlier it is presumed to underlie the development of some of the attributes of memory, such as the spatial attribute, the temporal attribute, and the various kinds of associative attributes, including those used in mnemonic systems. We should, of course, continue to search for the factor or factors which modify the role of contiguity in unusual situations. In our notion of contiguity we must also, of course, include the contiguity that results when two verbal units are brought together mentally.

REHEARSAL

The discussion now will revolve around a number of concepts with which we are already acquainted, these including incidental learning and maintenance rehearsal. The studies we will examine have all made use of free recall. In further studying the effects of rehearsal, we intend to see what happens when the conditions of learning are as barren as they can be made. There are two common factors in the studies to be reviewed (in addition to the use of free recall). First, the subject is made to rehearse items or to hold them "in mind" by saying them over and over, and second, there is no intent to learn on the part of the subject. How much learning will occur under such circumstances? It is believed that the results of these studies are important for understanding certain aspects of free-recall learning. More particularly, the results are believed to represent learning in which the context and the items become associated by contiguity. This matter will receive close attention at a later point in the chapter.

In an earlier chapter a study by Tulving (1966) was reported in which subjects pronounced a list of nouns six times at a one-second rate, and then unexpectedly they were given free-recall learning trials on the words. Their performance on the free-recall trials was no better than that for a control group which had been given pronouncing trials on a different list of words. Now, we do not know that the subjects could not have recalled some of the words immediately after the pronouncing trials, and we know that the Tulving finding does not occur when adjectives are used. Nevertheless, the fact that learning was low suggests that the mere pronouncing of words at a rapid rate does not produce much learning.

If a slight change is made in the Tulving procedure, a marked difference in the results occurs. Several investigators have shown that if subjects pronounce items rapidly under intent to learn, performance is substantial. Consider the study by Schwartz and Humphreys (1974). They presented forty nouns at a five-second rate for free-recall learning. The subjects in a C Group were free to study in any way they chose, those in the E Group were required to pronounce each word five times during the five seconds exposure interval. After a single study trial the C Group recalled an average of 12.75 words, the E Group, an average of 10.00. The difference was reliable. The mystery is why the recall of the E Group was as high as it was. It would seem that being required to say the words over and over would leave little time for encoding with semantic attributes. Is it possible that subjects can engage in rapid rote rehearsal (maintenance rehearsal) and at the same time carry out encoding activity which results in substantial learning? Or, if there is intent to learn, perhaps rote rehearsal may be quite effective in and of itself. We must grasp the fact that what appears to be rote rehearsal can be accompanied by quite rapid learning under intent to learn. However, our major interest at this point will be on the effects of rote rehearsal without intent to learn.

A preliminary statement is necessary before we look at studies in which maintenance rehearsal is involved. We will find that in some studies the amount of maintenance rehearsal is said to be unrelated to the number of items subsequently recalled. Some investigators have been inclined to overgeneralize these findings, perhaps leaving the reader with the belief that the amount of maintenance rehearsal has no influence on memory. Such a conclusion is erroneous. The amount of maintenance rehearsal is directly related to performance on recognition tests (e.g., Glenberg, Smith, & Green, 1977; Woodward, Bjork, & Jongeward, 1973). These findings not only show that maintenance rehearsal influences memory, but suggest again that the attributes functioning in recall are probably quite different from those mediating recognition decisions.

Some Studies

Mechanic (1964) presented his subjects twenty-four trigrams, some words and some nonwords, but all quite pronounceable. There were four groups of subjects, two incidental and two intentional. The second variable was the nature of the rehearsal required. Each trigram was presented for eleven seconds. Two of the groups (one incidental, one intentional) were told that the investigator was interested in the effects of repetition on the pronunciation of the units. As each of the twenty-four items occurred on a screen, the subjects were asked to pronounce it over and over into a microphone. The other two groups were told that the study dealt with extrasensory perception. Each trigram, the subjects were told, had been paired randomly with a number between zero and ninety-nine. The subjects were asked to look at each trigram for nine seconds and then during the last two seconds (during which period the screen was blank) they were to announce their guess over the microphone. After all twenty-four trigrams had been presented once, the subjects were given five minutes to recall as many items as possible.

The results are shown in Figure 11.2. Intent to learn made a large difference in amount learned when the extrasensory perception task (ESP) was carried out. On the other hand, when the subjects pronounced the items over and over during the eleven-second period, recall was equivalent for both the intentional and incidental groups. This is to say that pronouncing the trigrams over and over produced a considerable amount of learning, and intent to learn was of no consequence. Subjects in the ESP groups were not required to pronounce the items during the eleven seconds, but Mechanic observed that many subjects did pronounce the trigrams to themselves as they were figuring out what their ESP number should be. This pronouncing may have accounted for the fact that the incidental ESP subjects recalled as many as 3.50 trigrams. It would also indicate that the mean number of rehearsals is directly related to the amount recalled.

Figure 11.2.
Free recall as related to incidental and intentional learning instructions and when subjects are and are not (ESP) required to pronounce the words. Data from Table 1 of Mechanic (1964).

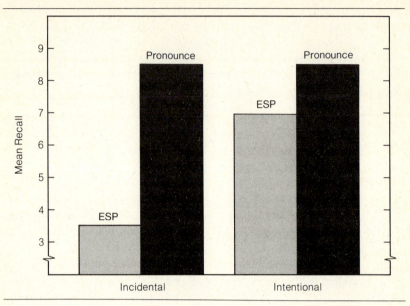

Meunier, Kestner, Meunier, and Ritz (1974) used twenty-four CCCs of 29 percent association value, with one intentional group and one incidental group. Each CCC was presented for two seconds following which was a blank interval of three, nine, or fifteen seconds. All subjects were instructed to write the trigrams as rapidly as possible over and over during the blank intervals. The ostensible purpose of the experiment, as reported to the subjects, was to measure the speed and accuracy of writing and the changes in writing which may take place with time. After the twenty-fourth CCC was presented, recall was requested, with five minutes allowed.

The numbers of rehearsals per item were approximately 2.5, 5.7, and 8.6 for the three blank intervals in order. As might be anticipated when CCCs are used, recall was low; the highest recall at any point was 15 percent. Nevertheless, there was some increase in recall as the rehearsal interval increased in length from three seconds to nine seconds, but no further increase beyond that. The relationship between rehearsal time and recall was of exactly the same nature for both groups, but recall was higher for the intentional group. But, again we see a positive relationship between rehearsal time and recall.

Earlier in this chapter we saw how Glenberg and Bradley (1979) tested whether the temporal contiguity of two words resulted in the formation of an association between the two. This was a case of maintenance rehearsal using the Brown-Peterson procedure, with the subjects given a four-place number to remember over the retention interval. During the retention interval the subjects said two words over and over. After a number of such trials the subjects were asked to recall the words. The result showed that the words did not become associated. It can be seen that this method can be adapted to maintenance rehearsal of single items, as was done by Glenberg, Smith, and Green (1977). They found no relationship between length of the rehearsal interval and recall. For rehearsal intervals of two, six, and eighteen seconds, the recall values were 11, 7, and 12 percent.

Craik and Watkins (1973) used quite a different procedure to institute maintenance rehearsal. A long list of words was presented and the subjects were to "hold in mind" a word beginning with a particular letter. The subject was to do this for the first word in the list having an appropriate first letter, and to continue holding the word in mind until a new word appeared with the appropriate first letter. At this point the subject was to "dump" the first word and substitute the new word in the holding state. To illustrate, suppose the words in a small segment of the list are *horse, desk, street, happy, radio, grass, car, fence, heaven*. Suppose further that the letter *h* is the designated letter for the list. When the word *horse* appeared the subjects must start holding this word in mind by saying it to themselves, and this must continue until the word *happy* appears and at which point *horse* is scratched and *happy* is held in mind until *heaven* appears at which time *happy* is replaced with *heaven*. It can be seen that by the appropriate spacing of the words beginning with *h*, the length of the maintenance rehearsal of the words can be varied. After a number of such lists, recall of all words is requested and the number recalled is related to the length of the rehearsal interval.

Craik and Watkins also varied exposure duration of each word (.5, 1.0, and 2.0 seconds). Recall increased by a small amount as duration increased, although there was no interaction between duration and length of the maintenance-rehearsal time. We will look only at the results for the two-second duration. There were nine maintenance-rehearsal intervals, varying from two to twenty-eight seconds. For these nine intervals the poorest recall was 10 percent, and the highest was 22 percent. Thus, although recall was not related to the amount of maintenance rehearsal beyond the shortest interval, the fact remains that a considerable amount of learning occurred even with the shortest interval (two seconds).

As a means of looking at a still different technique, as well as at a different finding, a study by Darley and Glass (1975) will be examined. Subjects were given a booklet and on each sheet was a list of forty words on the left-hand side and a single target word on the right-hand side. The task was to search down the list as rapidly as possible until the target word was found, at which time the word was checked, the page turned, and another list of words was searched for a new target. This was repeated for sixteen lists; the subjects were then unexpectedly asked to recall as many of the target words as possible. The independent variable was the position held by the target words in the lists; the further down the target word was in the list, the longer the subject had to hold the word in mind during the search, hence, the greater the amount of rehearsal. Actually, four target words occurred in each quarter of the list so that four levels of rehearsal constituted the independent variable. The results were clear; as the length of the rehearsal interval increased, the percentage recalled increased, the values being 25, 30, 33, and 39 percent.

Maki and Schuler (1980) also used a search procedure to vary rehearsal duration. A subject was shown a target word on a computer scope for two seconds. Then the word disappeared and a set of eight words appeared. The subject scanned this set for the target word. If no target word was found, a second set of eight words appeared and this set was searched, and so on. The greater the number of sets searched before the target word was found, the greater the rehearsal. After the thirty-two target words had been given, subjects were asked to recall them. In three experiments Maki and Schuler found a positive relationship between rehearsal time and recall.

There have been still other ways of studying the effect of rote rehearsal. For example, Nelson (1977) used an incidental learning procedure wherein the subjects answered a question about each word. The question, which was the same for twenty words, was "Does the word contain an r sound?" Some words occurred once, some twice. Nelson viewed this as being repetition at a shallow or phonemic level, and his primary interest was in the adequacy of the theoretical conception of depth of processing (see Chapter 5). Nelson found that recall was 25 percent after a single repetition and 33 percent after two. He concluded that this shallow processing had a clear effect on memory.

This review should be sufficient to give the flavor of the techniques and results of studies on maintenance rehearsal. We now must ask what we are to make of the results of these experiments.

Evaluation

With regard to the factual outcome of the studies we have reviewed on rote of maintenance rehearsal, it would seem that there are contradictions. Some studies have shown that recall is not related to the amount of maintenance rehearsal. There is, perhaps, a critical matter with respect to the studies reporting this lack of relationship. It is probably not correct to conclude that number of rehearsals is not related to recall when some minimum number of rehearsals produces recall that may be as high as 20 percent. The results of these studies can be more accurately described as showing that recall increases sharply as number of rehearsals increases from zero to some relatively small number (the minimum number used in the experiment). Thus, it is not that rehearsal has no effect; rather, it is that the effect it does have appears in some studies to be primarily restricted to the first few rehearsals.

Rundus (1980), in pondering the seeming contradiction among the results of some of the studies, concluded that perhaps the failure to find an influence of length of maintenance rehearsal occurred because the interval had not been long enough. He therefore increased the intervals up to sixty seconds using the Brown-Peterson technique, in which the subjects rehearse a word during the retention intervals for four-place numbers. For intervals of six, eighteen, thirty-six, and sixty seconds, the corresponding recall values were 13, 18, 23, and 36 percent. Thus, there was a near linear relationship between recall and length of time of maintenance rehearsal.

These results are clearly at odds with the earlier studies reviewed here in that there is no sensible way to extrapolate the results of these earlier studies to predict such high levels of learning for rehearsal intervals of thirty-six and sixty seconds. The reason for this discrepancy across experiments is not apparent; we can only say that under some conditions maintenance rehearsal leads to quite high levels of learning. As will be seen in the next study reviewed, Rundus had earlier produced results more in line with those of previous investigators.

Rundus (1977) used the Brown-Peterson procedure just as in his later study. The wrinkle was that he introduced the same word for rehearsal up to three times. Thus, the word X might be used three different times as the word to be rehearsed to fill the retention interval. The rehearsal time for each presentation was either four, eight, or twelve seconds. We may ask about the recall of words that had been used on only one trial, those that had been used on two trials, and those that had been used on three trials, each time for four, eight, or twelve seconds. The results are plotted in Figure 11.3, and the information there is somewhat surprising. We should note initially that the lower line is for a frequency of one and shows no effect of rehearsal time as this time increases from four to twelve seconds, although 20 percent of the items were correctly recalled as a consequence of four seconds of rehearsal. This lack of a relationship between rehearsal time and recall beyond the initial rapid rise is what had been found by others (using this technique) whose studies were reviewed earlier.

Still referring to Figure 11.3, we see that as frequency increases (where frequency refers to the number of different times that a word was introduced to fill the retention interval), recall increases to as high as 60 percent. We are dealing again with a spacing effect, apparently. More specifically, it would seem that during the first few seconds of maintenance rehearsal, attention begins to attenuate sharply, and the repetition beyond those few seconds adds very little. Essentially the subject may respond by echoing the words. Thus, the present author finds that he can read without too much difficulty while saying a word over and over.

Figure 11.3.

Free recall as a function of the length of time of maintenance rehearsal and as a function of the number of different times an item occurred in maintenance rehearsal ($f = 1, 2, 3$). Data from Table 2 of Rundus (1977).

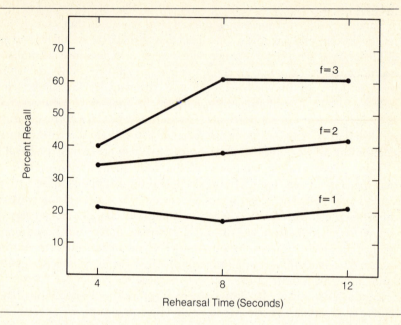

In an earlier chapter we saw that if the experimenter could devise ways to force subjects to make semantic responses to words, these words were learned as well as if the subject had been left to his own devices. Incidental learning was as good as intentional learning. The results we have examined on the recall of individual words in this section have shown that with a great variety of techniques used to produce rote or maintenance rehearsal, some learning occurs incidentally. Rote rehearsal may sometimes produce as much learning as intentional learning, but far more frequently the incidental learning that occurs under rote rehearsal is less than that which would occur with intentional learning, particularly when the materials to be learned have low meaningfulness and are difficult to pronounce. Spacing the rote rehearsal adds a great deal to the amount learned. Thus, while maintenance rehearsal may not be the most effective way to acquire unrelated items, it is a way. For what it is worth, subjects believe that maintenance rehearsal is quite an effective way to learn (Shaugnessy, 1981).

FREE-RECALL LEARNING

The studies we have just reviewed incorporating rehearsal made use of free recall. We concluded that even rote rehearsal can produce an appreciable amount of free-recall learning. That was the first step in trying to answer a more fundamental question, namely, what are the mechanisms by which items are acquired in free recall, whether after rote rehearsal or after rehearsal in which semantic attributes are emphasized.

In an earlier chapter we dealt with free-recall learning when IARs were the central mechanism of interest. In that discussion we never faced the problem posed just above. Rather, we assumed that recall was directly related to the frequency with which an item was rehearsed, and IAR theory was concerned with the ways in which rehearsal frequency differed under the various conditions of an experiment. The question remains as to how our subjects manage to recall any items and how frequency imparts its influence.

From a systematic point of view, the "nice" thing about the paired-associate task is that a cue for each response is provided. Because of stimulus selection and transformations, the nominal stimulus may not always be the functional stimulus, but we do know that our analysis must start with the nominal stimulus term and that the functional stimulus is likely very close at hand. In free-recall learning, such a starting point is not available. Rather, we must try to determine what the stimulus is for an item that is recalled. To hold to such a position would seem to require the assumption that some instigating stimulus is involved for every response that the subject produces. Again, to theorize about free recall would seem to theorize also about the stimuli which produce the responses. Such an approach would try to draw paired-associate learning and free-recall learning closer together. The remarks to be made represent an elaboration of those appearing in an earlier publication (Underwood, 1972a). As background, some data describing relevant aspects of free-recall learning are needed.

Background Facts

Paced Versus Unpaced Recall.   The test phase of free recall may be paced in that a neutral stimulus such as an asterisk or a tone occurs at a constant rate, with the subject being asked to recall a different word each time the stimulus occurs. For the unpaced procedure (which is far more frequently used than is the paced), a given period of time is allowed for the recall of the items. For example, for a paced test for a list of twenty words, the neutral stimulus would occur every two seconds, while with the unpaced test, forty seconds would be allowed for the recall of as many items as possible.

Studies show that the unpaced test generally produces a greater number of correct responses than does the paced test. However, the point to be emphasized here is that the difference between the two methods is relatively small. For example, in a study by McCullers and Haller (1972) in which several variables were manipulated, the paced tests produced 94 percent as many correct responses as did the unpaced test across the three study-test trials. The number of responses that can be produced under the pressure of pacing is only a little less than the number that can be given with an unpaced test where, presumably, the subjects can more easily organize recall.

Output Rate. Given an unpaced test with oral recall, what is the rate at which the words are emitted? Murdock and Okada (1970) measured the time between successive words emitted in oral recall in single-trial free recall. The time between the first few words recalled averaged about one second. They also noted that once ten seconds had passed since the last word was recalled, it was quite unlikely that any more words would be recalled. This rapid spewing of words initially has been noted by many experimenters and is emphasized here. If the subjects are given a long list with unpaced written recall, at the signal to recall the subjects write furiously; it is as if many words all try to come out of the pencil at the same time. These observations, plus the fact of paced versus unpaced recall, do not suggest that the act of free recall is based on any very complicated retrieval schemes when unrelated words are used, and our later comments will build on this idea.

Context Attributes

Context refers to background stimuli for the learning task. This may include the physical background of the room in which the experiment is conducted, the device on which the words are presented, the background on which the words are printed, or even the psychological state (such as the mood) of the subject (Bower, 1981). To determine if a given context is a part of a memory the usual procedure is to learn within a given context and then test in a different context. If performance is poorer with the change than with no change, it is spoken of as a context effect.

There is no doubt that context effects do occur. Perhaps one of the most unusual demonstrations was produced by Godden and Baddeley (1975). The subjects, who were members of a diving club, learned lists of words either underwater or on land. They then were tested for the lists on land and underwater. The data show rather striking differences; performance was better when the testing context was the same as the learning context. Although there are negative studies in the literature, we can say that under many conditions there is evidence for a context effect when recall is involved. What we cannot give are the reasons for the failures. Therefore, at this point we will simply assume that some of the words in a free-recall list become associated with the context, and that this allows for the recall of some of the words. There is no basis for trying to identify the context beyond that which is meant when we say the learning environment.

The context may be thought of as A, and to this stimulus a number of words may become associated. At first glance this might appear to be an interference paradigm in which the words are B, C, D, and so on. However, there is no interference in a within-list A-B, A-D paradigm (e.g., Bruce & Weaver, 1973), because there is no need to discriminate between the two response terms. Both response terms are correct in a within-list recall. In the previous chapter we saw that two free-recall lists of unrelated words given in a retroactive inhibition paradigm produced substantial interference. This may be attributed to the fact that items in successive lists become associated to the same context (at least in part), thus producing competition at the time of recall. Such a position has been stated by a number of investigators.

What is proposed, then, is that some of the words in a free-recall list become associated with the context. Under such conditions it would be anticipated that the words would be emitted rapidly because there is no search needed for independent cues for each response term. The subjects spew out the words.

As might have been inferred from some of the previous comments, context is not a happy concept to use if analysis is the goal, but we seem to need it in spite of its all-encompassing nature. In a paired-associate list each stimulus term might be thought of as the context for its response term. Further, it would not seem unreasonable to suppose that the stimulus terms dominate other contexts such as differences in the physical characteristics of the learning environment. In line with this notion is the finding that physical-context effects are absent or minimal in magnitude in a retroactive interference paradigm using paired-associates (Strand, 1970). In at least one case, memory for paired-associates did reflect associations between the task and the physical environment (Smith, Glenberg, & Bjork, 1978). Nevertheless, it seems worthwhile to assume that context effects are less likely to be found with paired associates than with free-recall lists.

In a study by Brown and Underwood (1974), the subjects were presented a thirty-six-pair list. The stimulus terms were three-letter words, the response terms concrete, two-syllable nouns. The independent variable was the number of different stimulus terms in the list, which ranged from one to thirty-six. Thus, at one extreme all thirty-six response terms had the same stimulus term, and at the other extreme, each response term had a unique stimulus term. The repeated stimulus terms were blocked. For example, when there were three different stimulus terms, the first twelve pairs had stimulus term X, the next twelve pairs stimulus term Y, and last twelve, term Z. This list was viewed as having three contexts, a different context for each stimulus term. By means that will not be reviewed here, subjects were required to associate the stimulus terms with the response terms, even though they were instructed that for some tests they would only have to recall the response terms.

In this experiment, in which stimulus terms are viewed as context stimuli, the subjects had to recall the context if they were to produce the response terms to it. The fewer the number of stimulus terms, the greater the probability of stimulus recall—hence, the greater the likelihood of response recall. The results conformed to this expectation, although the data were somewhat disorderly. With only one stimulus term (constant context throughout), nearly 30 percent of the response terms were recalled; when there were thirty-six stimulus terms (context change on every pair), about 18 percent of the response terms were recalled. Thus, it would appear that a constant context can provide a stable cue for free recall, and that is the supposition we are making. To repeat the overall assumption, some of the items in a free-recall list are recalled because they are associated with the context. These tumble out very rapidly at recall because they do not depend upon unique cues.

Interitem Associations

Slamecka (1968) carried out an unusual study using free recall. After having the subjects study a list, he gave the subjects in an E Group half the items and asked them to recall the remaining half. The subjects in a C Group were asked to recall all of the words. It would seem that if free recall associations are formed between items during the study phase, the recall of the E Group for the remaining half of the items would be better than that for the C Group. Certainly, it would seem that some of the items given the E Group would be associated with those not given, resulting in elevated recall as compared with the C Group. Slamecka did not find this. The E Group actually recalled a little less than the C Group.

Slamecka's results have sometimes been interpreted to mean that interitem associations are not formed in free recall. Such a conclusion is probably not warranted. We have seen that if pairs of words that are normatively associated are placed in a list, performance is better than if unrelated words are used. Of course, the critical test is to show that interitem associations develop between words on study and test trials when the words are unrelated initially. Evidence of a positive nature would be the order of recall of the so-called unrelated words becoming nonrandom as trials continue; this could indicate a form of subjective organization that may be based on ease of learning interitem associations. Tulving (1962) did in fact demonstrate that the order of recall of unrelated words becomes stable over trials.

Tulving did more than simply show stable recall protocols. In a further study (1965) he had subjects learn sixteen-item lists of unrelated words which other subjects had previously learned. From these previous subjects he identified two output orders. One of the orders was said to indicate high organization in that each word had followed the preceding word with relatively high frequency in the output. Similarly, in an order indicating low organization, successive words had followed each other infrequently in the output. These two lists (consisting of the same words and differing only in order) were given as serial lists to further groups of subjects. The group given the high-organization list required 8.2 trials to learn, the one given the low-organization list required 13.2 trials. Upon examination of the high list, it seems apparent that there are at best few pre-established associations between the successive words: *drumlin, pomade, quillet, hoyden, maxim, issue, accent, treason, barrack, office, finding, walker, garden, valley, lagoon, jungle.* Rather, it must be that the order of the words is such that new associations are relatively easily established as compared with the low list: *valley, issue, walker, accent, office, drumlin, jungle, quillet, lagoon, pomade, garden, maxim, treason, hoyden, finding, barrack.*

Relationships between successive items in a list may be quite subtle and still have an influence on the rate at which associations will be established. A study by Baddeley (1961) illustrates this point. Baddeley gave his subjects a list of paired associates to learn, the items all being CVCs. For some of the pairs the first letter of the response term was one which follows the last letter of the stimulus term with high probability as gauged by the frequency with which the two letters occur in that order in words. For other pairs the probability was low. For example, the pair QEM-POG was considered a high-probability pair because P follows M quite frequently in words. On the other hand, a pair such as ROG-QUT was considered a low-probability pair because G is followed by Q very infrequently in words. It was found that learning was more rapid for the first type of pairs than for the second type. It is highly unlikely that the subjects were aware of the reason why the pairs differed in difficulty; i.e., the differences in the pairs were subtle.

A great deal of learning takes place on test trials in free-recall learning. Indeed, given that there has been one study trial, test trials are almost as good as further study trials (e.g., Donaldson, 1971). It seems likely that test trials are effective because interitem associations may be formed during the test trials as well as during the study trials. As Wallace (1970) has argued, test trials allow items to become contiguous, attempting to recall may produce mental contiguity of items, and so on. The number of such effective associations would be minimal (although not absent) on the early trials, and would increase as trials continued. When recall becomes completely stable, it would appear that the subjects have essentially formed a serial list out of the free-recall list, probably mediated by the associations between items. At the same time, the dependence upon context has probably decreased.

In an earlier chapter evidence was given to show that serial learning usually does not involve the establishment of item-to-item associations. It might seem, therefore, that if a free-recall list becomes a serial list as trials proceed, such learning too would not consist of item-to-item associations. Two comments will be made about this apparent contradiction. First, there is evidence that item-to-item associations can occur in serial learning. Thus, if a paired-associate list is learned, and then the pairs are placed in serial order, learning of the serial list is markedly facilitated. Second, studies that have investigated transfer from free-recall learning to paired-associate learning, and the reverse, give every indication that interitem associations are involved in free-recall learning (Postman, 1971). If a free-recall list is learned and then the words are paired randomly to produce a paired-associate list, the learning of the paired-associate list will be inhibited. Apparently, the associations developed in free-recall learning interfere with the acquisition of the pairs. The reverse procedure produces positive transfer. That is, if after learning a paired-associate list the items are randomized in a free-recall list, performance on the free-recall list will be facilitated. Thus, going from a free-recall task to a paired-associate task made up of the items from the free-recall list produces negative transfer; the reverse order produces positive transfer. This is precisely what would be expected if interitem associations are formed during free-recall learning.

Other Possible Cues

We must consider the possibility that words in a free-recall list may be cued by other words outside the list. We know this happens when categorized lists are used so that the category name may serve as a cue. Furthermore, as Mandler (1967) has shown in a number of studies, subjects can sort a group of so-called unrelated words into categories of their own choosing. Whatever the category designations are, they could serve as retrieval cues. Children may categorize words that to the adult are not obvious members of the same category. Thus, a child may put a *clock* and a *house* together because a clock is found in a house. The point is that we must not sharply restrict the notion of what does and does not constitute a category, thereby restricting too sharply the range of possible cues which may be functioning in free recall.

There is no reason not to believe that words in a list also produce noncategory IARs and that these IARs have a potential to serve as cues for the recall of the words that produced them. Suppose, for example, a word in the free-recall list is *up* and the IAR "down" occurs. Perhaps at recall the subjects remember that a word in the list made them think of *down*. Therefore, they may generate responses (other words) to *down* and trust to recognition to tell which one was in the study list. This basic idea is often spoken of as the generate-recognize model (Watkins & Gardiner, 1979).

How does one test such a notion? One possibility, of course, is to give the subject various kinds of cues at recall and see if performance is aided. There have been a large number of such studies, but none have clearly told us what happens when the subjects are left to their own devices. There are also certain systematic issues that have never been resolved. For example, why should a subject remember an IAR and not the word that produced it?

Whatever the answer, we must hold open the possibility that noncategory IARs may cue the recall of some words.

Position of a word in a list very likely serves as a cue, and this cue should not be lumped with context. The position cues may be particularly important in single-trial free recall. The cue might be "beginning of the list" or "near end of list." There is evidence to show that subjects do use the first few items in a list as a rehearsal group and that these items receive more rehearsals than any others in the list (Rundus & Atkinson, 1970). Undoubtedly the primacy effect is due to this rehearsal.

The speculations about free recall have led to the conclusion that four types of stimuli are involved in the associations that presumably mediate free recall: context; interitem associations; IARs to words in the list, particularly conceptual IARs; and finally, the position held by an item in the list. The free-recall task is viewed as a paired-associate task in which the stimulus terms come from varying classes.

SUMMARY

The emphasis in this chapter on contiguity, rehearsal, and free-recall learning by no means exhausts the topics that could be called basic. If we asked other investigators for their opinions as to what constitute basic questions, without doubt the list would become very long. Consequently, this chapter cannot pretend to be representative, and certainly it is not complete. Some writers have a limit on the amount of speculation they can tolerate.

The critical question asked in this chapter concerned basic mechanisms of associative learning. It was concluded that contiguity is a necessary condition for learning and that in most situations it is a sufficient condition. Data do not allow this latter conclusion to be firm, but if one thinks about what would happen if associations were not limited by a law of contiguity, it becomes clear that contiguity is of fundamental importance in the formation of associations.

Free recall poses special interpretative problems because of the lack of control over potential stimulus units that evoke the responses at recall. The study of rote or maintenance rehearsal is judged basic to the understanding of free recall, and thus the literature on such rehearsal was evaluated. It was discovered that rote rehearsal has a surprisingly large influence on learning, particularly when the rehearsal is spaced.

Given the above, the problem of free recall revolves around the identification of the stimuli that are contiguous with the rehearsals. It was concluded that context stimuli formed associations with list items, that interitem associations evolve, that category names and other IARs may cue words in the list, and that position and items may become associated. Thus, four sources of stimuli were identified as being of importance for the free-recall learning of unrelated items.

EPILOGUE

As this book ends it might be useful to provide some general comments about theory and about the area of research covered. At various points throughout the text, we have noted the differences between recall and recognition. These differences were reflected in the theoretical approaches taken here. Recognition decisions have been explained as being due primarily to the frequency attribute, with phenomenal frequency differences in events being critical to the decisions. The frequency attribute is assumed to play only a minor role in the mastery of associative learning tasks as these tasks were described in Chapter 3. Of course, subjects must recognize the stimulus terms in a paired-associate list before correct responses can be given to them. Furthermore, the fact that intrusions are relatively rare in learning lists of unrelated words can be attributed to differences in the situational frequency for the words in the list and those not in the list. Associative learning between words, on the other hand, was assumed to have little role to play in recognition decisions.

It was proposed that associations between words develop as a consequence of the temporal contiguity of the verbal units. Free-recall learning was treated as a special case of paired-associate learning in which the critical explanatory problem was that of identifying the cues for recall. To make these statements is not to say that mnemonics have no role in associative learning. Rather, we have sought to emphasize the pre-mnemonic stage of associative learning. However, IAR theory assumed the presence of preestablished associations and that words in a learning task may produce associates implicitly as a result. Several different phenomena in different kinds of tasks seem to be encompassed by this type of theory.

Although serial learning was classed as an associative-learning task, this expressed a long-term faith that is probably not justified by the evidence. It is an irony that we know so little about the underpinnings of serial learning when this was the task developed by Ebbinghaus when he opened up the area of research a hundred years ago. Someone will soon bring a new approach to serial learning that will serve to refresh it. Whether with verbal or nonverbal tasks, sequential responding is a very important part of human behavior.

There are a number of unsolved problems at various levels of discourse. Some of these were pointed out at various places in the text. Perhaps the most disturbing of these has to do with forgetting. A relatively few years ago it seemed that a fairly comprehensive theoretical account of forgetting was close at hand, but that has slipped away. Some investigators have lost confidence in interference as a major cause of forgetting, but none of the proposed replacements thus far has created a feeling that things are on a productive new track. But that will surely come.

The above comments were not intended to reflect discouragement about the rate of development of knowledge in the area covered in the text.

How do we know whether our progress over the years has been slow, fast, or reasonable? If this book should be revised ten years from now it will beyond doubt show that our empirical facts of today have been sharpened and expanded, that some of the intractable puzzles of the present have been made tractable, and that our theories have become more comprehensive than they are currently. The cumulative nature of any experimental discipline must necessarily lead to the identification of such changes as representing steady progress.

References

Adams, J. A., Marshall, P. H., & Bray, N. W. Closed-loop theory and long-term retention. *Journal of Experimental Psychology*, 1971, *90*, 242–50.

Anderson, J. R. Interference: The relationship between response latency and response accuracy. *Journal of Experimental Psychology: Human Learning and Memory*, 1981, *7*, 326–43.

Anderson, R. C., & Myrow, D. L. Retroactive inhibition of meaningful discourse. *Journal of Educational Psychology Monograph*, 1971, *62*, 81–94.

Arkes, H. R., Schumacher, G. M., & Gardner, E. T. Effects of orienting tasks on the retention of prose material. *Journal of Educational Psychology*, 1976, *68*, 536–45.

Bach, M. J. Implicit response frequency and recognition memory over time. *Journal of Experimental Psychology*, 1974, *103*, 675–79.

Baddeley, A. D. Stimulus-response compatibility in the paired-associate learning of nonsense syllables. *Nature*, 1961, *191*, 1327–28.

Baddeley, A. D. The trouble with levels: A reexamination of Craik and Lockhart's framework for memory research. *Psychological Review*, 1978, *85*, 139–52.

Baddeley, A. D., & Hull, A. Prefix and suffix effects: Do they have a common basis? *Journal of Verbal Learning and Verbal Behavior*, 1979, *18*, 129–40.

Bahrick, H. P. Maintenance of knowledge: Questions about memory we forgot to ask. *Journal of Experimental Psychology: General*, 1979, *108*, 296–308.

Bahrick, H. P., Bahrick P. O., & Wittlinger, R. P. Fifty years of memory for names and faces: A cross-sectional approach. *Journal of Experimental Psychology: General*, 1975, *104*, 54–75.

Barnes, J. M., & Underwood, B. J. "Fate" of first-list associations in transfer theory. *Journal of Experimental Psychology*, 1959, *58*, 97–105.

Battig, W. F. Procedural problems in paired-associate learning research. *Psychonomic Monograph Supplements*, 1965, *1*, No. 1.

Battig, W. F., & Montague, W. E. Category norms for verbal items in 56 categories: A replication and extension of the Connecticut category norms. *Journal of Experimental Psychology Monograph*, 1969, *80* (3, Pt. 2).

Berkowitz, J. Verbal discrimination learning as a function of experimental frequency. *Psychonomic Science*, 1968, *13*, 97–98.

Björgen, I. A. *A re-evaluation of rote learning.* Universitetsforlaget, 1964.

Bloom, B. S. Time and learning. *American Psychologist*, 1974, *29*, 682–88.

Blumenthal, G. B., & Robbins, D. Delayed release from proactive interference with meaningful material: How much do we remember after reading brief prose passages? *Journal of Experimental Psychology: Human Learning and Memory*, 1977, *3*, 754–61.

Boulay, E. A., & Underwood, B. J. Simultaneous paired associate and verbal discrimination learning as a simulation of the double-function list. *Memory & Cognition*, 1976, 4, 298–301.

Bower, G. H. Interference paradigms for meaningful propositional memory. *American Journal of Psychology*, 1978, *91*, 575–85.

Bower, G. H. Mood and memory. *American Psychologist*, 1981, *36*, 129–48.

Bower, G. H., & Winzenz, D. Group structure, coding, and memory for digit series. *Journal of Experimental Psychology Monograph*, 1969, *80*, (2, Pt. 2).

Brewer, C. L. Presentation time, trials to criterion, and total time in verbal learning. *Journal of Experimental Psychology*, 1967, *73*, 159–62.

Brown, A. S. Catalog of scaled verbal material. *Memory & Cognition Supplement*, 1976, 4, 1–45.

Brown, A. S., & Underwood, B. J. Verbal context shifts and free recall. *Journal of Experimental Psychology*, 1974, *102*, 133–41.

Brown, J. Some tests of the decay theory of immediate memory. *Quarterly Journal of Experimental Psychology*, 1958, *10*, 12–21.

Brown, J. *Recall and recognition.* New York: Wiley, 1976.

Brown W. P., & Atkinson, J. T. O. Categories, subcategories, and the attenuation of proactive inhibition in free recall. *Memory & Cognition*, 1974, 2, 127–29.

Bruce, D., & Weaver, G. E. Retroactive facilitation in short-term retention of minimally learned paired associates. *Journal of Experimental Psychology*, 1973, *100*, 9–17.

Bugelski, B. R., & Rickwood, J. Presentation time, total time, and mediation in paired-associate learning: Self pacing. *Journal of Experimental Psychology*, 1963, *65*, 616–617.

Butter, M. J. Differential recall of paired associates as a function of arousal and concreteness-imagery levels. *Journal of Experimental Psychology*, 1970, *84*, 252–56.

Calfee, R. C., & Anderson, R. Presentation rate effects in paired-associate learning. *Journal of Experimental Psychology*, 1971, *88*, 239–45.

Cermak, L. S., & Craik, F. I. M. *Levels of processing in human memory*. Hillsdale, N.J.: Erlbaum Associates, 1979.

Cofer, C. N. Learning of content and function words in nonsense syllable frames: A repetition and extension of Glanzer's experiment. *Journal of Verbal Learning and Verbal Behavior*, 1967, *6*, 198–202.

Cofer, C. N., Bruce, D. R., & Reicher, G. M. Clustering in free recall as a function of certain methodological variations. *Journal of Experimental Psychology*, 1966, *71*, 858–66.

Cohen, R. L. Recency effects in long-term recall and recognition. *Journal of Verbal Learning and Verbal Behavior*, 1970, *9*, 672–78.

Conrad, R. Very brief delay of immediate recall. *Quarterly Journal of Experimental Psychology*, 1960, *12*, 45–47.

Cooper, E. H., & Pantle, A. J. The total-time hypothesis in verbal learning. *Psychological Bulletin*, 1967, *68*, 221–34.

Craik, F. I. M., & Lockhart, R. S. Levels of processing: A framework for memory research. *Journal of Verbal Learning and Verbal Behavior*, 1972, *11*, 671–84.

Craik, F. I. M., & Tulving, E. Depth of processing and the retention of words in episodic memory. *Journal of Experimental Psychology: General*, 1975, *104*, 268–94.

Craik, F. I. M., & Watkins, M. J. The role of rehearsal in short-term memory. *Journal of Verbal Learning and Verbal Behavior*, 1973, *12*, 599–607.

Cramer, P. *Word association*. New York: Academic Press, 1968.

Crouse, J. H. Retroactive interference in reading prose materials. *Journal of Educational Psychology*, 1971, *62*, 39–44.

DaPolito, F., Barker, D., & Wiant, J. The effect of contextual changes on component recognition. *American Journal of Psychology*, 1972, *85*, 431–40.

Darley, C. F., & Glass, A. L. Effects of rehearsal and serial list position on recall. *Journal of Experimental Psychology: Human Learning & Memory*, 1975, *104*, 453–58.

Deese, J. On the prediction of occurrence of particular verbal intrusions in immediate recall. *Journal of Experimental Psychology*, 1959, *58*, 17–22.

Deffenbacher, K. A., Platt, G. J., & Williams, M. A. Differential recall as a function of socially induced arousal and retention interval. *Journal of Experimental Psychology*, 1974, *103*, 809–11.

Deichmann, J. W., Minnigerode, F. A., & Kausler, D. H. Selection strategies and reversal-non-reversal shifts in verbal discrimination transfer. *Psychonomic Science*, 1970, *18*, 209–10.

Donaldson, W. Output effects in multitrial free recall. *Journal of Verbal Learning and Verbal Behavior*, 1971, *10*, 577–85.

Doten, G. W. The effects of rest periods on interference of a well-established habit. *Journal of Experimental Psychology*, 1955, *49*, 401–406.

Drewnowski, A. Attributes and priorities in short-term recall: A new model of memory span. *Journal of Experimental Psychology: General*, 1980, *109*, 208–50.

Duncan, C. P. Retrieval of low-frequency words from mixed lists. *Bulletin of the Psychonomic Society*, 1974, 4, 137–38.

Eckert, E., & Kanak, N. J. Verbal discrimination learning: A review of the acquisition, transfer, and retention literature through 1972. *Psychological Bulletin*, 1974, 81, 582–607.

Ekstrand, B. R., & Underwood B. J. Paced versus unpaced recall in free learning. *Journal of Verbal Learning and Verbal Behavior*, 1963, 2, 288–90.

Ekstrand, B. R., Wallace, W. P., & Underwood, B. J. A frequency theory of verbal-discrimination learning. *Psychological Review*, 1966, 73, 566–78.

Ellis, H. C., & Shaffer, R. W. Stimulus encoding and the transfer of stimulus differentiation. *Journal of Verbal Learning and Verbal Behavior*, 1974, 13, 393–400.

Epstein, W. Retention of sentences, anomalous sequences, and random sequences. *American Journal of Psychology*, 1972, 85, 21–30.

Epstein, W., Rock, I., & Zuckerman, C. B. Meaning and familiarity in associative learning. *Psychological Monographs*, 1960, 74 (4, Whole No. 491).

Finkenbinder, E. O. The course of forgetting. *American Journal of Psychology*, 1913, 24, 8–32.

Forrester, W. E. Distributed practice and retroactive inhibition in a minimal paired-associates task. *Journal of Verbal Learning and Verbal Behavior*, 1969, 8, 713–18.

Forrester, W. E., & Spear, N. E. Sound coding in verbal learning with and without restrictions on decoding. *Psychonomic Science*, 1969, 17, 91–92.

Galbraith, R. C. On the independence of attributes of memory. *Journal of Experimental Psychology: Human Learning & Memory*, 1975, 1, 23–30.

Galbraith, R. C., & Underwood, B. J. Perceived frequency of concrete and abstract words. *Memory & Cognition*, 1973, 1, 56–60.

Gardiner, J. M., & Cameron, P. C. Change in speaker's voice and release from proactive inhibition. *Journal of Experimental Psychology*, 1974, 102, 863–67.

Ghatala, E. S., & Levin, J. R. Phenomenal background frequency and the concreteness/imagery effect in verbal discrimination learning. *Memory & Cognition*, 1976, 4, 302–306.

Ghatala, E. S., Levin, J. R., & Subkoviak, M. J. Rehearsal strategy effects in children's discrimination learning: Confronting the crucible. *Journal of Verbal Learning and Verbal Behavior*, 1975, 14, 398–407.

Glenberg, A. M. Component-levels theory of the effects of spacing of repetitions on recall and recognition. *Memory & Cognition*, 1979, 7, 95–112.

Glenberg, A. M., & Adams, F. Type I rehearsal and recognition. *Journal of Verbal Learning and Verbal Behavior*, 1978, 17, 455–463.

Glenberg, A. M., & Bradley, M. M. Mental contiguity. *Journal of Experimental Psychology: Human Learning and Memory*, 1979, 5, 88–97.

Glenberg, A. M., Smith, S. M., & Green, C. Type I rehearsal: Maintenance and more. *Journal of Verbal Learning and Verbal Behavior*, 1977, *16*, 339–52.

Godden, D. R., & Baddeley, A. D. Context-dependent memory in two natural environments: On land and underwater. *British Journal of Psychology*, 1975, *66*, 325–31.

Goedel, G. D., & Englert, J. A. The imagery effect and phenomenal background frequency in verbal discrimination learning. *Memory & Cognition*, 1978, *6*, 209–16.

Goggin, J. P. Storage differences between pictures and words. In L. S. Cermak (Ed.), *Human memory and amnesia*. Hillsdale, N.J.: Erlbaum Associates, 1982.

Goulet, L. R., & Barclay, A. Comparison of paired-associate transfer effects between the A-B, C-A and A-B, B-C paradigms. *Journal of Experimental Psychology*, 1965, *70*, 537–39.

Green, D. M., & Swets, J. A. *Signal detection theory and psychophysics*. New York: Wiley, 1966.

Green, R. L., & Schwartz, M. Class of initial letter as a cue to correctness in verbal discrimination. *Bulletin of the Psychonomic Society*, 1976, *7*, 481–82.

Greenberg, R., & Underwood, B. J. Retention as a function of stage of practice. *Journal of Experimental Psychology*, 1950, *40*, 452–57.

Greitzer, F. L. Intracategory rehearsal in list learning. *Journal of Verbal Learning and Verbal Behavior*, 1976, *15*, 641–54.

Gunter, B., Clifford, B. R., & Berry, C. Release from proactive interference with television news items: Evidence for encoding dimensions within televised news. *Journal of Experimental Psychology: Human Learning & Memory*, 1980, *6*, 216–23.

Hall, J. W., & Kozloff, E. E. False recognitions as a function of number of presentations. *American Journal of Psychology*, 1970, *83*, 272–79.

Hall, J. W., & Pierce, J. W. Recognition and recall by children and adults as a function of variations in memory encoding instructions. *Memory & Cognition*, 1974, *2*, 585–90.

Harris, G., Begg, I., & Mitterer, J. On the relation between frequency estimates and recognition memory. *Memory & Cognition*, 1980, *8*, 99–104.

Harris, R. L., Gausepohl, J., Lewis, R. J., & Spoehr, K. T. The suffix effect: Post-categorical attributes in a serial recall paradigm. *Bulletin of the Psychonomic Society*, 1979, *13*, 35–37.

Hasher, L., & Zacks, R. T. Automatic and effortful processes in memory. *Journal of Experimental Psychology: General*, 1979, *108*, 356–88.

Heckelman, S. B., & Spear, N. E. Effect of interitem similarity on free learning by children. *Journal of Verbal Learning and Verbal Behavior*, 1967, *6*, 448–50.

Hess, J. L., & Simon S. Extra-list intrusions in immediate free recall as a function of associative strength in children. *Psychological Reports*, 1964, *14*, 92.

Hicks, R. E., & Young, R. K. Part-whole list transfer in free recall: A reappraisal. *Journal of Experimental Psychology*, 1972, *96*, 328–33.

Hinrichs, J. V., & Mewaldt, S. P. The Ranschburg effect: Modification of guessing strategies by context. *Bulletin of the Psychonomic Society*, 1977, *9*, 85–88.

Hintzman, D. L. Effects of repetition and exposure duration on memory. *Journal of Experimental Psychology*, 1970, *83*, 435–44.

Hintzman, D. L. Theoretical implications of the spacing effect. In R. L. Solso (Ed.), *Theories in cognitive psychology: The Loyola symposium*. Hillsdale, N.J.: Erlbaum, 1974.

Hintzman, D. L., Block, R. A., & Inskeep, N. R. Memory for mode of input. *Journal of Verbal Learning and Verbal Behavior*, 1972, *11*, 741–49.

Hopkins, R. H., & Epling, W. F. Pronunciation and the length of the study interval in verbal discrimination. *Journal of Experimental Psychology*, 1971, *88*, 145–46.

Howell, W. C. Representation of frequency in memory. *Psychological Bulletin*, 1973, *80*, 44–53.

Hunt, R. R., & Elliott, J. M. The role of nonsemantic information in memory: Orthographic distinctiveness effects on retention. *Journal of Experimental Psychology: General*, 1980, *109*, 49–74.

Hunt, R. R., Elliott, J. M., & Spence, M. J. Independent effects of process and structure on encoding. *Journal of Experimental Psychology: Human Learning and Memory*, 1979, *5*, 339–47.

Hunt, R. R., & Ellis, H. C. Recognition memory and degree of semantic contextual change. *Journal of Experimental Psychology*, 1974, *103*, 1153–59.

Hyde, T. S., & Jenkins, J. J. Recall for words as a function of semantic, graphic, and syntactic orienting tasks. *Journal of Verbal Learning and Verbal Behavior*, 1973, *12*, 471–80.

Ingison, L. J., & Ekstrand, B. R. Effects of study time, method of presentation, word frequency, and word abstractness on verbal discrimination learning. *Journal of Experimental Psychology*, 1970, *85*, 249–54.

Izawa, C. Massed and spaced practice in paired-associate learning: List versus item distributions. *Journal of Experimental Psychology*, 1971, *89*, 10–21.

Jacoby, L. L., Bartz, W. H., & Evans, J. D. A functional approach to levels of processing. *Journal of Experimental Psychology: Human Learning and Memory*, 1978, *4*, 331–46.

Jahnke, J. C. The Ranschburg effect. *Psychological Review*, 1969, *76*, 592–605.

Jahnke, J. C. The effects of intraserial and interserial repetition on recall. *Journal of Verbal Learning and Verbal Behavior*, 1972, *11*, 706–16.

Jahnke, J. C. Restrictions on the Ranschburg effect. *Journal of Experimental Psychology*, 1974, *103*, 183–85.

Jahnke, J. C. Stimulus and response prefixes interfere differentially with short-term recall. *Journal of Experimental Psychology: Human Learning and Memory*, 1975, *1*, 727–32.

Jenkins, J. J., Mink, W. D., & Russell, W. A. Associative clustering as a function of verbal association strength. *Psychological Reports*, 1958, *4*, 127–36.

Johnson, L. M. Similarity of meaning as a factor in retroactive inhibition. *Journal of General Psychology*, 1933, *9*, 377–89.

Johnson, M. K., Raye, C. L., Wang, A. Y., & Taylor, T. H. Fact and fantasy: The roles of accuracy and variability in confusing imaginations with perceptual experiences. *Journal of Experimental Psychology: Human Learning and Memory*, 1979, *5*, 229–40.

Jung, J. Effects of response meaningfulness (*m*) on transfer of training under two different paradigms. *Journal of Experimental Psychology*, 1963, *65*, 377–84.

Kasschau, R. A., & Pollio, H. R. Response transfer mediated by meaningfully similar and associated stimuli using a separate-lists design. *Journal of Experimental Psychology*, 1967, *74*, 146–48.

Kausler, D. H. Orthographic distinctiveness of homonyms and the feature-tagging hypothesis. *American Journal of Psychology*, 1973, *86*, 141–49.

Kausler, D. H., & Boka, J. A. Effects of double functioning on verbal discrimination learning. *Journal of Experimental Psychology*, 1968, *76*, 558–67.

Kausler, D. H., Erber, J. T., & Olson, G. A. Taxonomic instances as right or wrong items and selection strategies in verbal-discrimination learning. *American Journal of Psychology*, 1970, *83*, 428–35.

Kausler, D. H., & Farzanegan, F. Word frequency and selection strategies in verbal-discrimination learning. *Journal of Verbal Learning and Verbal Behavior*, 1969, *8*, 196–201.

Kausler, D. H., & Olson, R. D. Homonyms as items in verbal discrimination learning and transfer. *Journal of Experimental Psychology*, 1969, *82*, 136–42.

Kausler, D. H., Wright, R. E., & Bradshaw, G. L. Effects of imagery on individual item identifications and frequency judgments in multiple-item recognition learning. *Journal of Experimental Psychology: Human Learning and Memory*, 1979, *5*, 135–50.

Keppel, G. A reconsideration of the extinction-recovery theory. *Journal of Verbal Learning and Verbal Behavior*, 1967, *6*, 476–86.

Keppel, G., Postman, L., & Zavortink, B. Studies of learning to learn: VIII. The influence of massive amounts of training upon the learning and retention of paired-associate lists. *Journal of Verbal Learning and Verbal Behavior*, 1968, *7*, 790–96.

Kintsch, W. An experimental analysis of single stimulus tests and multiple-choice tests of recognition memory. *Journal of Experimental Psychology*, 1968, *76*, 1–6.

Kucera, H., & Francis, W. N. *Computational analysis of present-day American English*. Providence: Brown University Press, 1967.

Lachar, B., & Goggin, J. Effects of changes in word length on proactive interference in short-term memory. *Psychonomic Science*, 1969, *17*, 213–14.

Landauer, T. K., & Ross, B. H. Can simple instructions to use spaced practice improve ability to remember a fact?: An experimental test using telephone numbers. *Bulletin of the Psychonomic Society*, 1977, *10*, 215–18.

LaPorte, R., & Voss, J. F. Nonspecific transfer as a function of number of lists acquired and criterion of learning. *American Journal of Psychology*, 1974, *87*, 463–74.

LaPorte, R., Voss, J. F., & Bisanz, G. Nonspecific transfer with and without test trials on the first list. *American Journal of Psychology*, 1974, *87*, 475–79.

Laurence, M. W. Role of homophones in transfer learning. *Journal of Experimental Psychology*, 1970, *86*, 1–7.

Lee, C. L. Short-term recall of repeated items and detection of repetitions in letter sequences. *Journal of Experimental Psychology: Human Learning and Memory*, 1976, *2*, 120–27.

Levy, C. M., & Jowaisas, D. Short-term memory: Storage interference or storage decay? *Journal of Experimental Psychology*, 1971, *88*, 189–95.

Light, L. L., & Carter-Sobell, L. Effects of changed semantic context on recognition memory. *Journal of Verbal Learning and Verbal Behavior*, 1970, *9*, 1–11.

Light, L. L., & Schurr, S. C. Context effects in recognition memory: Item order and unitization. *Journal of Experimental Psychology*, 1973, *100*, 135–40.

Loftus, E. F., & Loftus, G. R. On the permanence of stored information in the human brain. *American Psychologist*, 1980, *35*, 409–20.

Long, D., & Allen, G. A. Relative effects of acoustic and semantic relatedness on clustering in free recall. *Bulletin of the Psychonomic Society*, 1973, *1*, 316–18.

Lovelace, E. A., & Pulley, S. J. Verbal-discrimination learning: Familiarization of common and uncommon words. *Canadian Journal of Psychology*, 1972, *26*, 97–105.

Lupker, S. J. The semantic nature of response competition in the picture-word interference task. *Memory & Cognition*, 1979, *7*, 485–95.

Lutz, W. J., & Scheirer, C. J. Coding processes for pictures and words. *Journal of Verbal Learning and Verbal Behavior*, 1974, *13*, 316–20.

Maki, R. H., & Hasher, L. Encoding variability: A role in immediate and long-term memory? *American Journal of Psychology*, 1975, *88*, 217–31.

Maki, R. H., & Schuler, J. Effects of rehearsal duration and level of processing on memory for words. *Journal of Verbal Learning and Verbal Behavior*, 1980, *19*, 36–45.

Mandler, G. Organization and memory. In K. W. Spence & J. T. Spence (Eds.), *The psychology of learning and motivation* (Vol. 1). New York: Academic Press, 1967.

Mandler, G. Recognizing: The judgment of previous occurrence. *Psychological Review*, 1980, *87*, 252–71.

Marshall, J. F., Rouse, R. O., Jr., & Tarpy, R. M. Acoustic versus associative models of short-term memory coding. *Psychonomic Science*, 1969, *14*, 54–55.

Martin, E., & Melton, A. W. Meaningfulness and trigram recognition. *Journal of Verbal Learning and Verbal Behavior*, 1970, *9*, 126–35.

Maskarinec, A. S., & Thompson, C. P. The within-list distributed practice effect: Tests of the varied context and varied encoding hypotheses. *Memory & Cognition*, 1976, *4*, 741–46.

Matthews, W. A. Continued word associations and free recall. *Quarterly Journal of Experimental Psychology*, 1966, *18*, 31–38.

Mayhew, A. J. Interlist changes in subjective organization during free-recall learning. *Journal of Experimental Psychology*, 1967, *74*, 425–30.

McCullers, J. C., & Haller, J. Another look at paced versus unpaced recall in free learning. *Journal of Experimental Psychology*, 1972, *92*, 439–40.

McFarland, C. E., Jr., Rhodes, D. D., & Frey, T. J. Semantic-feature variability and the spacing effect. *Journal of Verbal Learning and Verbal Behavior*, 1979, *18*, 163–72.

McGeoch, J. A. Forgetting and the law of disuse. *Psychological Review*, 1932, *39*, 352–70.

McNulty, J. A. Short-term retention as a function of method of measurement, recording time, and meaningfulness of the material. *Canadian Journal of Psychology*, 1965, *19*, 188–96.

Mechanic, A. The responses involved in the rote learning of verbal materials. *Journal of Verbal Learning and Verbal Behavior*, 1964, *3*, 30–36.

Melton, A. W. Repetition and retrieval from memory. *Science*, 1967, *158*, 532.

Melton, A. W., & Irwin, J. McQ. The influence of degree of interpolated learning on retroactive inhibition and the overt transfer of specific responses. *American Journal of Psychology*, 1940, *53*, 173–203.

Meunier, G. F., Kestner, J., Meunier, J. A., & Ritz, D. Overt rehearsal and long-term retention. *Journal of Experimental Psychology*, 1974, *102*, 913–14.

Mewaldt, S. P., & Hinrichs, J. V. Repetition and inference in short-term memory. *Journal of Experimental Psychology: Human Learning and Memory*, 1977, *3*, 572–81.

Meyer, D. R., & Miles, R. C. Intralist-interlist relations in verbal learning. *Journal of Experimental Psychology*, 1953, *45*, 109–15.

Moates, D. R., & Koplin, J. H. Convergent associations in mediated generalization. *American Journal of Psychology*, 1967, *80*, 81–87.

Morgan, R. L., & Underwood, B. J. Proactive inhibition as a function of response similarity. *Journal of Experimental Psychology*, 1950, *40*, 592–603.

Murdock, B. B., Jr. The immediate retention of unrelated words. *Journal of Experimental Psychology*, 1960, *60*, 222–34.

Murdock, B. B., Jr., & Okada, R. Interresponse times in single-trial free recall. *Journal of Experimental Psychology*, 1970, *86*, 263–67.

Murray, H. G. Incidental paired-associate learning as a function of interstimulus interval. *Journal of Verbal Learning and Verbal Behavior*, 1970, *9*, 642–46.

Nelson, D. L., & Davis, M. J. Transfer and false recognitions based on phonetic identities of words. *Journal of Experimental Psychology*, 1972, *92*, 347–53.

Nelson, D. L., Peebles, J., & Pancotto, F. Phonetic similarity as opposed to informational structure as a determinant of word encoding. *Journal of Experimental Psychology*, 1970, *86*, 117–19.

Nelson, D. L., Reed, V. S., & McEvoy, C. L. Encoding strategy and sensory and semantic interference. *Memory & Cognition*, 1977, 5, 462–67.

Nelson, D. L., Wheeler, J., & Bercov, S. Variations in item availability and distinctiveness and the role of temporal constancy cues in serial anticipation. *Journal of Experimental Psychology*, 1970, 86, 463–64.

Nelson, T. O. Repetition and depth of processing. *Journal of Verbal Learning and Verbal Behavior*, 1977, 16, 151–71.

Nelson, T. O., & Vining, S. K. Effect of semantic versus structural processing on long-term retention. *Journal of Experimental Psychology: Human Learning and Memory*, 1978, 4, 198–209.

Nodine, C. F., & Goss, A. E. Temporal parameters in paired-associate learning. *Psychonomic Monograph Supplement*, 1969, 3 (1, Whole No. 33).

Oldfield, R. C. Things, words and the brain. *Quarterly Journal of Experimental Psychology*, 1966, 18, 340–53.

Olton, R. M. The effect of a mnemonic upon the retention of paired-associate verbal material. *Journal of Verbal Learning and Verbal Behavior*, 1969, 8, 43–48.

Packman, J. L., & Battig, W. F. Effects of different kinds of semantic processing on memory for words. *Memory & Cognition*, 1978, 6, 502–508.

Paivio, A. Learning of adjective-noun paired associates as a function of adjective-noun word order and noun abstractness. *Canadian Journal of Psychology*, 1963, 17, 370–79.

Paivio, A. *Imagery and verbal processes*. New York: Holt, Rinehart, & Winston, 1971.

Paivio, A., Yuille, J. C., & Madigan, S. A. Concreteness, imagery, and meaningfulness values for 925 nouns. *Journal of Experimental Psychology Monograph Supplement*, 1968, 76 (1, Pt. 2).

Peterson, L. R., & Peterson, M. J. Short-term retention of individual verbal items. *Journal of Experimental Psychology*, 1959, 58, 193–98.

Plenderleith, M., & Postman, L. Individual differences in intentional and incidental learning. *British Journal of Psychology*, 1957, 48, 241–48.

Postman, L. Transfer of training as a function of experimental paradigm and degree of first-list learning. *Journal of Verbal Learning and Verbal Behavior*, 1962, 1, 109–118.

Postman, L. Short-term memory and incidental learning. In A. W. Melton (Ed.), *Categories of human learning*. New York: Academic Press, 1964. (a)

Postman, L. Studies of learning to learn II. Changes in transfer as a function of practice. *Journal of Verbal Learning and Verbal Behavior*, 1964, 3, 437–47. (b)

Postman, L. Experimental analysis of learning to learn. In G. H. Bower & J. T. Spence (Eds.), *The psychology of learning and motivation* (Vol. 3). New York: Academic Press, 1969.

Postman, L. Organization and interference. *Psychological Review*, 1971, 78, 290–302.

Postman, L., & Adams, P. A. Studies in incidental learning: VIII. The effects of contextual determination. *Journal of Experimental Psychology*, 1960, 59, 153–64.

Postman, L., Adams, P. A., & Phillips, L. W. Studies in incidental learning: II. The effects of association value and of the method of testing. *Journal of Experimental Psychology*, 1955, *49*, 1–10.

Postman, L., & Goggin, J. Whole versus part learning of paired-associate lists. *Journal of Experimental Psychology*, 1966, *71*, 867–77.

Postman, L., & Greenbloom, R. Conditions of cue selection in the acquisition of paired-associate lists. *Journal of Experimental Psychology*, 1967, *73*, 91–100.

Postman, L., & Hasher, L. Conditions of proactive inhibition in free recall. *Journal of Experimental Psychology*, 1972, *92*, 276–84.

Postman, L., & Keppel, G. Retroactive inhibition in free recall. *Journal of Experimental Psychology*, 1967, *74*, 203–11.

Postman, L., & Kruesi, E. The influence of orienting tasks on the encoding and recall of words. *Journal of Verbal Learning and Verbal Behavior*, 1977, *16*, 353–69.

Postman, L., & Riley, D. A. A critique of of Köhler's theory of association. *Psychological Review*, 1957, *64*, 61–72.

Postman, L,, & Riley, D. A. Degree of learning and interserial interference in retention: A review of the literature and an experimental analysis. *University of California Publications in Psychology*, 1959, *8*, 271–396.

Postman, L., & Stark, K. Studies of learning to learn: IV. Transfer from serial to paired-associate learning. *Journal of Verbal Learning and Verbal Behavior*, 1967, *6*, 339–53.

Postman, L., Thompkins, B. A., & Gray, W. D. The interpretation of encoding effects in retention. *Journal of Verbal Learning and Verbal Behavior*, 1978, *17*, 681–705.

Proctor, R. W. The relationship of frequency judgments to recognition: Facilitation of recognition and comparison to recognition-confidence judgments. *Journal of Experimental Psychology: Human Learning & Memory*, 1977, *3*, 679–89.

Puff, C. R. Clustering as a function of the sequential organization of stimulus word lists. *Journal of Verbal Learning and Verbal Behavior*, 1966, *5*, 503–506.

Puff, C. R. A consolidated theoretical view of stimulus-list organization effects in free recall. *Psychological Reports*, 1974, *34*, 275–88.

Putnam, V., Iscoe, I., & Young, R. K. Verbal learning in the deaf. *Journal of Comparative and Physiological Psychology*, 1962, *55*, 843–46.

Radtke, R. C., & Grove, E. K. Proactive inhibition in short-term memory: Availability or accessibility? *Journal of Experimental Psychology: Human Learning and Memory*, 1977, *3*, 78–91.

Radtke, R. C., & Jacoby, L. Pronunciation and number of alternatives in verbal-discrimination learning. *Journal of Verbal Learning and Verbal Behavior*, 1971, *10*, 262–65.

Raye, C. L. Recognition: Frequency or organization? *American Journal of Psychology*, 1976, *89*, 645–58.

Richardson, J. Latencies of implicit associative responses and positive transfer in paired-associative learning. *Journal of Verbal Learning and Verbal Behavior*, 1968, *7*, 638–46.

Richardson, J. Component selection in paired-associate learning: Research and theory. *American Journal of Psychology*, 1976, *89*, 3–49.

Roberts, W. A. Free recall of word lists varying in length and rate of presentation: A test of the total-time hypotheses. *Journal of Experimental Psychology*, 1972, *92*, 365–72.

Robinson, E. S. *Association theory to-day*. New York: Century Company, 1932.

Roediger, H. L., III. Inhibiting effects of recall. *Memory & Cognition*, 1974, *2*, 261–69.

Roediger, H. L., III., & Schmidt, S. R. Output interference in the recall of categorized and paired-associate lists. *Journal of Experimental Psychology: Human Learning and Memory*, 1980, *6*, 91–105.

Rothkopf, E. Z. Incidental memory for location of information in text. *Journal of Verbal Learning and Verbal Behavior*, 1971, *10*, 608–13.

Rothkopf, E. Z., & Coke, E. U. The prediction of free recall from word association measures. *Journal of Experimental Psychology*, 1961, *62*, 433–38.

Rowe, E. J., & Paivio, A. Word frequency and imagery effects in verbal discrimination learning. *Journal of Experimental Psychology*, 1971, *88*, 319–26.

Rowe, E. J., & Paivio, A. Effects of noun imagery, pronunciation, method of presentation, and intrapair order of items in verbal discrimination. *Journal of Experimental Psychology*, 1972, *93*, 427–29.

Rundus, D. Maintenance rehearsal and single-level processing. *Journal of Verbal Learning and Verbal Behavior*, 1977, *16*, 665–81.

Rundus, D. Maintenance rehearsal and long-term recency. *Memory & Cognition*, 1980, *8*, 226–30.

Rundus, D., & Atkinson, R. C. Rehearsal processes in free recall : A procedure for direct observation. *Journal of Verbal Learning and Verbal Behavior*, 1970, *9*, 99–105.

Runquist, W. N. Retention of verbal associates as a function of strength. *Journal of Experimental Psychology*, 1957, *54*, 369–75.

Runquist, W. N. Acoustic similarity among stimuli as a source of interference in paired-associate learning. *Journal of Experimental Psychology*, 1970, *83*, 319–22.

Runquist, W. N., & Runquist, P. A. Interference reduction with conceptually similar paired associates. *Journal of Experimental Psychology: Human Learning & Memory*, 1978, *4*, 370–81.

Russ-Eft, D. Proactive interference: Buildup and release for individual words. *Journal of Experimental Psychology: Human Learning & Memory*, 1979, *5*, 422–34.

Saegert, J. Retention interval and false recognition of implicit associative responses. *Journal of Verbal Learning and Verbal Behavior*, 1971, *10*, 511–15.

Sanders, M. S., & Dudycha, A. L. Learning a 720-item paired-associate list by a part method: Effect of list length on learning time per item. *Psychological Reports*, 1974, *35*, 199–206.

Saufley, W. H., Jr., & LaCava, S. C. Reminiscence and arousal: Replications and the matter of establishing a phenomenon. *Bulletin of the Psychonomic Society*, 1977, *9*, 155–58.

Savage, S., & Kanak, J. The effect of frequency and number of pairs in a verbal discrimination task. *Bulletin of the Psychonomic Society*, 1973, *2*, 278–80.

Schnorr, J. A., & Atkinson, R. C. Study position and item differences in the short- and long-term retention of paired associates learned by imagery. *Journal of Verbal Learning and Verbal Behavior*, 1970, *9*, 614–22.

Schulman, A. I. Declining course of recognition memory. *Memory & Cognition*, 1974, *2*, 14–18. (a)

Schulman, A. I. Memory for words recently classified. *Memory & Cognition*, 1974, *2*, 47–52. (b)

Schulman, A. I., & Lovelace, E. A. Recognition memory for words presented at a slow or rapid rate. *Psychonomic Science*, 1970, *21*, 99–100.

Schulz, L. S., & Lovelace, E. A. Interpair acoustic and formal similarity in verbal discrimination learning. *Journal of Experimental Psychology*, 1972, *94*, 295–99.

Schulz, L. S., & Straub, R. B. Effects of high-priority events on recognition of adjacent items. *Journal of Experimental Psychology*, 1972, *95*, 467–69.

Schulz, R. W., & Hopkins, R. H. Presentation mode and meaningfulness as variables in several verbal-learning tasks. *Journal of Verbal Learning and Verbal Behavior*, 1968, *7*, 1–13.

Schwartz, M. Effect of stimulus class on transfer and RI in the A-B, C-B paradigm. *Journal of Verbal Learning and Verbal Behavior*, 1968, *7*, 189–195.

Schwartz, M. The effect of constant vs. varied encoding and massed vs. distributed presentations on recall of paired associates. *Memory & Cognition*, 1975, *3*, 390–94.

Schwartz, R. M., & Humphreys, M. S. Recognition and recall as a function of instructional manipulations of organization. *Journal of Experimental Psychology*, 1974, *102*, 517–19.

Schwenn, E. A., & Underwood, B. J. The effect of formal and associative similarity on paired-associate and free-recall learning. *Journal of Verbal Learning and Verbal Behavior*, 1968, *7*, 817–24.

Seamon, J. G., & Virostek, S. Memory performance and subject-defined depth of processing. *Memory & Cognition*, 1978, *6*, 283–87.

Shaughnessy, J. J. Persistence of the spacing effect in free recall under varying incidental learning conditions. *Memory & Cognition*, 1976, *4*, 369–77.

Shaughnessy, J. J. Subjective rating scales and the control of encoding in incidental learning. *Bulletin of the Psychonomic Society*, 1979, *14*, 205–208.

Shaughnessy, J. J. Memory monitoring accuracy and modification of rehearsal strategies. *Journal of Verbal Learning and Verbal Behavior*, 1981, *20*, 216–230.

Shepard, R. N., & Teghtsoonian, M. Retention of information under conditions approaching a steady state. *Journal of Experimental Psychology*, 1961, *62*, 302–309.

Shuell, T. J. Retroactive inhibition in free-recall learning of categorized lists. *Journal of Verbal Learning and Verbal Behavior*, 1968, *7*, 797–805.

Shuell, T. J., & Koehler, R. Proactive inhibition in free recall. *Journal of Experimental Psychology*, 1970, *83*, 495–501.

Slamecka, N. J. Proactive inhibition in connected discourse. *Journal of Experimental Psychology*, 1961, *62*, 295–301.

Slamecka, N. J. An examination of trace storage in free recall. *Journal of Experimental Psychology*, 1968, *76*, 504–13.

Slamecka, N. J., & Barlow, W. The role of semantic and surface features in word repetition effects. *Journal of Verbal Learning and Verbal Behavior*, 1979, *18*, 617–27.

Smith, A. D. Output interference and organized recall from long-term memory. *Journal of Verbal Learning and Verbal Behavior*, 1971, *10*, 400–408.

Smith, E. D. Multiple-list specific and nonspecific transfer. *American Journal of Psychology*, 1974, *87*, 159–71.

Smith, S., & Jensen, L. Test of the frequency theory of verbal discrimination learning. *Journal of Experimental Psychology*, 1971, *87*, 46–51.

Smith, S. M., Glenberg, A., & Bjork, R. A. Environmental context and human memory. *Memory & Cognition*, 1978, *6*, 342–53.

Spence, J. T. Associative interference on paired-associate lists from extra-experimental learning. *Journal of Verbal Learning and Verbal Behavior*, 1963, *2*, 329–38.

Sternberg, S. Memory-scanning: Mental processes revealed by reaction-time experiments. *American Scientist*, 1969, *57*, 421–57.

Strand, B. Z. Change of context and retroactive inhibition. *Journal of Verbal Learning and Verbal Behavior*, 1970, *9*, 202–206.

Stroop, J. R. Studies of interference in serial verbal reaction. *Journal of Experimental Psychology*, 1935, *18*, 643–62.

Thorndike, E. L. *The fundamentals of learning*. New York: Bureau of Publications, Teachers College, 1932.

Thorndike, E. L., & Lorge, I. *The teacher's word book of 30,000 words*. New York: Teachers College Press, Columbia University, 1944.

Tulving, E. Subjective organization in free recall of "unrelated" words. *Psychological Review*, 1962, *69*, 344–54.

Tulving, E. The effect of order of presentation on learning of "unrelated" words. *Psychonomic Science*, 1965, *3*, 337–38.

Tulving, E. Subjective organization and effects of repetition in multi-trial free-recall learning. *Journal of Verbal Learning and Verbal Behavior*, 1966, *5*, 193–97.

Tulving, E. Theoretical issues in free recall. In T. R. Dixon and D. L. Horton (Eds.), *Verbal behavior and general behavior theory*. Englewood Cliffs, N. J.: Prentice-Hall, 1968.

Tulving, E., McNulty, J. A., & Ozier, M. Vividness of words and learning to learn in free-recall learning. *Canadian Journal of Psychology*, 1965, *19*, 242–52.

Turvey, M. T., & Egan, J. Contextual change and release from proactive interference in short-term verbal memory. *Journal of Experimental Psychology*, 1969, *81*, 396–97.

Twedt, H. M., & Underwood, B. J. Mixed vs. unmixed lists in transfer studies. *Journal of Experimental Psychology*, 1959, *58*, 111–16.

Underwood, B. J. The effect of successive interpolations on retroactive and proactive inhibition. *Psychological Monographs*, 1945, *59* (3, Whole No. 273).

Underwood, B. J. Associative transfer in verbal learning as a function of response similarity and degree of first-list learning. *Journal of Experimental Psychology*, 1951, *42*, 44–53.

Underwood, B. J. Degree of learning and the measurement of forgetting. *Journal of Verbal Learning and Verbal Behavior*, 1964, *3*, 112–29. (a)

Underwood, B. J. The representativeness of rote verbal learning. In A. W. Melton (Ed.), *Categories of human learning*. New York: Academic Press, 1964. (b)

Underwood, B. J. Individual and group predictions of item difficulty for free learning. *Journal of Experimental Psychology*, 1966, *71*, 673–79.

Underwood, B. J. Attributes of memory. *Psychological Review*, 1969, *76*, 559–73. (a)

Underwood, B. J. Some correlates of item repetition in free-recall learning. *Journal of Verbal Learning and Verbal Behavior*, 1969, *8*, 83–94. (b)

Underwood, B. J. Are we overloading memory? In A. W. Melton and E. Martin (Eds.), *Coding processes in human memory*. Washington, D.C.: Winston & Sons, 1972.(a)

Underwood, B. J. Word recognition memory and frequency information. *Journal of Experimental Psychology*, 1972, *94*, 276–83. (b)

Underwood, B. J. The role of the association in recognition memory. *Journal of Experimental Psychology Monograph*, 1974, *102*, 917–39.

Underwood, B. J. *Temporal codes for memories: Issues and problems*. Hillsdale, N. J.: L. Erlbaum Associates, 1977.

Underwood, B. J. Recognition memory as a function of length of study list. *Bulletin of the Psychonomic Society*, 1978, *12*, 89–91.

Underwood, B. J., Boruch, R. F., & Malmi, R. A. Composition of episodic memory. *Journal of Experimental Psychology: General*, 1978, *107*, 393–419.

Underwood, B. J., Broder, P. K., & Zimmerman, J. Associative matching and cumulative proactive inhibition. *Bulletin of the Psychonomic Society*, 1973, *1*, 48.

Underwood, B. J., & Ekstrand, B. R. An analysis of some shortcomings in the interference theory of forgetting. *Psychological Review*, 1966, *73*, 540–49.

Underwood, B. J., & Ekstrand, B. R. Effect of distributed practice on paired-associate learning. *Journal of Experimental Psychology Monograph Supplement*, 1967, *73* (4, Pt. 2).

Underwood, B. J., & Ekstrand, B. R. Differentiation among stimuli as a factor in transfer performance. *Journal of Verbal Learning and Verbal Behavior*, 1968, *7*, 172–75. (a)

Underwood, B. J., & Ekstrand, B. R. Linguistic associations and retention. *Journal of Verbal Learning and Verbal Behavior*, 1968, *7*, 162–71. (b)

Underwood, B. J., Ekstrand, B. R., & Keppel, G. An analysis of intralist similarity in verbal learning with experiments on conceptual similarity. *Journal of Verbal Learning and Verbal Behavior*, 1965, *4*, 447–62.

Underwood, B. J., & Erlebacher, A. H. Studies of coding in verbal learning. *Psychological Monographs*, 1965, *79* (13, Whole No. 606).

Underwood, B. J., & Freund, J. S. Further studies on conceptual similarity in free-recall learning. *Journal of Verbal Learning and Verbal Behavior*, 1969, *8*, 30–35. (a)

Underwood, B. J., & Freund, J. S. Verbal-discrimination learning with varying numbers of right and wrong terms. *American Journal of Psychology*, 1969, *82*, 198–202. (b)

Underwood, B. J., & Freund, J. S. Testing effects in the recognition of words. *Journal of Verbal Learning and Verbal Behavior*, 1970, *9*, 117–25. (a)

Underwood, B. J., & Freund, J. S. Word frequency and short-term recognition memory. *American Journal of Psychology*, 1970, *83*, 343–51. (b)

Underwood, B. J., & Goad, D. Studies of distributed practice: I. The influence of intra-list similarity in serial learning. *Journal of Experimental Psychology*, 1951, *42*, 125–134.

Underwood, B. J., & Humphreys, M. Context change and the role of meaning in word recognition. *American Journal of Psychology*, 1979, *92*, 577–609.

Underwood, B. J., Kapelak, S. M., & Malmi, R. A. Integration of discrete verbal units in recognition memory. *Journal of Experimental Psychology: Human Learning & Memory*, 1976, *2*, 293–300. (a)

Underwood, B. J., Kapelak, S. M., & Malmi, R. A. The spacing effect: Additions to the theoretical and empirical puzzles. *Memory & Cognition*, 1976, *4*, 391–400. (b)

Underwood, B. J., & Lund, A. M. Retention differences as a function of the number of verbal lists learned simultaneously. *Journal of Experimental Psychology: Human Learning and Memory*, 1979, *5*, 151–59.

Underwood, B. J., & Lund, A. M. Incidental development of associations in simultaneous learning. *Bulletin of the Psychonomic Society*, 1980, *16*, 411–13. (a)

Underwood, B. J., & Lund, A. M. Semantic encoding and the effects of formal intralist similarity. *American Journal of Psychology*, 1980, *93*, 235–45. (b)

Underwood, B. J., & Lund, A. M. Transfer effects from single-task learning to simultaneous learning. *Bulletin of the Psychonomic Society*, 1980, *16*, 391–93. (c)

Underwood, B. J., & Lund, A. M. Attenuation of attention in simultaneous learning. Unpublished manuscript, 1980.

Underwood, B. J., & Lund, A. M. The effect of degree of learning on within-list competition. *American Journal of Psychology*, 1981, *94*, 195–208.

Underwood, B. F., Lund, A. M., & Malmi, R. A. The recency principle in the temporal coding of memories. *American Journal of Psychology*, 1978, *91*, 563–73.

Underwood, B. J., & Malmi, R. A. An evaluation of measures used in studying temporal codes for words within a list. *Journal of Verbal Learning and Verbal Behavior*, 1978, *17*, 279–93. (a)

Underwood, B. J., & Malmi, R. A. The simultaneous acquisition of multiple memories. In G. H. Bower (Ed.), *The psychology of learning and motivation*, New York: Academic Press, 1978. (b)

Underwood, B. J., & Reichardt, C. S. Contingent associations and the double-function, verbal-discrimination task. *Memory & Cognition*, 1975, *3*, 311–14.

Underwood, B. J., Reichardt, C. S., & Malmi, R. A. Sources of facilitation in learning conceptually structured paired-associate lists. *Journal of Experimental Psychology: Human Learning & Memory*, 1975, *104*, 160–66.

Underwood, B. J., & Richardson, J. Some verbal materials for the study of concept formation. *Psychological Bulletin*, 1956, *53*, 84–95.

Underwood, B. J., & Schulz, R. W. *Meaningfulness and verbal learning*. Philadelphia: Lippincott, 1960.

Underwood, B. J., & Schulz, R. W. Studies of distributed practice: XXI. Effect of interference from language habits. *Journal of Experimental Psychology*, 1961, *62*, 571–75.

Underwood, B. J., & Shaughnessy, J. J. *Experimentation in psychology*, New York: Wiley, 1975.

Underwood, B. J., Shaughnessy, J. J., & Zimmerman, J. Learning-to-learn verbal-discrimination lists. *Journal of Verbal Learning and Verbal Behavior*, 1972, *11*, 96–104. (a)

Underwood, B. J., Shaughnessy, J. J., & Zimmerman, J. List length and method of presentation in verbal discrimination learning with further evidence on retroaction. *Journal of Experimental Psychology*, 1972, *93*, 181–87. (b)

Underwood, B. J., & Zimmerman, J. The syllable as a source of error in multisyllable word recognition. *Journal of Verbal Learning and Verbal Behavior*, 1973, *12*, 701–706.

Underwood, B. J., Zimmerman, J., & Freund, J. S. Retention of frequency information with observations on recognition and recall. *Journal of Experimental Psychology*, 1971, *87*, 149–62.

Vereb, C. E., & Voss, J. F. Perceived frequency of implicit associative responses as a function of frequency of occurrence of list items. *Journal of Experimental Psychology*, 1974, *103*, 992–98.

Vogt, J., & Kimble, G. A. False recognition as a function of associative proximity. *Journal of Experimental Psychology*, 1973, *99*, 143–45.

von Wright, J. M. Forgetting and interference. *Soc. Sci. Fennica, Comm. Hum. Litt.* 1959, *26*, 1–124.

von Wright, J. M., & Salminen, H. Retention as a function of previous learning. *Nature*, 1964, *204*, 301–302.

Wallace, W. P. Implicit associative response occurrence in learning with retarded subjects: A supplementary report. *Journal of Educational Psychology*, 1967, *58*, 110–14.

Wallace, W, P., Consistency of emission order in free recall. *Journal of Verbal Learning and Verbal Behavior*, 1970, *9*, 58–68.

Wallace, W. P. On the use of distractors for testing recognition memory. *Psychological Bulletin*, 1980, *88*, 696–704.

Wallace, W. P., Sawyer, T. J., & Robertson, L. C. Distractors in recall, distractor-free recognition, and the word-frequency effect. *American Journal of Psychology*, 1978, *91*, 295–304.

Wallace, W. P., & Underwood, B. J. Implicit responses and the role of intralist similarity in verbal learning by normal and retarded subjects. *Journal of Educational Psychology*, 1964, *55*, 362–70.

Walsh, M. F., & Schwartz, M. The Ranschburg effect: Tests of the guessing-bias and proactive interference hypotheses. *Journal of Verbal Learning and Verbal Behavior*, 1977, *16*, 55–68.

Ward, L. B. Reminiscence and rote learning. *Psychological Monographs*, 1937, *49* (4, Whole No. 220).

Watkins, M. J., & Gardiner, J. M. An appreciation of generate-recognize theory of recall. *Journal of Verbal Learning and Verbal Behavior*, 1979, *18*, 687–704.

Weeks, R. A. Auditory location as an encoding dimension. *Journal of Experimental Psychology: Human Learning and Memory*, 1975, *104*, 316–18.

Wenger, S. K. The within-list distributed practice effect: More evidence for the inattention hypothesis. *American Journal of Psychology*, 1979, *92*, 105–13.

Whitely, P. L. The dependence of learning and recall upon prior intellectual activities. *Journal of Experimental Psychology*, 1927, *10*, 489–508.

Whitely, P. L., & Blankenship, A. B. The influence of certain conditions prior to learning upon subsequent recall. *Journal of Experimental Psychology*, 1936, *19*, 496–504.

Whitely, P. L., & McGeoch, J. A. The curve of retention for poetry. *Journal of Educational Psychology*, 1928, *19*, 471–79.

Wickelgren, W. A. Acoustic similarity and retroactive interference in short-term memory. *Journal of Verbal Learning and Verbal Behavior*, 1965, *4*, 53–61.

Wickens, D. D. Encoding categories of words: An empirical approach to meaning. *Psychological Review*, 1970, *77*, 1–15.

Wickens, D. D., & Clark, S. Osgood dimensions as an encoding class in short-term memory. *Journal of Experimental Psychology*, 1968, *78*, 580–84.

Wike, S. S. The effects of feedback, guessing and anticipation rate upon verbal discrimination learning. *Psychological Record*, 1970, *20*, 171–78.

Williams, M. D. Retrieval from very long-term memory. Doctoral dissertation, University of California, San Diego, 1976.

Williams, O. A study of the phenomenon of reminiscence. *Journal of Experimental Psychology*, 1926, *9*, 368–87.

Wipf, J. L., & Webb, W. B. Supplementary report: Proactive inhibition as a function of the method of reproduction. *Journal of Experimental Psychology*, 1962, *64*, 421.

Wood, G. Implicit responses and conceptual similarity: A repetition. *Journal of Verbal Learning and Verbal Behavior*, 1968, *7*, 838–46.

Wood, G., & Underwood, B. J. Implicit responses and conceptual similarity. *Journal of Verbal Learning and Verbal Behavior*, 1967, *6*, 1–10.

Woodward, A. E., Jr., Bjork, R. A., & Jongeward, R. H., Jr. Recall and recognition as a function of primary rehearsal. *Journal of Verbal Learning and Verbal Behavior*, 1973, *12*, 608–17.

Young, R. K. A comparison of two methods of learning serial associations. *American Journal of Psychology*, 1959, *72*, 554–59.

Young, R. K. Tests of three hypotheses about the effective stimulus in serial learning. *Journal of Experimental Psychology*, 1962, *63*, 307–13.

Young, R. K., & Thomson, W. J. Retention of single- and double-function lists. *Journal of Verbal Learning and Verbal Behavior*, 1967, *6*, 910–15.

Zacks, R. T. Long-term retention after acquisition under different conditions of practice. *Journal of Experimental Psychology*, 1972, *94*, 340–42.

Zechmeister, E. B. Orthographic distinctiveness. *Journal of Verbal Learning and Verbal Behavior*, 1969, *8*, 754–61.

Zechmeister, E. B. Orthographic distinctiveness as a variable in word recognition. *American Journal of Psychology*, 1972, *85*, 425–30.

Zechmeister, E. B., & McKillip, J. Recall of place on the page. *Journal of Educational Psychology*, 1972, *63*, 446–53.

Zechmeister, E. B., McKillip, J., & Pasko, S. Verbal discrimination learning of items read in textual material. *Journal of Experimental Psychology*, 1973, *101*, 393–95.

Zechmeister, E. B., & Shaughnessy, J. J. When you know that you know and when you think that you know but you don't. *Bulletin of the Psychonomic Society*, 1980, *15*, 41–44.

Zechmeister, E. B., & Underwood, B. J. Acquisition of items and associations in verbal discrimination learning as a function of level of practice. *Journal of Experimental Psychology*, 1969, *81*, 355–59.

Zimmerman, J. Free recall after self-paced study: A test of the attention explanation of the spacing effect. *American Journal of Psychology*, 1975, *88*, 277–91.

Name Index

A

Adams, F., 243
Adams, J. A., 240
Adams, P. A., 90, 91, 97
Allen, G., 59
Anderson, J. R., 185, 186
Anderson, R., 75
Anderson, R. C., 228
Arkes, H. R., 97
Atkinson, R. C., 76, 181, 222, 223, 261

B

Bach, M. J., 143, 144, 145
Baddeley, A. D., 97, 204, 256, 259
Bahrick, H. P., 213, 216, 219, 220
Bahrick, P. O., 213, 216
Barclay, A., 188
Barker, D., 114
Barlow, W., 164
Barnes, J. M., 237
Bartz, W. H., 97
Battig, W. F., 38, 94, 148
Begg, I., 108
Bercov, S., 170, 171
Berkowitz, J., 122
Berry, C., 50, 51
Bisanz, G., 182
Björgen, I. A., 92
Bjork, R. A., 113, 249, 257
Block, R. A., 61, 65

Bloom, B. S., 76
Blumenthal, G. B., 234, 235
Boka, J. A., 126
Boruch, R. F., 35, 43, 52, 106, 120
Boulay, E. A., 127
Bower, G. H., 65, 228, 229, 256
Bradley, M. M., 242, 250
Bradshaw, G. L., 117
Bray, N. W., 240
Brewer, G. L., 75
Broder, P. K., 234
Brown, A. S., 257
Brown, J., 33, 46, 141
Brown, W. P., 181
Bruce, D., 187, 257
Bruce, D. R., 150
Bugelski, B. R., 76
Butter, M. J., 221, 222

C

Calfee, R. C., 75
Cameron, P. C., 66
Carter-Sobell, L., 114
Cermak, L. S., 94
Clark, S., 66
Clifford, B. R., 50, 51
Cofer, C. N., 150, 177
Cohen, R. L., 36
Coke, E. U., 145
Conrad, R., 203

Cooper, E. H., 73, 74, 85
Craik, F. I. M., 94, 95, 96
Cramer, P., 133
Crouse, J. H., 228

D

DaPolito, F., 114
Darley, C. F., 251
Davis, M. J., 173
Deese, J., 147
Deffenbacher, K. A., 220, 221
Deichmann, J. W., 119
Donaldson, W., 259
Doten, G. W., 197, 198
Drewnowski, A., 57
Dudycha, A. L., 80
Duncan, C. P., 159

E

Ebbinghaus, Hermann, 2, 41, 194, 211, 262
Eckert, E., 120
Egan, J., 66
Ekstrand, B. R., 99, 116, 128, 148, 169, 175, 177, 194, 232
Elliott, J. M., 60, 97, 163
Ellis, H. C., 114, 194
Englert, J. A., 128
Epling, W. F., 121
Epstein, W., 177, 224
Erber, J. T., 119
Erlebacher, A. H., 224
Evans, J. D., 97

F

Farzanegan, F., 119
Finkenbinder, E. O., 211, 212
Forrester, W. E., 59, 230
Francis, W. N., 101
Freund, J. S., 108, 123, 125, 142, 154, 212, 214
Frey, T. J., 89

G

Galbraith, R. C., 128, 164
Gardiner, J. M., 66, 260
Gardner, E. T., 97
Gausepohl, J., 204

Ghatala, B. S., 120, 128, 131
Glass, A. L., 251
Glenberg, A. M., 89-90, 113, 242, 243, 247, 249, 250, 251, 257
Goad, D., 174
Godden, D. R., 256
Goedel, G. D., 128
Goggin, J. P., 80, 169
Goggin, R., 60, 61, 235
Goss, A. E., 74
Goulet, L. R., 188
Gray, W. D., 97
Green, C., 249, 251
Green, D. M., 16
Green, R. L., 119
Greenberg, R., 232, 233
Greenbloom, R., 166
Greitzer, F. L., 154
Grove, E. K., 236
Gunter, B., 50, 51

H

Hall, J. W., 116, 140
Haller, J., 255
Harris, G., 108
Harris, R. L., 108, 204
Hasher, L., 62, 87, 231
Heckelman, S. B., 146
Hess, J. L., 147
Hicks, R. E., 196
Hinrichs, J. V., 202, 203
Hintzman, D. L., 61, 65, 90, 112
Hopkins, R. H., 121, 128
Howell, W. R., 103
Hull, A., 204
Humphreys, M. S., 113, 114, 248
Hunt, R. R., 60, 97, 114, 163
Hyde, T. S., 92

I-J

Ingison, L. J., 128
Inskeep, N. R., 61, 65
Iscoe, I., 130
Izawa, C., 79
Jacoby, L. L., 97
Jahnke, J. C., 202, 203, 204
Jenkins, J. J., 92, 145, 146
Jensen, L., 122

Subject Index

A

A–B, A–Br paradigm, 188
A–B, A–D paradigm, 185–87
A–B, C–B paradigm, 187–88
Abstract versus concrete words
  effect of, on recognition, 115, 128–29
  as task variable, 166–69
Acoustic attribute, 57–59
Adjective-noun list, versus noun-adjective list, 177, 248
Anticipation learning
  and paired-associate learning, 37–38, 159
  and serial learning, 42, 170
  and verbal-discrimination learning, 25, 117, 118
Arbitrary event classes, use of, 26
Arousal, effect of, on forgetting, 221–23
Association values, effect of, on recognition, 114–15
Associative learning, 80, 98, 127, 262. *See also* Paired-associate learning
Attention theory, 85–87
Attenuation-of-attention theory, 85–87
Attributes of memory, 56–57
  acoustic, 57–59
  affective, 66
  class, 67–68
  context, 66
  frequency, 62
  modality, 65–66
  orthographic, 59–62
  spatial, 62–63
  temporal, 63–65
  transformational, 68–70
  verbal associative, 67–68

B

Bach study, 144–45
Background frequency, 101, 110
  effect of, on recognition, 115, 127–28, 141–45
Beta, 16
Bidirectional learning, 37, 127
Blocked-random effect, 148, 151, 153
Brown-Peterson procedure/task, 46–51, 181, 234–36, 242, 251

C

Ceiling effects, 78
Class attributes, 67–68
Clustering, 36–37
Conceptual implicit associative responses, 134–38
Conceptual relatedness, 147–55
Concrete versus abstract words
  effect of, on recognition, 115, 128–29
  as task variable, 166–69
Context attributes, 66
  in free-recall learning, 256–58

O

Old-new recognition, 10–11
  application of frequency theory to, 106–11
  association values, 114–15
  background frequency, 115
  concrete versus abstract words, 115
  context manipulations, 113–14
  deductive consequences, 108–11
  exposure duration, 111–12
  forced choice, 11–14
  individual differences, 106
  instructional procedures, 116
  length of list, 116
  orthography, 116
  parallel manipulations, 106–8
  recognition errors, 112–13
  repeated items in testing, 108–10
  running recognition, 21–22
  similarity between items, 113
  syllable as a unit, 110–11
  two-category classification task, 25–26
  verbal discrimination learning, 22–25
  yes-no trials, 14–21
Original learning (OL), 225
Orthographic attributes, 59–62
Orthography, 116, 163
Output interference, 199–201

P

Paced recall, versus unpaced recall, 34–35, 255–56
Paired-associate learning, 37–41, 69, 127, 194–96
  conceptual IARs, 134–38
  crossed associates, 138
  effect of meaningfulness on, 164
  and mixed versus unmixed lists, 158–59
  and natural language mediators, 69–70
  and task variables in, 176, 177
  verbal-discrimination learning, 160–61
Paradigms. *See* Identity paradigms; Similarity paradigms
Parallel associates, 67

Parallel manipulations, in old-new recognition, 106–8
Perception, effect of, 196–97
Performance, learning, memory and, 7–8
Positive transfer, failures to find, 192–97
Prefix effects, as interference phenomenon, 203–5
Primacy effect, 35
Proactive inhibition, 48, 61, 231–36
  release from, 49–51, 60, 63, 66
Probability matching, 19–20
Probe recall procedures, 27–29, 54
Processing, depth of, 94
Processing model of frequency theory, 117–20

Q-R

Ranschburg effect, 201–3
Recall learning
  free recall, 34–37
  miniaturized tasks, 46–53
  paired-associate, 37–41
  serial learning, 41–43
  serial syntactical, 43–46
  versus recognition memory, 4, 262
Recency effect, 35, 55
Recency judgments, 64
Recognition memory, 10, 99
  application of, to old-new recognition, 10–11, 106–11, 113
  association values, 114–15
  background frequency, 115, 141–45
  concrete versus abstract words, 115
  context manipulations, 113–14
  differences between recall and, 262
  errors in, 112–13
  exposure duration, 111–12
  false alarms, 138–40
  forced-choice procedures, 11–14
  frequency information on, 99–103
  frequency theory, 103–32
  implicit associative responses, 138–40
  instructional procedures, 116
  length of list, 116
  miniature tasks, 26–32
  orthography, 116

probe technique, 27
running recognition, 21–22
string matching, 30–32
two-category classification task, 25–26
and verbal-discrimination learning, 22–25, 116–30
versus recall memory, 4, 262
yes-no tests, 14–21, 262
Rehearsal, 248–49
studies of, 249–52
evaluation of, 252–54
Relearning, as measure of retention, 211
Release-from-proactive inhibition (PI) technique, 49–51, 60, 63, 66
Repetition, effect of, on recognition, 108–10
Representational response (RR), 133
Response learning, 187
Response measures, 55
Retroactive inhibition, 225–31
Reverse associations, 147
Rote rehearsal, 251–52
Running recall task, 54
Running recognition tests, 21–22

S

Sense-impression responses, 153
Sensory codes, presence of, in memory, 172–74
Sentential facilitation, 69
Serial learning, 41–43, 170, 194–96, 262
Serial probe task, 54
Serial syntactical, 43–46
Similarity paradigms, 189–92
Simultaneous learning, and forgetting, 205–7, 221
Single task learning, 205–7
Single-list situation, 215
arousal, 221–23
interfering tasks, 223–25
level or degree of learning, 216–18
simultaneous learning, 221
spaced learning, 218–21
Situational frequency, 101, 104, 123, 127

Spaced learning, and forgetting, 218–21
Spacing effect, 78–79
kind of task, 79–81
list construction, 81–82
testing procedures, 82–84
theory of, 85, 89–90
attention, 85–87
context, 87–89
variable-encoding, 87–89
Spatial attribute, 62–63
Stimulus discrimination, 192–94
Stimulus selection, 166
String matching, 30–32
Stroop effect, 197–99
Study time, 72–73
incidental learning, 90–98
spacing effect, 78–90
total-time hypothesis, 73–78
Study-test method
and amount of study time, 74
and paired-associate learning, 38, 74, 76
and serial learning, 42
and serial syntactical, 44–45
and verbal-discrimination learning, 23, 117
Subjective organization, 36–37
Suffix effects, as interference phenomenon, 203–5
Syllables as units, effect of, on recognition, 110–11

T

Task variables, 157
concrete words versus abstract words, 166–69
form class, 177
meaningfulness, 161–66
mixed versus unmixed lists, 157–61
noun-adjective versus adjective-noun, 177
vividness, 177–78
within-list similarity, 169–76
Temporal attribute, 63–65
Test trials
forced choice, 11–14
yes-no tests, 14–20
Total-time hypothesis, 73